# Italy's
# Great Chefs
## and their secrets

ACADEMIA
BARILLA

WHITE STAR PUBLISHERS

TEXT
ACADEMIA BARILLA
GIANCARLO GONIZZI
MARIA GRAZIA VILLA

INTRODUCTIONS
GUIDO, LUCA AND PAOLO BARILLA
GIANLUIGI ZENTI

PHOTOGRAPHS
LUCIO ROSSI

ACADEMIA BARILLA EDITORIAL COORDINATION
CHATO MORANDI
ILARIA ROSSI

PHOTOGRAPHY ASSISTANT
ALESSANDRO DELCANALE

# CONTENTS

# A THOUSAND ITALIAN CUISINES

There's no such thing as one national gastronomy in Italy. However, there's a food and wine scene that is so vast, in terms of its infinite variations and local abundance, that it can proudly represent this unique situation around the world.

There are different reasons for this, which are essentially of an historical and geographical nature.

History paints a picture of a country that, after the decline of the Roman Empire, was divided into courts, principalities, and small states for centuries, which were often influenced by foreign rulers.

Due to an absence of unitary guidelines, each city and territory therefore laid down its own independent paths in the kitchen, often working and adapting exotic influences into its own culture which still remain and are preserved today, after the country's unification in the nineteenth century.

However, the real reasons for our gastronomic good fortune are based on an even more deep-seated reality. Cuisine in Italy is created using genuine and delicious products, proffered by the generosity of nature in its many forms and enhanced by one hundred percent innate Italian creativity and ingenuity, which motivated our peoples to identify ways in which to "salvage" every foodstuff that was available (even the less noble parts) through suitable, varied,

and complicated recipes, capable of turning even the simplest of fare into a unique gastronomic experience.

Our cooking is therefore based on a myriad of products determined by the climate and terrain of the land. The seas and mountains, market gardens and forests, lakes and plains have all marked the birth of unique ingredients, as unique as our land. This gives rise to a cuisine that is deeply anchored to tradition and the characteristics of the regions. The Italy of a thousand bell towers is also the Italy of a thousand cuisines and just as many products, once the offspring of instinctive knowledge, handed down by generations and in harmony with the culture of the place, now envied – and copied – all over the world. This is the reason why Barilla, which has distributed one of our country's most characteristic products – pasta – all over the world, decided to found the *Academia Barilla* to enhance the Italian gastronomic tradition.

*Academia Barilla* promotes courses to spread the knowledge of our gastronomy, distributes the best of Italy's products, and spreads our culture of flavors through publications such as this, which recounts the wealth of food and wine in our country through the voices of thirty of the most valued Italian chefs and the extraordinary heritage of products par excellence which past generations left us as an heirloom. *Academia Barilla* is situated in Parma, the heart of the Food

VALLEY, A CITY MUCH APPRECIATED FOR ITS FOOD PRODUCTS – FROM PARMIGIANO-REGGIANO CHEESE TO PROSCIUTTO DI PARMA, PASTA, AND NUMEROUS SPECIALTIES – A STONE'S THROW AWAY FROM THE CITY CENTER, WITH THE STONEWORK OF THE BAPTISTERY BY BENEDETTO ANTELAMI AND THE DOMES FRESCOED BY DA CORREGGIO, THE TEATRO REGIO, THE TEMPLE TO OPERA, WHICH HAS CONSECRATED THE GENIUS OF VERDI AND TOSCANINI OVER TIME.

CROSSING THE THRESHOLD OF *ACADEMIA BARILLA* MEANS ENTERING A STATE-OF-THE-ART ESTABLISHMENT IN TERMS OF ITS EQUIPMENT AND MATERIALS USED: FROM THE 90-SEAT AUDITORIUM TO THE SENSORY ANALYSIS LABORATORY, FROM THE HALL USED FOR PRACTICAL TRAINING TO THE MULTIPURPOSE SPACES, AND FINALLY THE GASTRONOMIC LIBRARY, AN EXCEPTIONAL TOOL OF KNOWLEDGE ON THE EVOLUTION OF GASTRONOMY AND TASTE, WITH A PATRIMONY OF OVER 8,500 VOLUMES AND PERIODICALS (FROM THE SIXTEENTH CENTURY TO THE PRESENT DAY), THOUSANDS OF HISTORICAL MENUS (FROM THE NINETEENTH CENTURY ONWARDS) AND HUNDREDS OF GASTRONOMY-RELATED PUBLICATIONS (FROM THE SIXTEENTH CENTURY ONWARDS).

NEVERTHELESS, *ACADEMIA BARILLA* REACHES OUT TO THE WORLD ESPECIALLY THROUGH ITS PRODUCTS, PUBLICATIONS, AND CULTURAL INITIATIVES, AN UNTIRING AMBASSADOR OF THIS COUNTRY WHERE THE BEST INGREDIENTS MAKE SURE THAT EVERY FLAVOR IS TRANSFORMED INTO A MEMORABLE EXPERIENCE. IT'S UNIQUE, JUST LIKE ITALY.

GUIDO, LUCA, AND PAOLO BARILLA

# A JOURNEY TO ITALY:
# WHERE BEAUTY MEETS GOODNESS

ITALY IS A TRULY UNIQUE COUNTRY: A LONG STRIP OF LAND THAT STRETCHES OUT OF THE EUROPEAN CONTINENT FOR OVER 800 MILES (1,300 KILOMETERS) INTO THE WATERS THE MEDITERRANEAN SEA. IN THIS SEA-KISSED LAND, MANY POPULATIONS HAVE LEFT THEIR MARK OVER THE CENTURIES. SO MUCH SO THAT TODAY ITALY IS CONSIDERED – AND RIGHTLY SO – A TRUE OPEN-AIR MUSEUM: MONUMENTS AND WORKS OF ART, ARCHITECTURE AND SCULPTURE, LANDSCAPE AND NATURE ALL BLEND INTO ONE COMPLETE AND TOTALLY FASCINATING ENTITY.

BUT THE MARK LEFT BY THE VARIOUS POPULATIONS – ETRUSCANS, GREEKS, ROMANS, LONGOBARDS, BYZANTINES, SPANISH, FRENCH, AUSTRIANS, JUST TO NAME THE MOST FAMOUS – IS EVIDENT NOT ONLY IN AESTHETIC TASTES BUT ALSO, AND ABOVE ALL, IN CULINARY TASTES. THERE ARE MORE THAN 170 "TYP-ICAL" PRODUCTS THAT ARE LINKED TO A SPECIFIC GEOGRAPHICAL AREA AND TO CERTAIN INGREDIENTS, AND DOZENS OF FOOD "REGIONS" CHARACTERIZE THE COUNTRY, MAKING IT A REAL TROVE OF TRADI-TIONS AND FLAVORS. THUS THE "JOURNEY TO ITALY" - THAT GRAND TOUR WHICH, FOR THE EUROPEAN ARISTOCRACY, WAS CONSIDERED SINCE THE 17TH CENTURY AN INDISPENSABLE PART OF A YOUNG PER-SON'S EDUCATION – BECAME AN UNREPEATABLE EXPERIENCE IN WHICH BEAUTY AND GOODNESS MERGED, MAKING THE ANCIENT GREEK IDEAL OF PERFECTION A REALITY.

SINCE MEDIEVAL TIMES THE JOURNEY TO THE MILD MEDITERRANEAN CLIMATE REPRESENTED A FUN-DAMENTAL EXPERIENCE; ARTISTS IN SEARCH OF WORK, MERCHANTS LOOKING FOR NEW MERCHANDISE AND NEW MARKETS AND PILGRIMS SEARCHING FOR THEIR OWN SPIRITUALITY OR FOR FORGIVENESS ON THE TOMB OF PETER THE APOSTLE, TRAVELED ALL OVER THE COUNTRY. OVER THE CENTURIES, THE MOTIVES VARIED AND, BEGINNING IN THE 17TH CENTURY, THE JOURNEY ACQUIRED ADDED VALUE DUE TO ITS OWN INTRINSIC QUALITIES. A TRIP TO ITALY WAS LONGER MADE FOR SPECIFIC ENDS, BUT AS A UNIQUE AND SOLE OBJECTIVE IN ITSELF, TO SATISFY A BOLD CURIOSITY. IT WAS NOT JUST A JOURNEY TAKEN IN THE NAME OF KNOWLEDGE AND AWARENESS, BUT ALSO FOR DIVERSION AND PURE DELIGHT. THUS, THE SONS AND DAUGHTERS OF THE EUROPEAN ARISTOCRACY EMBARKED FOR ITALY, INTENT ON MATURING AN EDUCATION THAT DERIVED FROM THAT LOST CLASSICISM OF WHICH ITALY HELD THE LAST VESTIGE AND MEMORY. THEY FOUND, ALONG WITH OTHER YOUNG TOURISTS, COLORS SO RARE IN THEIR COLD NATIVE LANDS--WARM HUES AND UNEXPECTED TASTES IN A PALETTE OF EMOTIONS,

EXPERIENCES THAT WOULD ALWAYS REMAIN IN THE MEMORY AND THE EDUCATION OF THE TRAVELER.

THE CENTURIES OLD STRATIFICATION OF TRADITIONS AND CUSTOMS AND THE CREATIVITY OF THE ITALIAN PEOPLE HAVE GIVEN RISE TO AN EXTREMELY VARIED CULINARY HERITAGE, SO DIFFERENT FROM THE UNIFIED CUISINE OF THE EUROPEAN NOBILITY WHICH WAS INFLUENCED VERY LITTLE BY LOCAL CUSTOM AND CHARACTERIZED BY AN ABUNDANCE OF MEAT AND FISH AND COMPLEX PREPARATION IN WHICH DECORATION TOOK PRECEDENCE OVER TASTE.

THIS BOOK, TAKING UP THE *"GRAND TOUR"* TRADITION ONCE AGAIN, SEEKS TO PROPOSE A LONG JOURNEY THROUGH THE VARIOUS CUISINES OF THE ITALIAN PENINSULA. A JOURNEY, FROM NORTH TO SOUTH, FROM THE MOUNTAINS TO THE SEA, DIVIDED INTO THIRTY SECTIONS, WHICH IS THE NUMBER OF "CUISINES" OF A STRONG CHARACTER THAT CAN STILL BE IDENTIFIED TODAY IN ITALY AND WHICH DO NOT ALWAYS COINCIDE WITH THE ADMINISTRATIVE REGIONS (OF WHICH THERE ARE ONLY TWENTY) INTO WHICH THE TERRITORY IS DIVIDED.

YOUNG COOKS WERE CHOSEN TO MAKE THESE TRADITIONS COME TO LIFE THROUGH STORIES AND RECIPES, BECAUSE THEY ARE PASSIONATE ABOUT THEIR MISSION AND VERY MUCH IN LOVE WITH THEIR OWN LAND. THEY ARE CAPABLE OF TRANSMITTING ANCIENT FLAVORS WITH FRESH EYES AND A SENSITIVITY TOWARDS TODAY. THE RESULT IS A BOOK THAT IS FILLED WITH SPECIFIC AND UNIQUE INGREDIENTS AND PRODUCTS, BUT ALSO DEMONSTRATES HOW THE COLORS, HISTORY AND MONUMENTS OF EVERY ITALIAN REGION "PLAY THEIR PART" IN THE KITCHEN, BLENDING VISION AND FLAVOR IN A CREATIVE, INTENSELY EMOTIONAL EXPERIENCE THAT HIGHLIGHTS THE TASTE OF QUALITY.

ACCORDING TO THE STYLE AND THE *MISSION* OF THE "ACADEMIA BARILLA."

THE ACADEMIA BARILLA WAS FOUNDED IN PARMA IN 2004 WITH THE OBJECTIVE OF BEING AN INTERNATIONAL CENTER DEDICATED TO ITALIAN GASTRONOMIC CULTURE, WITH THE CAPABILITY OF PROVIDING TRAINING, SERVICES AND PRODUCTS THAT HAVE BEEN SELECTED WITH GREAT CARE FROM THE ITALIAN GASTRONOMIC HERITAGE.

GIANLUIGI ZENTI
DIRECTOR ACADEMIA BARILLA

# ACADEMIA BARILLA

## AN AMBASSADOR OF ITALIAN
## GASTRONOMY AROUND THE WORLD

ACADEMIA BARILLA IS THE INTERNATIONAL CENTER DEDICATED TO THE DEVELOPMENT AND PROMOTION OF ITALIAN GASTRONOMIC CULTURE OFFERING TRAINING, SERVICES, AND RIGOROUSLY SELECTED PRODUCTS, WHICH HAVE BEEN CHOSEN AS PART OF THE ITALIAN GASTRONOMIC HERITAGE. ACADEMIA BARILLA WAS FOUNDED IN 2004 WITH ITS HEADQUARTERS IN PARMA, THE CAPITAL OF ITALIAN CUISINE FAMOUS WORLDWIDE FOR THE QUALITY OF ITS LOCAL PRODUCTS AND ITS PRESTIGIOUS FOOD INDUSTRY, AND IS THE IDEAL MEETING POINT BETWEEN THE LEADING REPRESENTATIVES OF FOOD AND WINE AND LOVERS OF THE ITALIAN FOOD CULTURE.

ACADEMIA BARILLA WAS SET UP WITH THE MISSION OF DEFENDING AND SAFEGUARDING ITALIAN FOOD PRODUCTS FROM FORGERIES AND IMPROPER USES OF ORIGINAL TRADE NAMES AND BRANDS, PROMOTING AND SPREADING THE UNDERSTANDING OF THESE PRODUCTS AND ITALIAN COOKING WITH SPECIAL EVENTS ORGANIZED IN PARTNERSHIP WITH LEADING INSTITUTIONS AND ENDORSERS, AS WELL AS DEVELOPING AND SUPPORTING ITALIAN GASTRONOMY BY INVESTING IN THE RESTAURANT INDUSTRY AND THE IMPLEMENTATION OF SPECIAL SERVICES FOR ITS OPERATORS.

THE HEADQUARTERS OF ACADEMIA BARILLA ARE LOCATED IN THE OLD BARILLA PASTA-MAKING FACTORY AREA, RE-DESIGNED BY RENZO PIANO, AND UNITES THE SAFEGUARDING OF TRADITION WITH THE UTMOST IN MODERN INNOVATION. IT IS EQUIPPED WITH AN AUDITORIUM, A SENSORY ANALYSIS LABORATORY, A HALL USED FOR PRACTICAL TRAINING, MULTIPURPOSE SPACES, AND AN EXTREMELY COMPREHENSIVE GASTRONOMIC LIBRARY.

ACADEMIA BARILLA ALSO HOLDS A RANGE OF TRAINING COURSES THAT IS VAST ENOUGH TO SATISFY A WHOLE ARRAY OF DIFFERENT NEEDS: FROM GASTRONOMIC EXPERTS TO SIMPLE FOOD LOVERS, FROM PROFESSIONAL CHEFS TO AMATEUR COOKS. THE TEACHING STAFF OF ACADEMIA BARILLA IS MADE UP OF A TEAM OF INTERNATIONALLY RENOWNED CHEFS AND WITH THE CONTRIBUTION OF LEADING VISITING CHEFS, INCLUDING MORENO CEDRONI, SCOTT CONANT, GIANCARLO PERBELLINI, CARLO CRACCO, ETTORE BOCCHIA, ALFONSO IACCARINO, VALENTINO MERCATILLII, GIADA DE LAURENTIIS, ANDREA ZANIN, IGINIO MASSARI, AND MANY OTHERS.

ACADEMIA BARILLA IS ALSO WELL-POSITIONED IN THE FIELD OF CORPORATE SERVICES, OFFERING SOLUTIONS FOR SALES MEETINGS, PRESS CONFERENCES, AND PRODUCT PRESENTATIONS, INCENTIVE PROGRAMS, MEETINGS AND CONVENTIONS, THEMED SEMINARS AND CONVENTIONS, CULINARY-RELATED MANAGEMENT TRAINING COURSES, TEAM BUILDING, AND MUCH MORE.

ACADEMIA BARILLA ALSO OFFERS GOURMET TOURS: PERSONALIZED FOOD AND WINE EXPERIENCES LASTING FROM ONE TO SEVEN DAYS. THE FOOD AND WINE TOURS ALLOW ONE TO EXPERIENCE THE BEST OF ITALIAN CULTURE AND GASTRONOMY: FROM THE TRADITIONAL ACETAIE (VINEGAR AGEING ESTABLISHMENTS) OF MODENA AND REGGIO EMILIA TO THE RENOWNED WINE AND SALAMI CELLARS, FROM OPERA CONCERTS TO SHOPPING IN STORES AND OUTLETS SELLING QUALITY ITALIAN PRODUCTS, FROM DINNERS ORGANIZED IN CASTLES AND HISTORIC HOMES TO TOTAL RELAXATION AND FITNESS IN OUR DAY SPAS.

ACADEMIA BARILLA DISTRIBUTES AND APPENDS ITS SIGNATURE TO A RANGE OF HIGH-QUALITY ITALIAN SPECIALTIES, SELECTED BY LEADING CHEFS AND CATERING EXPERTS, PRODUCED BY SMALL ITALIAN ARTISAN COMPANIES.

THE SELECTION INCLUDES MATURE CHEESES (PARMIGIANO REGGIANO PDO, PECORINO TOSCANO PDO, PECORINO GRAN CRU SARDO, AND PECORINO DOLCE), PROSCIUTTO DI PARMA, SALAME DI PARMA, PDO EXTRA-VIRGIN OLIVE OILS FROM A RANGE OF ORIGINS, ACETO BALSAMICO TRADIZIONALE DI MODENA, COMPOTES AND PRESERVES (GOURMET CHIANTI WINE JELLY; SPICY FIG COMPOTE; AND FRESH PEARS WITH BALSAMIC VINEGAR OF MODENA) AND SICILIAN SEA SALT FLAVORED WITH BLACK OLIVES OR WITH FRESH ORANGE ZEST.

ACADEMIA BARILLA WAS AWARDED WITH THE IMPRESA–CULTURA AWARD IN 2007 FOR THE PROMOTION OF ITALIAN GASTRONOMIC CULTURE AND CREATIVITY AROUND THE WORLD.

# Gaetano Alia

## LA LOCANDA DI ALIA RESTAURANT
### Castrovillari (Cosenza)

or Chef Gaetano Alia, co-owner of the restaurant *La Locanda di Alia* with his wife Daniela who is the head of the dining room with Biagio Durante, in Castrovillari, Cosentino, every-thing is expressed in an understandable language. "Every morning, among the market stalls, the vegetables speak to me, as do the fish and the meats", he says. "I just 'listen' to the products to select the best, and get ideas for a dish...."

This culinary talent knows the combination of raw materials to perfection, judging from the restaurant, which is one of the most famous not just in Calabria but in Southern Italy. Located a few minutes from the city center, in the beautiful scenery of the National Park of Pollino, the restaurant "is located in an old country house that is owned by our family. Over time we have renovated it and today it is a relais immersed in a lush and fragrant Mediterranean garden of about a hectare, covered with ancient local varieties of fruit trees."

The restaurant, founded in 1952, is among the oldest in Calabria. "It was just after the war when my father Antonio, a tailor, and my mother Lucia, a housewife, decided to open a modest restaurant to offer a simple cuisine with excellent raw materials and ingredients." In 1978 when his father died, Gaetano and his brother were forced – him in the kitchen flanked by his mother, and Pinuccio in the dining room – to manage the business which slowly became a restaurant. "We began to understand, without changing the original philosophy of the regional cuisine offered by mamma, that the future was in true, but restated flavors: emphasizing the quality of the raw materials, cooked simply and with basic combinations. We attempt to put in the pot not just the main product, but the idea behind it." And soon we became successful: "The first food guides began to come out showing interest in our work, declaring our restaurant one of the most beautiful areas in Southern Italy." Meanwhile the Alia brothers invested in the tavern, "which today is quite impressive."

Great dishes are born only of respect and knowledge, and so is the food offered by *La Locanda di Alia* for over thirty years. Gaetano's cuisine can be defined as a "regional creation." In Calabria, "you can still find traditional cooking and there is an attachment to the typical dishes: for this reason it makes sense to offer local dishes with a new twist." The quality of the raw materials naturally is fundamental. And for Gaetano "they should be found at most at five kilometers from the restaurant door." Finding excellent raw materials nearby is reflected in an elegant cuisine, even if it stems from basic products. As the 'New York Times' wrote about *Locanda da Alia*: *"*Here simplicity is the authentic choice for a refined Mediterranean cuisine*."*

Gaetano developed into a great chef when he was still very young: "I went to hotel school, but more than anything I attended my mother's school. She cooked marvelous, enjoyable and balanced dishes, a gift of nature, so much so that many people still have not forgotten her dishes. She never studied, but she knew the culture of life."

The book menu is in the spirit of the region. As appetizer, *guanciale di maiale nero* (black pork cheeks) of Calabria, tuna roe from Pizzo Calabro, nuts, and licorice oil. "These three flavors are the synthesis of the land of Calabria: in Italy I think there is no other region that better understands the boar of Calabria, our tuna fish is known as the 'pork of the sea' because nothing is thrown away, and the licorice which is found everywhere in Calabria, is the best in the world."

For first course, 'candles with a spicy sauce of Spilinga *'nduja* and shredded Crotone pecorino, aged in caves'. A traditional pasta of southern Italy, made by hand and topped with the delicious *"'nduja",* a typical Calabrian sausage with a spicy flavor. Second is 'cod with fresh onions marinated in sweet peppers, flavored with mint and wild fennel'. And finally the dessert: 'figs in chocolate', a reinvention of a traditional sweet. All the families of Calabria are used to gathering the figs, let them dry in the sun, stuff them with nuts or almonds and cover them with chocolate. "My idea was to take the dried figs, cut them in thin slices, top them with toasted almonds, walnuts, a little cinnamon, cloves and orange zest or candied citron, a typical product of Calabria. Then I serve them with a sauce of white chocolate and mint and a sprinkle of *diavolilli*, or colored sugar."

---

## Black Calabrese pork cheek,
dried and salted tuna roe from Pizzo Calabro,
walnuts, and licorice oil

P.**22**

---

## Candele pasta with *'nduja*

P.**24**

---

## Salt cod
with fresh green onions marinated
in sweet pepper, mint,
and wild fenne

P.**26**

---

## Chocolate figs

P.**27**

---

# Black Calabrese pork cheek, dried and salted tuna roe from Pizzo Calabro, walnuts, and licorice oil

### Ingredients for 4 people
Preparation time: 15' - Sauce: 2 days

3 1/2 oz (100 g) lamb's lettuce
1 1/2 oz (40 g) dried, salted tuna roe (bottarga) from Pizzo Calabro
4 walnuts, shelled and coarsely chopped
8 slices of black Calabrese pork cheek (bacon)

SAUCE
Generous 1 tablespoon (20 g) extra-virgin olive oil
Licorice stick

### Method

Two days before, coat the licorice stick with the extra-virgin olive oil and keep in a dark place. Clean the lamb's lettuce. Thinly shave the tuna roe using a mandolin.
Slice the pork cheek.

### Serving

Arrange the lamb's lettuce on a plate. Arrange the dried, salted tuna roe and 2 slices of pork cheek on top.
Dress with the flavored oil and sprinkle with the walnuts.

# Candele pasta with *'nduja*

## Ingredients for 4 people
Preparation time: 30'

2 small, round green bell peppers
1 1/3 lb (600 g) fresh San Marzano tomatoes
1 1/2 oz (40 g) Pecorino di Crotone
1 small bunch of parsley
4 tablespoons extra-virgin olive oil
1 clove garlic
1 basil leaf
Pinch salt
2 3/4 oz (80 g) *'nduja* (typical Calabrese salami)
14 oz (400 g) candele pasta

## Method

Wash the bell peppers and cut into little stripes lenghtwise.
Clean the tomatoes and cut a cross into the bottom. Blanch in boiling water for
2 minutes. Let cool in ice water and dice them.
Thinly shave the Pecorino and chop the parsley. Set aside.
To make the sauce, combine the oil, tomatoes, garlic, bell peppers, basil, and salt in an
aluminum frying pan.
Simmer for about 15 minutes. Add the *'nduja* and mix well. Cook for another 3 minutes.
Meanwhile, cook the pasta "al dente" in plenty of salted water. Drain and transfer to
the pan with the sauce. Toss well.

## Serving

Serve with a sprinkling of Pecorino di Crotone and parsley.

# Salt cod with fresh green onions marinated in sweet pepper, mint, and wild fennel

### Ingredients for 4 people
Preparation time: 25'

1 fillet of Norwegian salt cod, already soaked
4 fairly large fresh green onions, thinly sliced
Scant 1/3 cup (20 g) fennel, fronds only

SAUCE
Generous 3 tablespoons (50 g) extra-virgin olive oil
20 mint leaves and fennel stalks, thinly sliced
2 tablespoons (30 g) sweet chile powder
1/4 teaspoon (2 g) wild fennel seeds

### Method

Steam the salt cod with the green onions and fennel fronds for 7 minutes.
Break up the fish into pieces.
Mix all the ingredients for the sauce in a bowl. Add the salt cod and set aside for at least 2 hours before serving.

# Chocolate figs

### Ingredients for 4 people
Preparation time: 25'

Generous 3 tablespoons (50 g) milk
1 sprig of fresh mint
5 oz (150 g) white chocolate
12 almond-stuffed dried figs
1 teaspoon anisette

8 walnuts
10 toasted almonds
Ground cinnamon and cloves
Handful of colored sugar sprinkles
Zest of 1 orange, for serving

### Method

Heat the milk with the mint in a small saucepan. Let infuse for 10-15 minutes.
Add the chocolate, broken up into pieces, and mix until it has melted completely.
Cut the figs into slices.

### Serving

Cover the plate with the hot chocolate. Arrange the figs on top. Sprinkle with the
cinnamon and cloves. Finish by sprinkling with the sugar sprinkles.
Garnish with a grating of orange zest.

# Manolo Allochis

## IL VIGNETO RESTAURANT
### fraz. Ravinali, Roddi (Cuneo)

nstead of going out for pizza with friends or a night at the disco, while attending hotel school, Manolo Allochis, the talented chef at *Il Vigneto* in Ravinali in the heart of Piedmont's Langhe, used all the money he earned in the summers and winters to eat in the best restaurants. He would travel a hundred to a hundred and fifty kilometers, just to get a table. "My parents thought it was a waste of money and there were frequent arguments", he says. "They came from another world - they were not artistic, both mom and dad worked in the health industry - they didn't understand what drew me to it." Still, it was a great investment for the future.

He has always had a passion for cooking: "Right after the eighth grade I went to a restaurant close to home to wash dishes. To become a chef, I believe one should go through all the stages first: to be able to direct others, you should do the job yourself, first..." After three years of studies and passing the qualifying examination he went to work for various restaurants and also served some internships between seasons, such as one internship in Florence's *Enoteca Pinchiorri*, "where I even paid in order to work with them", and a series of courses at the Higher Institute of Culinary Arts, Etoile of Sottomarina in Chioggia. He started to get steady work in hotels and restaurants, first in Val d'Aosta, Liguria and then later in Lyon, France, under Jean -Paul Lacombe, the second chef of the city under chef Bocuse. Finally, he arrived at a restaurant in the Langhe with a Michelin star where he worked for five years: "My dream was exactly to work there and become a chef. Once my goal was fulfilled, I had another dream to: to open a restaurant of my own..."

And so it started. On a cold evening in January 2005, he came across the restaurant *Il Vigneto*, where he knew the owner. It was love at first sight: "It was dark and snowing, but I really liked the old place…" He had the insight to see the potential that the *Genius Loci* could offer. He took some time and in April decided to take over the local, offering his brother Rossano, who was working on a private yacht as hotel manager, the opportunity to manage it with him. In record time they renovated it into its original style and officially opened in September, keeping the same name.

*Il Vigneto* is a short walk from Alba, the delightful walled capital of the famous white truffle. It is an old farmhouse surrounded by a unique landscape of peace and quiet. A staff of young men runs the restaurant: "We are the oldest. I am 36 years old and my brother Rossano, wine steward and manager of the dining room, is 38." It is a good team: "The kitchen works like a clock: the assistant chef is second in command. A second in itself is nothing, but seconds add up to minutes, that is the chef-de-partie and minutes to an hour, that is the chef."

Manolo keeps things lively, "A kitchen that has fun, creating dishes that, while remaining tied to tradition, are very stimulating." If on the one hand his cooking is nicely bound to traditional dishes, "because people who come to the Langhe, come here to experience wine and food", on the other hand it tries not to overwhelm the uniqueness of the taste, "looking for pairings that may be rather unique, without making blunders." In short, a kitchen inspired by this generous land is a veritable mine of flavors, but make sure to revisit, personalize and not lose the relationship with tradition.

In the menu chosen for the book, the appetizer is "veal with tuna sauce… a new generation recipe that presents a new way of understanding and following tradition: although it looks like the traditional dish, it is not made of one piece of meat, but rather a pocket is made in a veal fillet and filled with a marinated tuna." Next is potato gnocchi, a first course characteristic of Cuneo, prepared with Alta Langa potatoes "I make them as big as ping pong balls, then I put in a quail egg inside and toss them in a pan with butter and white truffles, one of our regional products." Second course is a "*Fassone* pillow typical of *Piedmont*, veal braised in *Barolo* wine, combined with the sweet part of Piedmont-style *Fritto Misto* (mixed fried vegetables). This also contains pieces of meat, fish and vegetables: amaretto, semolina and apples." And, for dessert, a "hazelnut mousse, which uses our Piedmonts' chocolate and *Tonda Gentile* delle Langhe hazelnuts" a gourmand and worthy seal of a beautiful friendship with the land.

## Veal with tuna
for the new generation
P.32

## Alta Langa potato gnocchi
filled with runny quail's egg
and served with butter
and white Alba truffle
P.34

## Fassone cheeks
braised in Barolo wine
with sweet fried morsels
P.36

## Gianduja mousse
with Langhe hazelnuts
P.38

# Veal with tuna for the new generation

### Ingredients for 4 people
Preparation time: 2 h 30' – Marinating: 2 h

14 oz (400 g) fresh tuna fillet
1 1/3 lb (600 g) lean veal
Extra-virgin olive oil, for sauteing

#### TUNA MARINADE
2/3 cup (100 g) coarse sea salt
1/3 cup (50 g) table sea salt
Scant 3 tablespoons (40 g) brown sugar
Zest of 1 lemon
Zest of 1 organic orange
3/4 oz (20 g) parsley leaves
5 juniper berries
5 cloves
4 lemongrass leaves
Small bunch of herbs (such as dill, rosemary, thyme, sage, marjoram, and tarragon)

#### TUNA SAUCE
2 fresh egg yolks
Generous 3/4 cup (200 ml) extra-virgin olive oil
1 teaspoon (5 ml) lemon juice
1 hard-cooked egg yolk
2 salt-cured anchovy fillets
1 tablespoon (15 g) salt-cured capers
1/4 cup (40 g) tuna in oil
Salt and pepper

#### GARNISH
10 oz (300 g) mixed salad greens
4 quail's eggs, hard-boiled
4 capers
1/4 cup (50 g) mullet roe

## Method

Trim the tuna to obtain a cylinder-shaped fillet that is about 7 inches (18 cm) long with a diameter of approximately 1 1/2 inches (4 cm).

Place all the marinade ingredients in a food processor and blend for about 1 minute. Spread a layer of marinade to make one square on a sheet of parchment that is doubled up. Arrange the tuna on top and wrap it in the paper. Chill for 2 hours.

By doing this, the water that comes out of the tuna is absorbed by the paper and it is marinated dry.

Meanwhile, prepare a mayonnaise by emulsifying the egg yolks with the oil drizzled in very slowly and whisking energetically; add the lemon juice a little at a time. Separately chop the hard-cooked egg yolk, anchovies, capers (which have been rinsed well in cold water), and tuna in oil, drained and oil discarded. Add the chopped mixture to the mayonnaise and season with salt and pepper.

Wash the tuna fillet well under cold running water and dry with kitchen paper.

Cut a 1-inch (3-cm) thick slice from the widest side of the lean veal. Trim to make an evenly sized 8-inch (20 cm) log. Use a knife to cut a slit inside the veal, making a pocket. Insert the tuna fillet into the meat and secure tightly with kitchen string. Sauté in a non-stick frying pan, let rest and then remove the string.

Cut four slices of cold veal with tuna crosswise about 3/4-inch (2-cm) thick. Arrange a slice in the center of a plate and garnish with a little mixed greens, a caper, hard-boiled quail's egg, sliced in half, and a little roe. Finish the dish with a quenelle of tuna sauce in front of the veal with tuna.

# Alta Langa potato gnocchi filled with runny quail's egg and served with butter and white Alba truffle

## Ingredients for 4 people
Preparation time: 45'

FILLING
16 quail's eggs

GNOCCHI
2.5 lb (1.2 kg) potatoes from Alta Langa
2 cups (300 g) all-purpose flour
2 whole eggs
2 tablespoons (30 g) butter, softened
1/3 cup (40 g) grated Parmesan
Salt
Nutmeg

SERVING
2 tablespoons (50 g) butter
2 tablespoons (50 g) beef stock
2 oz (60 g) white Alba truffle (*Tuber Magnatum Pico*)

## Method

FILLING
Break the quail's eggs and beat well. Pour the beaten eggs into the plastic trays they came in (so that they form half-spheres of egg). Freeze for a couple of hours.

GNOCCHI
Boil the potatoes in their skins in plenty of salted water. Peel and mash them with a potato masher or fork on a wooden surface, mixing them with the remaining ingredients to make the gnocchi.
Divide the mixture into shapes that are slightly smaller than ping pong balls. Insert half a ball of frozen egg in each gnocco and smooth over with the mixture so that the egg isn't on the outside.
Cook the gnocchi in plenty of salted water until they rise to the surface. Wait a couple of minutes before draining them.

## Serving

Toss the gnocchi in the pan with the butter and beef stock.
Serve four gnocchi per portion, keeping them soft with some of the cooking juices.
Finish the dish by grating with plenty of white truffle.

# Fassone cheeks braised in Barolo wine with sweet fried morsels

**Ingredients for 4 people**
Preparation time: 1 h – Cooking time: 2 h – Marinating: 24 h

4 Piedmontese veal cheeks

MARINADE
3 1/2 oz (100 g) carrots
3 1/2 oz (100 g) celery
3 1/2 oz (100 g) onions
5 cloves
1 teaspoon (5 g) juniper
cinnamon stick
1 small bunch of herbs, consisting of bay leaves, rosemary, and sage
2 quarts (2 liters) Barolo wine

BATTER
2/3 cup (100 g) flour
3 tablespoons (45 g) water
2 tablespoons (45 g) Maraschino
2 egg yolks
2 teaspoons (10 g) melted butter

2 teaspoons (10 g) sugar
Pinch of brewer's yeast for desserts
Vanilla

SWEET FRIED MORSELS
8 dry amaretti cookies
1 2/3 cups (250 g) all-purpose flour
6 whole eggs
4 cups (500 g) breadcrumbs
4 Golden Delicious apples

SEMOLINA
Generous 2 3/4 cups (700 g) milk
1/2 cup (100 g) sugar
Generous 1 tablespoon (20 g) salt
2/3 cup (100 g) semolina
1 egg yolk

## Method

Coarsely chop the marinade vegetables. Arrange the veal cheeks in a large container and add the marinade spices, herbs, and vegetables. Cover with the wine and let infuse for at least 24 hours.

### BATTER

Place all the ingredients in a food processor and blend until smooth. Let rest in the refrigerator.

Meanwhile, dip the amaretti first in the flour and then in the egg. So sandwich them together, then dip in egg, then breadcrumbs, then egg, then breadcrumbs. Reserve any leftover flour, egg, and breadcrumb for dipping the semolina cubes.

### SEMOLINA

Bring the milk to a boil with the sugar and salt. Sift in the flour and beat with a handheld blender to make sure that no lumps form. Let simmer for a couple of minutes, remove from the heat, and beat in the egg yolk. Pour the semolina in a deep baking pan and spread the mixture out to about 1-inch (3-cm) thick. Let cool. Once it has cooled, cut into small cubes. Dip them into the flour, egg, and breadcrumbs. Reserve any leftover flour, egg, and breadcrumb for battering the apples.

### CHEEKS

Drain the meat from the marinade and dry it well. Place the cheeks in a saucepan with a little oil over medium heat and sear. Add all the ingredients needed for cooking, reserving some stock.

As soon as the wine comes to a boil, ignite it with a match so that the alcohol in the wine does not remain during cooking. Continue cooking over low heat for a couple of hours, adding stock if needed. Blend the cooking juices in a food processor with the herbs and vegetables to obtain a smooth sauce.

### SWEET FRIED MORSELS

Remove the core and peel from the apples and cut them into ¾-inch (2-cm) thick slices. Dip the apples in the batter and deep fry them. Also fry the amaretti and semolina.

## Serving

Arrange the cheek in the center of the plate, cover with the sauce, and serve with a couple of pieces of the fried apple, amaretto, and semolina.
Garnish with the bunch of the same herbs (fresh) used for cooking.

# Gianduja mousse with Langhe hazelnuts

## Ingredients for 4 people
Preparation time: 30' – Cooking time: 30' – Resting: 6 h

### TORTE
Generous 1/4 cup (70 g) egg whites
Generous 1 tablespoon (20 g) sugar
Generous 1/3 cup (40 g) toasted ground
Langhe hazelnuts
Generous 1/3 cup (40 g) toasted ground
almonds
Scant 1/4 cup (40 g) chopped semisweet
chocolate

### MOUSSE
1 cup (250 g) milk
1 cup (250 g) cream
Scant 1/2 cup (100 g) Langhe hazelnut paste
2/3 cup (150 g) egg yolks
1 teaspoon (5 g) potato starch
3 1/4 cups (800 g) chocolate gianduja
3 1/4 cups (800 g) lightly whipped cream
1/2 cup (100 g) sugar

### DECORATION
4 white chocolate and gianduja cigarette
Custard, for serving
4 physalis, for garnish

## Method

### TORTE
Whip the egg whites with the sugar until stiff peaks. Meanwhile, sift together all the remaining ingredients and gradually fold them into the beaten whites. Spoon into the individual cylindrical silicon molds. Bake in the oven at 275°F (140°C/gas mark 1) for about 30 minutes.

### MOUSSE
Boil the milk, cream, sugar and hazelnut paste. Slowly beat in the egg yolks and starch. Cook in the top of a double boiler for a couple of minutes without letting mixture come to a boil. Add the chocolate gianduja and let all the chocolate melt. Let cool slightly. Fold in the whipped cream to lighten. Let rest in the refrigerator for at least 6 hours.

## Serving

Position the torte in the center of the plate. Spread with a thin layer of chocolate and arrange a quenelle of gianduja mousse on top. Decorate the plate with a little custard, a physalis, and a white chocolate and gianduja cigarette.

# Michele Biagiola

## ENOTECA LE CASE RESTAURANT
### Mozzavinci (Macerata)

This is a thoughtful, but not rhetorical cuisine, tied to the past but fragrant with new emotions. This is the cuisine of Michele Biagiola, chef of the *Enoteca Le Case* in Mozzavinci, a small area of Macerata. "My cuisine is thoughtful, without necessarily resorting to the science of culinary art that is so used today", he explains. "Learning a new technique does not excite me for example as much as when I rework a dish from my land, made using basic techniques." He understands his land as a patrimony of tradition. "I was born in Macerata and my cooking is related to all the flavors that I can summon in my mind, because I know them so well from when I was a child."

Inaugurated in 2005, the *Enoteca* is nestled in the charming landscape of the Marche hills. Already granted a Michelin star, the restaurant has become one of the best in the Marche. "I take credit for achievements regarding my cuisine, but there is an entire organization, without which I could not have achieved this: Mrs. Elvia Pelagalli and her husband Marcello Giosuè, who are the entrepreneurial spirit, and their daughter Francesca, the true soul of the complex as a whole, managing the dining room beautifully with enthusiasm and determination. And there is second chef Giacomo Messi, the people who work with me every day, contributing their energy and their passion, and all the people that over the years with their work and contributions have helped the growth and success of the restaurant." Sometimes he feels like he is learning from his staff: "I consult with them and if a new dish does not pass the test of every one, then I may well decide not to include it on the menu."

After graduating from the *istituto alberghiero* (Hotel School), Michele, intrigued and interested in the opportunity to learn and discover new raw materials, gained some "important experience from Vincenzo Cammerucci in the *Lido* di Cesenatico restaurant, from Marc Veyrat at Megève in Haute-Savoie, and David Zuddas at the Digion in Burgundy." He continues with internships even now, that he has been heading the *Le Case* kitchen for over ten years.

When the *Enoteca* was first opened, Michele was already working in the restaurant which offered both traditional as well as innovative dishes, but always tied to the region. "At a certain point the management decided to separate the two types of restaurants in order not to mix the ambient and the clientele." Today, the clients of the *Enoteca* want a traditional but creative cuisine, "prepared using the same high quality raw materials: organic vegetables with a special focus on herbs growing naturally and ingredients of the past." Michele's credo is to "be guided by the seasons, combining culture, personal experience and love for the products of our land." With a Pythagorean spirit: "Francesca and I have the same taste, preferring to make vegetarian dishes: occasionally you can overdo it with meats and fish, a type of lust at the table... Over time we have designed a vegetarian menu that we prepare with the same – if not more – care as others."

The menu in this book is the happy success of a rethought tradition. The 'sandy seafood salad seasoned ancient style' – the appetizer – "born of a memory of the seafood salad with pickles that I ate as a child, sold from small kiosks along the beach." Prepared in the traditional form, and presented on a bed of edible 'sand' made of semolina, tapioca flour and wheat, oil and kelp. "It represents our sandy bed, but it is also our revenge for all those times that we could not enjoy a plate of fish because of the sand between the teeth..."

In the 'spaghetti with broth between Porto Recanati and San Benedetto', the chef has merged the recipe for *brodetto di pesce* (fish broth) from these two ports on the Marche coast, typical seaside dishes. "In Porto Recanati this is made with *zafferanella*, a sort of wild saffron, and with tomatoes, while in San Benedetto del Tronto it's made with green tomatoes and peppers." For the second course we have 'stuffed pigeon as served by Ermete', an historic Macerata shopkeeper who died in 1983. The full flavor of the filling which features *ciaùscolo* (traditional soft salami of Macerata), eggs and local flavors such as winter savory, "is added the acidity of wild strawberries and the ferrous flavor of wild spinach."

And for dessert we have the 'apple tart of soft pink apples', where the fruit, an ancient variety of Marche apple, is caramelized and topped with pastry cream, crystals of vanilla-flavored crushed ice and cinnamon, and crumbled vanilla shortbread.

# Sandy seafood salad
with old-fashioned dressing

P.44

# Spaghetti
with Porto Recanati and San Benedetto chowder

P.46

# *Pistacoppu* with stuffing, stuffed pigeon
inspired by the recipe of Ermete,
a master shopkeeper in Macerata

P.48

# Upside-down Rosa gentile
apple tart

P.50

# Sandy seafood salad with old-fashioned dressing

## Ingredients for 4 people
Preparation time: 40'

### SAND
1 tablespoon (15 g) semolina
1 tablespoon (15 g) durum wheat flour
1 tablespoon (15 g) tapioca starch
2 teaspoons (10 g) dried seaweed, finely chopped
1 tablespoon (15 g) extra-virgin olive oil

### PICKLED VEGETABLES
1 quart (1 liter) white wine vinegar
1/4 cup (50 g) sugar
3 tablespoons (50 ml) extra-virgin olive oil
Scant 3 tablespoons (40 g) salt
1/3 oz (10 g) asparagus, washed and cut into short lengths
1/3 oz (10 g) red bell peppers, washed and diced small
1/3 oz (10 g) yellow bell peppers, washed and diced small
1/2 oz (15 g) shallot, washed and cut into wedges
1/3 oz (10 g) eggplant peel, washed and diced
1/2 oz (15 g) green beans, washed and cut in half lengthwise

### FISH
4 mantis shrimp, or other large shrimp
4 medium scampi
8 oz (250 g) small-medium cuttlefish, cleaned

### TO SERVE
Small pieces of seaweed
Extra-virgin olive oil
1/4 oz (2 g) chopped parsley

## Method

### SAND
Mix together all the ingredients to make a smooth mixture.
Wrap it in a piece of parchment paper and freeze to -0.4°F (-18°C).
Break up the frozen mixture, scraping it with the blade of a knife. Bake in the oven at 350°F (180°C/gas mark 4) for 12 minutes.

### PICKLED VEGETABLES
Bring the vinegar, sugar, oil, and salt to a boil in a saucepan. Cook each vegetable separately, keeping them crunchy.
Remove each vegetable with a slotted spoon and let cool in ice water. Drain and dry with a cloth.

### FISH
Steam the mantis shrimp and scampi for 3-4 minutes. Shell them and set the flesh aside. Boil the cuttlefish for 10 minutes and cut into strips.

## Serving

Mix together the fish, pickled vegetables, parsley, the seaweed, oil, and crispy sand.

# Spaghetti with Porto Recanati and San Benedetto chowder

**Ingredients for 4 people**
Preparation time: 1 h 30'

1/2 oz (15 g) yellow bell peppers, blanched, peeled and diced small
1/2 oz (15 g) red bell peppers, blanched, peeled, and diced small
5 1/2 oz (160 g) green tomatoes, peeled, seeded, and diced
5 1/2 oz (160 g) red tomatoes, peeled, seeded, and diced
40 mussels, cleaned
3 1/2 oz (100 g) cuttlefish, cleaned and diced
3 1/2 oz (100 g) green onions, cleaned and chopped
2 teaspoons (10 g) garlic, chopped (peeled and green central part removed)
2 dried chile peppers

4 sprigs of parsley, washed
Generous 3 tablespoons (50 g) extra-virgin olive oil for the sauce
Salt to taste
4 oz (120 g) weever fish (or other chowder-appropriate fish), filleted, reserving bones
25 wild saffron strands
4 mantis shrimp, or other large shrimp
4 medium scampi
9 3/4 oz (280 g) spaghetti
2 fresh basil leaves
3/4 oz (20 g) fresh marjoram, washed
1 tablespoon (15 g) extra-virgin olive oil, for finishing

## Method

Open the mussels, and remove the beards that grow between the half-shells. Scrape the mussels well to remove any barnacles and calcium deposits. Wash well, changing the water several times. Cook the mussels in a little water in a saucepan, covered, over the heat. As soon as the mussels open, remove from the heat and remove the half-shells.

Cook the cuttlefish, chopped onion, garlic, chile peppers, parsley, and the diced tomatoes and bell peppers in the oil in a large saucepan over medium heat for about 6-7 minutes. Season with salt and pour in 3 cups (750 ml) of cold water. Add the weever fish bones and bring to a boil.

Remove the bones and add the mussels, saffron strands, mantis shrimp, scampi, and weever fish fillets at the same time. Cook for another 2-3 minutes.

Remove and set aside all the fish, apart from the cuttlefish.

Cook the spaghetti in plenty of salted boiling water until three-quarters cooked. Drain and transfer to the chowder and cook for another 3-4 minutes. Add the reserved fish at the end, as well as the basil, marjoram leaves. Drizzle with oil to finish.

# *Pistacoppu* with stuffing, stuffed pigeon inspired by the recipe of Ermete, a master shopkeeper in Macerata

### Ingredients for 4 people
Preparation time: 45'

4 pigeons

SAUCE
1 green onion
1 carrot
2 tablespoons (30 g) extra-virgin olive oil
1 quart cold water
2 sprigs of mountain savory, or regular savory
12 wild strawberries
Cooking juices of the cooked pigeon

ROASTED STUFFED PIGEON
Breasts, legs, wings, hearts, and livers of the pigeons
1 teaspoon (5 g) prosciutto
1/4 cup (60 g) extra-virgin olive oil

Scant 1/2 cup (100 ml) vino cotto
2 teaspoons (10 g) ciauscolo salami, or other salami
8 sprigs of mountain savory or regular savory
1 egg
Pinch of ground nutmeg
16 thin slices of pork cheeks
Salt to taste

TO SERVE
3 1/2 oz (100 g) wild spinach, blanched in plenty of salted water for 1 minute
2teaspoons (10 g) extra-virgin olive oil
12 wild strawberries
Salt to taste

## Method

SAUCE
Use a sharp knife to bone the pigeons, splitting up the legs, breasts, and wings; set aside. Brown the green onion, carrot, and the pigeon bones and cavities in the oil in a saucepan over medium heat. Turn up the heat and cook over high heat for about 7–8 minutes. Pour in cold water and the sprigs of savory. Bring to a boil, reducing it all to make a thick sauce. Add the wild strawberries. Strain through a fine-mesh sieve and reserve the liquid (you will combine it later with the pigeon cooking juices).

PIGEONS
Cook the livers, hearts, and prosciutto in the oil over high heat for 2 minutes. Add the vino cotto and let it evaporate. Add the ciauscolo, savory leaves, and egg. Cook for 1 minute. Add the nutmeg and let cool. Chop them up finely with a knife. Stuff the legs with the filling, wrapping them with the slices of pork cheek. Bake in the oven at 350°F (180°C/gas mark 4) for about 12 minutes. Brown the pigeon wings in oil in a separate frying pan. Add the breasts and cook for another 2 minutes. Season with salt. Bake in the oven at 350°F (180°C/gas mark 4) for 4 minutes.

## Serving

Arrange the wild spinach on the bottom of the plate and dress with oil and salt. Top with the various pieces of pigeon, fresh strawberries, and the natural cooking juices combined with the pigeon sauce.

# Upside-down Rosa gentile apple tart

## Ingredients for 4 people
Preparation time: 2 h - Freezing granita: 2 h

### SHORTCRUST PASTRY
2 3/4 cups (400 g) flour
1 egg yolk
1/4 cup (50 g) sugar
1/2 cup (75 g) all-purpose flour
Scant 2 tablespoons (25 g) butter

### CARAMELIZED APPLES
Scant 1/3 cup (70 ml) water
3/4 cup (150 g) sugar
2 tablespoons (30 g) butter
1 3/4 lb (800 g) Rosa gentile apples,
peeled and diced
1/2 teaspoon (3 g) powdered agar agar

### VANILLA AND CINNAMON GRANITA
Generous 1 tablespoon (18 g) sugar
Generous 3 tablespoons (50 ml) water
1/5 cinnamon stick
1/5 vanilla pod

### PASTRY CREAM
Scant 1/2 cup (100 ml) milk
1 teaspoon (5 g) lemon zest
1 egg yolk
Scant 1/2 cup (70 g) all-purpose flour
Scant 2 tablespoons (25 g) sugar

## Method

### CRUMBLED SHORTCRUST PASTRY
Mix the flours, eggs, butter and sugar together until crumbly. Bake at 350°F (170°C) for about 30 minutes.

### CARAMELIZED APPLES
Warm the water and sugar in a small saucepan over medium heat to 275°F (135°C). Turn off the heat, add the butter and let it melt. Add the apples and return to the stovetop over low heat for 2-3 minutes, mixing constantly. Remove from the heat and finish with the agar agar, mixing it well. Divide the apples, placing them in 4 molds of the desired size. Let cool in the refrigerator for at least 30 minutes.

### GRANITA
Mix the sugar and water in a small saucepan. Bring to a boil and add the cinnamon and vanilla. Remove from the heat, cover, and let cool to room temperature. Strain through a fine-mesh sieve and pour the liquid into a container to about 1/3-inch (1-cm) thick. Freeze to -0.4°F (-18°C). Break it up into small pieces just before serving.

### PASTRY CREAM
Bring the milk to a boil with the lemon zest. Meanwhile, beat the egg yolk with the flour and sugar. Slowly whisk the boiling milk into the egg mixture. Return to the pan in which the milk was boiled and cook cream gently to 180°F (82°C) over low heat, whisking constantly, until it has thickened. Let cool to 37.5°F (+3°C).

## Serving

Turn the apples out in the center of the plate. Serve with the cream, granita, and the crumbled pastry.

# Beppe (Giuseppe) Bologna

## TRATTORIA I BOLOGNA
### Rocchetta Tanaro (Asti)

f you could take a picture of the old Piedmontese cuisine today, it would not have the appearance of a robust and austere lady, who aged gracefully, but the friendly and genuine face of young chef Beppe Bologna, owner, with his restaurant family of *I Bologna* in Rocchetta Tanaro, in the province of Asti. He would not only wear "fall" clothing in line with the regional wine and food of the season, with hearty reds with the flavors of game and truffles. The tastes and aromas he embodies would last all year long creating a soft and sumptuous tapestry from the Alps to the rice fields. A true and proper paradise for lovers of good food.

"My country's life style moves me," he says. "Because we don't follow fashion. We like to eat and drink with friends and to keep things simple. My goal is to offer my guests a cuisine that will always leave a good memory." His is a generous spirit that does not miss a chance to give something to those who enter his dining room, whether it be a smile, a look, a flavor, an emotion, or a greeting from the heart.

The restaurant, which is housed in an old farmhouse in the Asti countryside, was completely renovated a couple of years ago, is actually a long family tradition. "My grandmother Caterina had a restaurant and passed it on to her son Carlo, my dad. He in turn handed it down to me. I took over in 1992, but my parents still work there. My mother Mariucca is in the kitchen with me and takes care of fresh pasta, my father and my wife Cristina are in the dining room."

Beppe serves excellent local cuisine accompanied by first-class wines, especially *Barbera* from the local winery "Braida", which belongs to his family. "My cuisine is typical of the Piedmont region, particularly the making of fresh pasta." Beppe has a gentle but strong touch typical of the Po Valley, as far as local dishes. "I always lighten the recipes, because they are all a bit 'heavy' and I do not want my guests to rise up from the table with an 'over eaten' feeling ..."

In some cases, he changes or removes some ingredients from a traditional dish to carry them out with more innovative techniques. "I trust my taste when I make these changes, but I also look to my mother who worked with my grandmother, and who 'stole' the secrets of the old Piedmontese cuisine. My grandmother, in turn, said they had been 'stolen' from a cook in the castle …"

A native of Rocchetta Tanaro, with just over a thousand inhabitants, Beppe was one of the last children born in the house, although you might say he was born directly in the kitchen. Always intrigued by the stove, when it was time to choose between accounting and hotel school, he had no doubt and chose the passion of his grandmother and mother. "After graduation, I started my internship. I had seven years of experience working in large restaurants, both in my region and then in other regions, such as the *San Domenico* in Imola, and abroad. Then, to be honest, I was confronted by my father who had bought this place… I wanted to continue to run loose for a while…" So he came back and, assisted by his mother, "who is the pillar of the family, the one with the fine details, the feminine touch", he created his own restaurant.

Beppe has chosen to create a menu that is in harmony with this land and its old world charm, in many ways still untouched. The appetizer is a classic from Asti (in the Piedmont region): raw meat, served in a salad with celery and Parmesan cheese cut into very thin slices. As a first course, he chose the typical Piedmontese *agnolotti*, called *del plin* for the pinch that is given when preparing the dough: candy shaped *ravioli* with a filling of veal, pork and rabbit, dressed with butter, sage and Parmesan (representative of the traditional cuisine of Monferrato, including the *tajarin* or thin egg noodles that are made strictly by hand, with basil cream). The second course is what we call a 'horse jowl' "even though at this time I am serving my guests three other local dishes: veal tripe stew with potatoes, local roasted rabbit with thyme and crispy pork with glazed onions." Last but not least, is the traditional *bunèt* Asti style, once popular in Monferrato. An ancestor of today's pudding, it owes its name to the molded copper tin in the form of a cap in which it is boiled. A delicious sweet and a worthy tribute to the Piedmont region, which proves this pastry is a reciprocated love.

# Raw veal salad

## Ingredients for 4 people
Preparation time: 20'

14 oz (400 g) lean veal (fillet)
2 tablespoons (30 ml) extra-virgin olive oil
Salt and pepper to taste
1 lemon
2 celery hearts
3 1/2 oz (100 g) Parmesan (preferably Parmigiano Reggiano)

## Method

Prepare the veal: lean the veal, removing any nerves and connective tissues using a sharp knife. Finely chop it with a knife, then season it with the oil, salt, pepper, and lemon juice.
Clean the celery, only keeping the hearts. Wash and cut them finely.

## Serving

Arrange the meat on the plate. Garnish with 2 hearts from 2 heads of celery and shaved Parmesan.

# Agnolotti

Ingredients for 4 people
Preparation time: 45' – Resting time: 20'

FILLING
7 oz (200 g) roasted veal
7 oz (200 g) pork
1 onion
1 clove red garlic
1 carrot
1 celery stalk
Extra-virgin olive oil
Rosemary
Generous 1/3 cup (100 ml) red wine
3 1/2 oz (100 g) sausage
7 oz (200 g) rabbit (loin meat, if possible)

3 1/2 oz (100 g) spinach
2 tablespoons Parmesan
Nutmeg
4 eggs
Salt and pepper

PASTA
1 1/3 cups (200 g) flour
2 whole eggs
2 tablespoons (30 ml) water
Melted butter, for serving
Fresh sage, for serving
Grated Parmesan cheese, for serving

## Method

FILLING
Cut up the veal, pork, and vegetables into small pieces.
Sauté it all in a saucepan in the oil with the rosemary. Add
the wine and let it evaporate. Add the sausage and cook
for 30 minutes.
In a separate pan, sauté the rabbit over medium heat.
When all the meat is well cooked, mince it using a meat
grinder. Add the boiled and chopped spinach, Parmesan,
and nutmeg and mix it all with the eggs. Season with salt
and pepper to taste.

PASTA
Sift the flour onto a wooden surface and shape into a
mound. Make a well in the center. Pour the eggs with the
water into the hollow and knead until the dough is smooth
and even. Let rest for 20 minutes. Roll out a very thin
sheet of pasta using a pasta machine.
Arrange small mounds of filling at 1/3 inch (1 cm) intervals
about 1/3 inch from the edge of the pasta.
Fold the edge of the pasta over the filling, sealing it by
pressing down slightly with your finger.
Use a ravioli cutter to cut the row of agnolotti and seal
them one at a time pressing down slightly with your fingers
(pinching them). Separate the agnolotti using the ravioli
cutter.
Cook the agnolotti in plenty of salted water for 3-4
minutes. Drain, then and serve with melted butter, sage,
and Parmesan cheese. Serve hot.

# Horse cheeks braised in red wine

### Ingredients for 4 people
Preparation time: 3 h

1 tablespoon (20 g) extra-virgin olive oil
5 or 6 horse cheeks
Salt and pepper to taste
2 cloves garlic
3 bay leaves
750 ml bottle of red wine
Flour, as much as needed
Water, as needed

### Method
Place a saucepan over medium heat. Add the oil and sauté the cheeks. Season with salt and pepper.
After a few minutes, add the garlic and bay leaves and sauté for 1 minute.
Pour in the red wine and let it evaporate.
Sprinkle with a little flour and add water to cover. Cover with a lid and simmer over low heat for 3 hours. If necessary, add more water during the cooking time.

## Bunèt

### Ingredients for 4 people
Preparation time: 40'

5 whole eggs
Generous 1/2 cup (120 g) sugar
2 tablespoons (30 g) cocoa
1 2/3 cups (400 g) milk
3 tablespoons (50 g) light cream
5 Mombaruzzo amaretti cookies, crumbled
Rum

### Method

Beat the eggs, sugar, and cocoa together in a bowl. Whisk in the milk, cream, and amaretti.
Prepare the caramel for the mold. Place the sugar in a copper pan over low heat. When the sugar melts and turns amber brown, pour it into a mold, followed by the amaretti mixture.
Place the mold in a roasting pan filled halfway with hot water and cook in a uncovered bain-marie at 285°F (140°C) for about 30 minutes.

# Francesco Bracali

## DA BRACALI RESTAURANT
### Massa Marittima (Grosseto)

Chef Francesco Bracali lacks neither imagination nor courage. Chef and co-owner, with his brother Luca, dining room manager of the *Da Bracali* restaurant in Ghirlanda, a small village in Massa Marittima, in the Tuscan Maremma. The structural complexity and daring combinations of his recipes are reminiscent of the unusual points of view from the splendid Piazza del Duomo in the center of Massa.

"My cuisine – he states – is quite creative: I put four or five ingredients in the same dish. It's not simple, but I think that the technique exclusively, and when used in the right amount, to a great degree gives a traditional dish new life, more appropriate for our times and our eating habits." Interpreting a dish "does not mean breaking contact with the region and with tradition, but to find ways to offer it in a way that is more elegant and original, without eradicating it." On the one hand his dishes reflect the origins of Maremma, on the other hand they have innovative aspects: "I love to experiment with new culinary pairings, combining flavors, textures, cooking methods. The end result may be a little complicated, but able to blend into a unique flavor with no need for too much explanation: everyone must understand he message of a great cook, like that of a great artist..."

The restaurant which from the outside looks like an English villa immersed in the thickly wooded hills of Grosseto, was started by Francesco's parents when he was just a child. At the time it was the classic country trattoria with bar that sold tobacco products. The first step towards haute cuisine coincided with the first remodeling of the restaurant (the second occurred in 2004) in 1997 when Francesco and his brother took over management of the restaurant. "Our parents, despite the many difficulties, have always supported us and were justifiably proud when we received a Michelin star in 1999."

Francesco is "one hundred per cent self-taught": no hotel school, no courses or internship in

Italy or abroad. "I've always been very involved in my parents' work, becoming absorbed is inevitable when the restauranti is a family affair..." In the beginning it was his mother who let him learn the basic of the craft and then gave him some recipes form the area. "Even as a boy, though, I knew that if I did this job I would do it in a more personal way..."

Francesco sees the dishes in his mind. In fact the menu in this book is born of intuition. The appetizer is a trio made of raw *chianina* beef with three sauces. "The *chianina* have a traditional way of cutting and dressing the beef, which is then served in three different ways: served on dry bread crumbs with chopped olives, accompanied by a sauce of chives; as dumplings, with a center of *brunoise* pears and dried tomatoes, served in a green sauce; and topped with dry mango powder and a roll of phyllo dough, flavored with ginger and accompanied by a classic mayonnaise."

The first course is rigatoni stuffed with *capocollo*, accompanied by a spelt sauce typical of Lucca. Pasta in typical Neapolitan shape, but dressed in Tuscan form. "The uniqueness of the dish is that when the rigatoni comes out of the oven, piping hot, it is spread over a thin layer of raw scallops with a drizzle of olive oil and licorice. The salty flavor of the sea goes very well with the filling, important for the pasta." The sauce is a spelt soup, the flagship of local cuisine, blended and then dressed with our extra virgin olive oil.

Second course is a chicken roasted in two separate occasions: one is a re-make of the classic roast chicken, typical Sunday lunch of Tuscan families. "The thigh is stuffed with the classic Tuscan herbs, I put it in a vacuum bag and I cook it all night. After this I put it under the *sala-mandra* a special device for browning foods. This gives a thigh that is still soft and juicy inside, but with a crunchy skin. Same goes for the breast, which I oil with *Cinta Senese* pork cheek and finally put it in the pan. Then from the chicken bones I prepare a double broth, which I use to make a puree of celeriac and an extra virgin olive oil."

For dessert, a Tuscan classic: *zuccotto*. In this case filled with a white chocolate mousse and raspberry jelly, and served with a dill sauce. "The *zuccotto* is a bit heavy in terms of calories, but dill, a classic grass in my area, helps to make it lighter and easier to digest."

# A new take on
Chianina beef carpaccio

P.**66**

# Rigatoni filled
with *capocollo*
and Lucchesia spelt sauce

P.**68**

# Roasted chicken
cooked in two ways

P.**72**

# White chocolate
and raspberry mousse zuccotto with dill sauce

P.**74**

## A new take on Chianina beef carpaccio

### Ingredients for 4 people
Preparation time: 1 h

12 oz (350 g) sirloin steak
4 tablespoons soy sauce
Salt and pepper, to taste
4 tablespoons extra-virgin
olive oil

GREEN SAUCE
4 oz (120 g) parsley
3 anchovy fillets
2 cloves garlic
1 tablespoon salt-cured
capers
Scant 1 cup (50 g) fresh
breadcrumbs
Generous 3 tablespoons
(50 g) vinegar
Scant 1/2 cup (100 g) extra-
virgin olive oil
Pepper to taste
2 hard-cooked egg yolks
Pinch of sugar

THREE TYPES
OF MAYONNAISE
•Classic
1 egg yolk
Pinch salt
1 tablespoon cider vinegar
Scant 1/2 cup (100 g) oil
•Chive
Classic + 2 chive stalks,
chopped
•Green
Classic + green sauce

GINGER-FLAVORED
PHYLLO PASTRY
8 phyllo pastry squares,
measuring
1 1/2-inches (4-cm) on each
side
Ginger-infused oil

FRIED BREAD WITH OLIVES
1 3/4 oz (50 g) bread
4 olives, chopped
1 clove garlic
1 bay leaf

TOMATO TARTARE
4 quenelles of tomato
tartare

TO SERVE
Herbs, such as chives,
Dried ground mangoes
2 teaspoons (10 g) pear,
diced
1 teaspoon (5 g) sun-dried
tomatoes in oil
Pane carasau (Italian
flatbread)
4 whole Pachino or cherry
tomatoes

## Method

Cut up the sirloin with a knife. Drizzle in the soy sauce and oil. Season with salt. Use your hands to work the meat and create three different shapes for each portion: a cone, cylinder, and square.

### GREEN SAUCE

Prepare the parsley, removing the large stalks and only keeping the best leaves. Wash, dry, and chop it finely with a *mezzaluna*. Chop the anchovies (having already removed the bones and washed them if salt-cured), garlic, and capers (rinsing them well to remove any excess salt).

Dampen the breadcrumbs with the vinegar. Squeeze out any excess and push through a strainer. Mix all these ingredients together well with the oil. Season with salt and pepper to taste. Add, if desidered, the hard-cooked egg yolks, which have also been pureed.

### THREE TYPES OF MAYONNAISE

Beat the egg yolk with a pinch of salt and some of the vinegar. Gradually pour in the oil, whisking until the desired consistency is reached. Season with salt and add more vinegar to taste.

Divide the mixture into three parts. Leave 1 portion plain, add the chopped chives to the second part, and add a teaspoon of green sauce to the last portion.

### GINGER-FLAVORED PHYLLO PASTRY

Spread 4 squares of phyllo pastry with the oil infused with the ground ginger and top each square with another pastry square.

Wrap the phyllo pastry around cylinders used to make four small cannelloni. Bake in the oven at 350°F (180°C/gas mark 4) for 5 minutes.

### FRIED BREAD WITH OLIVES

Grate the bread. Brown in the oil with the garlic and bay leaf in a frying pan for 10 minutes. Season with salt and pepper. Turn the mixture out onto kitchen paper to remove the excess oil. Add the chopped olives.

### TOMATO TARTARE

Cut a cross into the bottom of each tomato; blanch them in boiling water for several seconds. Cool them immediately in ice water and remove the skins and seeds.

Chop the pulp finely with a knife. Season with salt and sugar. Let drain in a strainer for 10 minutes.

Use two teaspoons to shape the drained tomatoes into small quenelles.


## Serving

Dip the carpaccio cylinder in the fried bread with olives. Arrange on a plate, accompanied with the chive mayonnaïse, a chive and a tomato quenelle to decorate.

Arrange a carpaccio cone on the plate and sprinkle with the dried ground mangoes. Drizzle with the plain mayonnaise and serve with a small roll of ginger-flavored phyllo pastry.

Cut a small pocket in the center of the carpaccio square and insert a pear and some chopped sundried tomatoes. Garnish with wild fennel and spoon the green mayonnaise into the remaining space on the plate.

Serve the carpaccio with the pane carasau in the center of the plate and a whole tomato to garnish.

# Rigatoni filled with *capocollo* and Lucchesia spelt sauce

Ingredients for 4 people
Preparation time: 1 h 40'

24 durum wheat rigatoni pasta tubes
4 scallops
Salt

FILLING
5 oz (150 g) Tuscan *capocollo*
5 oz (150 g) Mozzarella di Bufala or Burrata

SPELT SAUCE
1 cup (100 g) *farro lucchese* (spelt)
2 onions
2 stalks celery
2 carrots
1 clove garlic
1 bay leaf
1 sprig of rosemary
1/3 oz (10 g) Cinta Senese pork cheek
Scant 3 tablespoons (40 ml) extra-virgin olive oil
2 cups (500 ml) vegetable stock, as needed
Salt

ORANGE REDUCTION
1 orange
2 peppercorns
1 bay leaf

LICORICE OIL
Scant 2 tablespoons (25 g) extra-virgin olive oil
1/2 teaspoon (3 g) Amarelli powdered licorice

TO GARNISH
2 stalks celery
Extra-virgin olive oil
Salt and pepper
Orange zest

## Method

### FILLING
Grind the capocollo with the Mozzarella or Burrata cheese in a meat grinder and mix well. Cover with plastic wrap and keep in the refrigerator.

### SPELT SAUCE
Soak the spelt in cold water overnight.
The next day, drain. Cook the spelt in water with whole 1 carrot, 1 celery stalk, 1 onion, garlic, bay leaf, rosemary, and salt for 2 1/2 hours.
Drain the spelt and reserve the cooking water.
Brown the diced pork cheek in a little oil. Add the finely chopped carrot, celery, and onion left. Sauté over medium heat for 5 minutes.
Add the drained spelt. Cook for a few minutes. Add half the cooking water and vegetable stock to cover the spelt. Cook for about 40 minutes. Puree in a blender and season to taste, adding water, if needed, to reach the desired consistency.

### ORANGE REDUCTION
Cook the orange juice with the peppercorns and bay leaf in a small saucepan over low heat until it has reduced to one-third.

### RIGATONI
Cook the pasta in unsalted boiling water for 10 minutes.
Let cool and stuff them with the filling. Heat them in a steam oven for 4–5 minutes.

### CELERY
Cut the celery into small diamonds. Blanch in boiling water for 1 minute. Cool immediately under cold running water. Sauté in a little oil with a pinch of salt.

## Serving

Cover each hot rigatoni with a slice of raw scallop and drizzle with a little licorice-flavored oil.
Pour the spelt soup in the bottom of the plate and position the rigatoni in a spoke-like pattern radiating out from the center. Between one piece of pasta and another, add a drop of the orange reduction and two celery diamonds.
Garnish with the orange zest in the center and a drizzle of extra-virgin olive oil.

# Roasted chicken cooked in two ways

**Ingredients for 4 people**
Preparation time: 2 h

1 chicken, weighing about 4
to 4 1/2 lb (1.8–2 kg)

BREASTS
Salt and pepper
1 small branch of rosemary
2 sage leaves
10 slices of Cinta pork cheek
Extra-virgin olive oil, for
sauteing

LEGS
Salt and pepper
1 small branch of rosemary
1 small branch of marjoram
2 sage leaves
1/3 cup (80 g) chicken stock
Generous 1 tablespoon (20 g)
Marsala
2 teaspoons (10 g) white
wine
2 tablespoons (30 ml)
extra-virgin olive oil

ROASTED POTATOES
2 potatoes
Extra-virgin olive oil
Salt and pepper

CHICKEN STOCK
Chicken bones and leftovers
1 onion
1 carrot
1 stalk celery
2 stalks parsley
1 bay leaf
Peppercorns
Ice
Salt

CELERY ROOT PUREE
1 celery root
1/2 onion
Generous 1 tablespoon (20
ml) extra-virgin olive oil
Generous 3/4 cup (200 ml) milk
Concentrated chicken stock

Salt and white pepper

LEMON OIL
1 bunch of lemon balm
Generous 3 tablespoons
(50 g) extra-virgin olive oil

TOMATO TARTARE
1 tomato
1 teaspoon chopped green
onions
8 capers
4 black olives
2 basil leaves
Generous 1 tablespoon (20
ml) extra-virgin olive oil
alt and pepper

CHILE PEPPER TEMPURA
2 green chile peppers
Ice-cold water
Flour (for tempura)
Oil, for frying
Salt, to taste

## Method

Bone the chicken and separate the breasts from the legs. To cook the breasts, season with salt and pepper. Arrange the skinless breasts on top of the herbs and wrap in the pork cheek slices. Place in a vacuum pack for sous vide cooking. Cook in a steam oven at 143°F (62°C) for 4 hours. When the time has passed, remove the breasts from the pack, reserving the cooking liquid. Sauté the chicken in a little oil in a frying pan until the pork cheek becomes crispy. Keep warm.

### LEGS

Divide the two legs into quarters. Season with salt and pepper. Add the chopped herbs. Make a marinade with the stock, Marsala, and white wine, and a little extra-virgin olive oil. Place the legs in a vacuum pack with the marinade. Cook at 143°F (62°C) for 12 hours. At the end of the cooking time, remove the legs from the pack, reserving the cooking liquid. Bake the chicken legs in the oven with the potatoes cut into 1/3-inch (1-cm) cubes, seasoned with salt, pepper, and oil, at 375°F (190°C/gas mark 5) for 15 minutes. Adjust the flavor of the cooking liquid in a small saucepan over low heat and reduce if needed.

### CHICKEN STOCK

Brown the vegetables with the herbs in a little extra-virgin olive oil. In a separate pan, brown the chicken bones and leftovers. Add the vegetables and ice. Cook for 2 hours, skimming the foam occasionally. Strain and let cool.

### CELERY ROOT PUREE

Peel and dice the celery root. Sauté 1/2 chopped onion in the oil in a small saucepan. Add the celery root. Season with salt and pepper. Cover with the milk and bring to a boil. Drain and puree in a blender. Spread out the puree on a sheet of parchment paper. Let dry in the oven at 175°F (80°C) for about 2 hours. Transfer the dried mixture to a bowl. Re-hydrate with the chicken stock and puree with a handheld immersion blender, gradually adding the extra-virgin olive oil.

### LEMON OIL

Blanch the lemon balm in boiling water for 10 seconds. Let cool immediately in ice water. Drain, dry, and puree with the oil. Emulsify in a bowl using a handheld immersion blender.

### TOMATO TARTARE

Cut a cross in the bottom of the tomatoes; blanch them in boiling water for a few seconds. Remove the skins and seeds. Cut up the pulp with a knife. Season with salt and sugar. Add the remaining ingredients. Shape the tomatoes into 4 small quenelles.

### CHILE PEPPERS

Cut the chile peppers in half lengthwise. Dip in the flour and cold water mixture. Fry in very hot oil. Drain and dry on kitchen paper. Season with salt and arrange the tomato quenelles on top.

## Serving

Arrange the legs and 1/2 breast in the center of each plate. Pour the reserved cooking sauce over the top. Place the chile pepper on the side with the roasted potatoes. Finish with the celery root puree and lemon oil.

# White chocolate and raspberry mousse zuccotto with dill sauce

Ingredients for 4 people
Preparation time: 1 h + 1 night resting

### SPONGE CAKE
5 oz (150 g) egg yolks
1/3 cup (70 g) sugar
Generous 1 cup (270 g) egg whites
Scant 1 cup (135 g) all-purpose flour, sifted

### DIP
Generous 3 tablespoons (50 g) water
1/3 cup (70 g) sugar
2 teaspoons (10 g) Maraschino

### WHITE CHOCOLATE MOUSSE
1 sheet gelatin
4 oz (125 g) white chocolate
Generous 3/4 cup (200 g) cream

### RASPBERRY JELLY
1 sheet gelatin
Generous 1/3 cup (100 g) raspberry puree
Generous 1 tablespoon (20 g) sugar

### DILL SAUCE
5 egg yolks
Generous 1/3 cup (85 g) sugar
Generous 3/4 cup (200 g) milk
1 small bunch of dill

### TO DECORATE
1 tray of fresh raspberries
Small chocolate or caramel decorations

## Method

### SPONGE CAKE

Beat the egg yolks with half of the sugar. Beat the egg whites with the remaining sugar to stiff peaks. Fold the beaten whites into the egg yolk mixture. Fold in the sifted flour. Spoon the mixture into a pastry bag fitted with a smooth tip. Pipe out in lines on parchment paper to form a solid rectangle.

Bake in the oven at 400°F (200°C/gas mark 6) for 6-8 minutes.

Remove from the oven and immediately cut out 4 rounds using a pastry cutter for the base of the dessert.

### DIP

Make a syrup by heating the water and sugar. When it comes to a boil, remove from the heat and let cool. Add the Maraschino.

### MOUSSE

Soak the gelatin in cold water. Drain and squeeze dry.

Melt the chocolate in the top of a double boiler.

Heat half the cream in a separate pot and stir in the gelatin until dissolved.

Add the remaining cream to the melted chocolate, whisking. Add the cream and gelatin mixture and let mousse rest in the refrigerator for at least 1 hour.

At the end of this time, the mixture will have set. Whip until it forms a soft mousse.

### RASPBERRY JELLY

Soak the gelatin in cold water. Drain and squeeze dry. Heat 3 tablespoons of raspberry puree with the sugar. Stir in the gelatin until dissolved. Add the remaining puree and spread out on a baking sheet to form a film. Set in the refrigerator.

### SAUCE

Beat the egg yolks with the sugar until foamy.

Bring the milk to a boil and gradually pour over the beaten yolks, whisking constantly.

Return the mixture to the heat and heat to 185°F (85°C).

Remove from the heat, add the dill; let marinate for 10 minutes.

Transfer to a blender and puree; strain through a fine-mesh sieve.


## Serving

Dip the sponge cake rounds in the Maraschino syrup. Use them to line the zuccotto molds. Fill the molds, alternating with layers of mousse, raspberry jelly circles, and fresh raspberries. Top the zuccotto with the white chocolate mousse.

Leave overnight in the refrigerator.

Turn the zuccotto out upside-down onto a plate. Serve with the dill sauce, some fresh raspberries, and the chocolate and caramel decorations.

# Davide Brovelli

## IL SOLE RESTAURANT
### Ranco (Varese)

"If you have a heart and a shirt, sell the shirt and visit the surroundings of Lake Maggiore", wrote the French writer Stendhal. Well, if you have the desire to taste a creative cuisine of traditional flavors, there is a house of unspeakable beauty. This is *Il Sole* in Ranco in the province of Varese, a restaurant whose class and excellence have been recognized by the most prestigious Italian and international culinary associations.

The area, on the Lombardy side of Lake Maggiore, has been one of the favorite destinations of Milanese nobility since the 19th century, both for its beautiful natural scenery as well as its hunting and fishing, and for the presence of the *Sacro Monte* di Varese, a place of art and worship.

"My great-grandmother Emilia opened an inn here in 1850" says Davide Brovelli, the current chef and co-owner with his family of *Il Sole* di Ranco. At the time the village had a handful of houses and a small church, and guests came from the city in horse-drawn carriages to find accommodations and food in this cozy, restful place, nestled in a lush but peaceful garden with a serene view of the lake, then as now bathed in sunlight from dawn to dusk. The kitchen even back then, produced the best quality food made with free-range products, eggs, and fresh milk straight from the cow. "It was my grandmother Marina with my grandfather Augusto who continued the business of owning and running the inn. In the summer under the pergola, hikers and families would enjoy the specialties of the house." In the fifties his son Carlo, "*my father*", took over the kitchen, supported by years of studies and a series of experiences abroad, along with his wife Itala. "I remember when I was little, during the summers and on the weekends, my parents would churn out setting after setting. But it was a limited three month seasonal victory." For this reason in the seventies Davide's parents felt the need to focus on the restoration. It was not a clear break, but it has resulted in a slow change in the philosophy of cooking, with a careful refinement and care in the presentation of the dishes, the aesthetic aspect of the course and the professionalism of the dining room. "After some initial difficulties we begun to receive new customers from outside Varese and Milan, and at any time of the year." This was due to Carlo Brovelli becoming a Michelin two stars winning chef, with an international clientele and the completion of the renovations. And that quality is confirmed today with the passing of the baton to his capable son David.

The ambiance of the restaurant is very elegant with a touch of retro style that enhances the charm, but seems familiar. "Guests of the *Il Sole* take in the family spirit. It's a big enough company, but it has been run like a family for over a century, and you can feel that."

Davide began working in the *Sole*'s kitchen at age 16, but has been managing it himself for approximately fifteen years. "My training as a chef was born in the field: I never went to a hotel school, I chose to go to work immediately and get a little practical experience." In the mid- eighties he was at Vergé, in France at the *Moulin de Mougin*, in those years at the top of the catering business. Then he went to Los Angeles, in the United States, where he visited some of the restaurants that in that period were all the rage - restaurants like *Citrus* or *Valentino*, and then he returned home. "It was not hard to discover who I was." This was also because he had already been cooking with the family in the restaurant. "I think we should respect the history of our own cuisine, otherwise we will all end up with all the same dishes..." His motto is to honor the land where he was born and where he has lived for over forty years. "My cuisine could certainly be defined as local cuisine. First of all, I try to use and enhance freshwater fish like pike, trout, carp, eel, perch and whitefish; and then all the products of the area, from the delicious cheeses like the famous goat cheese from Valcuvia and *Bettelmatt* from the nearby Formazza Valley, to the great meats."

The lake is the connecting thread of the sections of the book, which speak of times past but in today's terms. As a starter, a freshwater sea urchin and caviar. As a first course, green noodles with smoked whitefish, scented with basil. For the second course we have pike breaded with pistachios, hazelnuts and almonds with mustard ice cream. And for dessert we have peaches from nearby Lake Monate, an *brutti e buoni soufflé* made with the famous hazelnut macaroons from two typical villages of the inner region, Cittiglio and Gavirate, and Vin Santo ice cream.

## Lake carpaccio
with sea urchins and caviar

P.**80**

## Green tagliolini pasta
with smoked whitefish
and basil

P.**82**

## Pistachio, hazelnut,
and almond-crusted black bass
with mustard ice-cream

P.**84**

## Peaches from Lago di Monate,
ugly-but-good cookie soufflé
and Vin Santo ice-cream

P.**86**

# Lake carpaccio with sea urchins and caviar

## Ingredients for 4 people
Preparation time: 25'

1 3/4 oz (50 g) cherry tomatoes
1 3/4 oz (50 g) small zucchini
1 3/4 oz (50 g) green beans
1 3/4 oz (50 g) green asparagus
1 3/4 oz (50 g) shelled peas
1 3/4 oz (50 g) eggplant
1 pike fillet
3 1/2 oz (100 g) mixed greens
Extra-virgin olive oil
Salt
Pepper
12 sea urchins
Soy sauce
3 tablespoons (40 g) Beluga caviar

## Method

Blanch the cherry tomatoes. Remove the skin and seeds and dice the flesh.
Dice the remaining vegetables, and blanch them, one type of vegetable at a time, keeping them crunchy. Set them aside.
The simplest thing to do is to ask for a pike fillet from your fishmonger, originally at least 15-22 lb (7-10 kg). (The larger the pike, the more tender and sweeter the meat). You can remove the fine fishbone that's usually among the fish meat.
Arrange the salad greens on individual plates, dressing them with oil and salt.
Cut the raw white pike meat very finely to make a carpaccio. Arrange it on the salad and season with salt and pepper.
Arrange the sea urchin flesh and all the blanched vegetables on top. Process the oil with the soy sauce using a handheld immersion blender. Drizzle the soy oil over the dish.
Garnish with caviar in the center and serve.

# Green tagliolini pasta with smoked whitefish and basil

## Ingredients for 4 people
Preparation time: 20' – 1 h – Marinating time: 1 h

### PASTA
3 1/4 cups (500 g) all-purpose flour
2 whole eggs
2 egg yolks
1 tablespoon extra-virgin olive oil
7 oz (200 g) spinach leaves
Salt

### BASIL MOUSSE
2 sheets of gelatin
fish fumet
16 basil leaves
cream
Salt
Pepper

### SERVING
200 Pachino or cherry tomatoes
Salt
Pepper
3 1/2 oz (100 g) wild arugula
1 3/4 oz (50 g) shallots
Parsley
1 clove garlic
2 smoked whitefish, each weighing 7 oz (200 g)
4 tablespoons extra-virgin olive oil
Generous 1 tablespoon (20 g) Belgian caviar (20 g)

## Method

### PASTA
Sift the flour onto a cutting board and shape into a mound. Make a well in the center. Pour the eggs and egg yolks and oil into the hollow. Add the spinach, which has been blanched, squeezed dry, and finely chopped, and salt. Knead until the dough is smooth and even. Let rest for about 1 hour in a cool place.

### MOUSSE
Soak the gelatin in cold water. Drain and squeeze out. Blend the fish fumet with the gelatin, basil leaves, and cream in a food processor. Let rest and set in a bowl in the refrigerator.

### PASTA SAUCE
Blanch and peel the cherry tomatoes. Put them in a bowl and season with salt and pepper, crushed in a mortar. Add the arugula and finely chopped shallot. Let marinate for about 1 hour. Finely chop a large handful of parsley with the garlic and put this in the bowl.

## Serving

In a saucepan, cook the ingredients for the pasta sauce over low heat with a little oil, keeping them slightly crunchy.
Cook the pasta in salted water. Drain and toss in the prepared sauce in the pan.
Arrange the pasta in the center of a deep plate with a fairly large brim. Garnish with the fillets of smoked whitefish that have been broken up roughly and a dollop of caviar. Serve with the basil mousse.

# Pistachio, hazelnut, and almond-crusted black bass with mustard ice-cream

Ingredients for 4 people
Preparation time: 1 h

### BLACK BASS
2/3 cup (100 g) hazelnuts
2/3 cup (100 g) pistachios
2/3 cup (100 g) blanched almonds
1 black bass, weighing about 2 1/2 lb (1.2 kg)
1 egg

### JERUSALEM ARTICHOKES PUREE
2 shallots, finely chopped
Generous 1/3 cup (100 ml) extra-virgin olive oil
10 oz (300 g) Jerusalem artichokes
5 oz (150 g) firm, ripe pumpkin
Generous 3/4 cup (200 ml) white wine
Water
Salt and Pepper

### CELERY ROOT PUREE
1 lb (500 g) celery root
1 quart (1 liter) whole milk
Water
Salt
Pepper

### MUSTARD ICE-CREAM
5 egg yolks
2 cups (500 ml) whole milk
Scant 2 tablespoons (25 g) wine vinegar
Generous 3 tablespoons (50 g) Pommery
Whole Grain Mustard de Meux
Fleur de sel, for serving
Toasted bread slices, for serving

## Method

### BLACK BASS

Spread the hazelnuts, pistachios, and almonds on a parchment-lined baking sheet. Toast at 400°F (200°C/gas 6) for about 10 minutes.

Place the nuts on a marble surface and let cool. Transfer to a food processor and grind well.

Scale and gut the black bass, removing the backbone and skin. Remove the stomach from the fillets and cut the fish at the back into 2 1/3 x 1-inch (6 x 3-cm) fingers (or ask your fishmonger to do this for you).

Dip the fish fingers in the ground nut mixture, followed by the beaten egg.

Heat the oil in a saucepan and fry the black bass fingers until golden brown all over.

### JERUSALEM ARTICHOKE PUREE

Brown the shallots in the oil in a frying pan. Add the Jerusalem artichokes and pumpkin, cut into cubes. Add the white wine and let it evaporate. Pour in the water and season with salt and pepper.

When the vegetables are tender, remove them with a slotted spoon, reserving the cooking water. Blend the vegetables in a food processor to obtain a smooth puree. Gradually add the cooking water, until you reach the desired consistency. Keep warm.

### CELERY ROOT PUREE

Clean and peel the celery root, dicing it. Place the celeriac in a large pot and cover with the milk and water. Cook over medium heat until tender. Repeat the method used above to make the Jerusalem artichoke puree, blending the vegetable until pureed. Keep warm.

### MUSTARD ICE-CREAM

Use a whisk to beat the egg yolks in a bowl, adding the cold milk.

In a saucepan, gently heat the mixture to 180°F (82°C).

Remove from the heat and let cool. Use a whisk to carefully add the vinegar and mustard. Pour into an ice-cream machine and churn according to the manufacturer's instructions.

## Serving

Arrange the Jerusalem artichoke puree and celery root puree on warm plates, using a spoon to draw a line of squid ink. Arrange a whole fish finger on top, as well as another one cut at three-quarters, so you can see the white of the fish. Sprinkle with *fleur de sel* and place a quenelle of mustard ice-cream on a slice of toasted bread.

# Peaches from Lago di Monate, ugly-but-good cookie soufflé and Vin Santo ice-cream

### Ingredients for 4 people
Preparation time: 30' – Resting: 3 h

PEACH PUREE
4 Peaches, pitted
Generous 3 tablespoons (50 ml) lemon juice
Generous 3 tablespoons (50 ml) sugar syrup

UGLY-BUT-GOOD COOKIE SOUFFLÉ
5 sheets of gelatin
1/4 cup (60 ml) water
3/4 cup (150 g) sugar
6 egg yolks
2 cups (500 g) Lago di Monate peach puree
2 cups (260 g) Tuscan ugly-but-good cookies (*brutti e buoni*), crumbled
Generous 2 3/4 cups (700 g) cream, whipped

VIN SANTO ICE-CREAM
4 egg yolks
Generous 1/4 cup (60 g) sugar
1 2/3 cups (400 ml) Vin Santo
Scant 1/4 cup (50 ml) whipping cream, whipped

### Method

PEACH PUREE
In a blender, puree the fresh Lago di Monate peaches and add the lemon juice and syrup.

UGLY-BUT-GOOD COOKIE SOUFFLÉ
Soak the gelatin in water. Drain and squeeze out.
Bring the water and sugar to a boil in a copper pot, heating it to 248°F (120°C). Beat the egg yolks in a small electric mixer beat in the hot syrup, a little at a time.
Warm the peach puree in the microwave and mix in the gelatin.
Mix the beaten egg mixture into the peach puree and add the crumbled ugly-but-good cookies. Fold in the whipped cream.
Pour the mixture into a mold and freeze.

VIN SANTO ICE-CREAM
Place the egg yolks, sugar, and Vin Santo in a metal bowl. Use a whisk to beat the mixture in a bain-marie (in the top of a double boiler) until heated to 158–167°F (70–75°C).
When it has cooled, fold in the whipped cream. Pour the mixture into an ice-cream machine and churn according to the manufacturer's instructions.

# Franca Checchi

## ROMANO RESTAURANT
### Viareggio (Lucca)

What moves this chef is also the epicenter of her cuisine. "It is so exciting in spring or in the first days of autumn to walk or cycle to the top of the pier and turn around to admire the sight of the Apian Alps, especially at sunset", confides Franca Checchi, chef and co-owner together with her husband Romano Franceschini, of the *Da Romano* restaurant in Viareggio, the elegant and worldly capital of Versilia. For Franca, the merger of products from the plains and mountains with those of the sea is the *summa*, the best of the regional cuisine.

"– A beautiful family, a loving and enthusiastic staff, a smashing cellar and above all a delicious cuisine –. The director of a well-known gourmet guide began a review of our restaurant with those words, filling us with satisfaction and with pride. We believe that those few words represent exactly our 48 years of history." Riding the crest of the wave is no trick, but testimony to a passion. *Da Romano* opened its doors on December 15, 1996. "It was named that because it was the custom to use the name of the person who managed a restaurant: when we opened it, my husband and I, we were two 'kids'; he was 23, I was barely 16." Romano had previously worked in different restaurants of Viareggio, where he acted as if they were his own. "He never looked at the clock or asked for a raise, because the most important thing for him was to learn how to run a restaurant." From the beginning he worked in the dining room, while Franca worked the kitchen. Today he has the help of his son Roberto, an expert wine steward, who works in the dining room with his father.

*Da Romano*, a Michelin star and member of the prestigious circle of 'Le Soste', offers a kitchen made of the aromas and flavors of Versilia, with old and new dishes alternating on the table. Franca does nothing to impress: "I don't believe in tricks; instead I try to get the food on the table through a series of transformations that are easily identified, and that speak through all their simplicity and transparency." This does not mean that it is a 'simple' cuisine, but that simplicity is the primary purpose of her research. "Basically everything that is put on the table owes its success to the great appeal that I can offer through the very highest quality of the products that I use. Ours is a traditional cuisines, tasty, light and in certain aspects innovative: just as it appears on the table and for the unusual combinations of ingredients that aim to attract customers."

The Viareggio tradition does not offer many traditional dishes: "of course many cannot be prepared because some of the ingredients today are 'illegal' according to the standards of the European Community, such as date shells and dried dolphin." Among the dishes that have survived, *Da Romano* offers some as tradition demands, with no changes. Some examples? The *maruzzelle* (sea snails) in stew, the *cicale di mare* (shrimp) soup and spaghetti with a sauce of *coltellacci* (razor clams). Desserts include the *scarpaccia viareggina,* a sweet cake with zucchini, and an Easter cake made of rice and chocolate.

Franca's training was as quick as her talent. "At first I had a period of time with a cook who had hired Roman when he opened his restaurant. We worked in tandem. I was still very young; I had to get the right rhythm. When the first chef left after a couple of years, after trying different chefs, I decided to take charge of the situation." She never studied or interned at any other restaurant. "I consider Franco Colombani, father and creator of *Linea Italia in Cucina* (Italian Cuisine Line) one of the top restaurant associations in all Italy, as a master. We are part of the association, which united the elite of Italian restaurants of those years, in 1980. We were the only restaurant under the Po. We met every month, to exchange experiences and to spread the 'creed' of quality regional cooking. I listened to my colleagues as if they were older brothers and I compared with them cooking techniques and practices, the ingredients used, and I learned a lot even if I was not working in other restaurants."

The dishes chosen for the book are all closely tied to the region. As an appetizer is squid stuffed with vegetables and shellfish. The first course is spaghetti with clams, and second is Viareggio fried fish. Dessert is a parfait with Tuscan-style cookies and cream with Vin Santo di Carmignano.

# Baby squid stuffed
with vegetables and shellfish

P.**92**

# Spaghetti
with arselle

P.**94**

# Viareggio-style
fish stew

P.**96**

# Tuscan cantuccini semifreddo
with Vin Santo di Carmignano custard

P.**98**

# Baby squid stuffed with vegetables and shellfish

### Ingredients for 4 people
Preparation time: 40'

2 lb (1 kg) baby squid
5 oz (150 g) carrots
5 oz (150 g) zucchini
8 mantis shrimp, or other large shrimp
Extra-virgin olive oil
2 clove garlic
Chile pepper, salt, and pepper, to taste
2 basil leaves
5 large calamint or mint leaves
2 slices of bread, crumbs removed

### Method

Clean the baby squid carefully, removing the eyes and the quills, but leaving the tentacles attached. Clean the carrot and zucchini and chop them finely; set aside.
Clean the mantis shrimp carefully, peeling and deveining them (but leaving heads and tails on). Saute the shellfish in a pan with 2 tablespoons of extra-virgin olive oil, 1 colve of garlic, and chile pepper for a few minutes.
Remove the shellfish from the pan, and remove the heads and tails, leaving only the meat; reserve the cooking oil in the pan.
Place the carrots, zucchini, basil leaves, calamint, and garlic in the shrimp cooking oil. Sauté over low heat until the vegetables have softened. Add the bread, cut into small pieces, and cook until they have softened and absorbed the liquid from the vegetables.
Process the shellfish meat briefly in a food processor. Add the vegetable, bread, and oil mixture from the pan and blend for several seconds.

# Spaghetti with arselle

## Ingredients for 4 people
Preparation time: about 30'

2 lb (1 kg) live arselle clams
1 clove garlic, crushed
Extra-virgin olive oil
1 chile pepper, seeded and finely chopped
Calamint or mint
1/4 cup (60 ml) good-quality dry white wine
14 oz (400 g) spaghetti
1 sprig of parsley, finely chopped

## Method

Carefully clean and wash the arselle under running water after having soaked them beforehand for 24 hours in seawater, or very salty water.
Sauté the garlic in the oil in a deep frying pan for 1 minute.
Add the chopped chile, calamint leaves, and arselle.
Cover the pan and cook for 3 minutes, shaking the pan occasionally to open the arselle.
Add the white wine and cook, uncovered, for 5 minutes until it has evaporated.
Meanwhile, cook the spaghetti in boiling water until not quite al dente. Drain; add pasta and parsley to the pan with the clams; saute until pasta is al dente.

# Viareggio-style fish stew

Ingredients for 4 people
Preparation time: 1 h

1 1/2 lb (700 g) mollusks, such as cuttlefish, octopus, and baby squid
8 spottail mantis shrimp, or other large shrimp
3 1/3 lb (1.5 kg) fish with bones, such as gurnard, weaver, scorpion fish, stargazer, dogfish, or conger
1 piece of spicy chile pepper
2 cloves garlic, lightly crushed
1/3 cup (80 g) extra-virgin olive oil
Scant 1/2 cup (100 ml) white wine
1 1/4 cups (300 g) fresh tomatoes
Salt
Freshly ground black pepper
Chopped parsley
Fish stock or water, as needed
8 slices of farmers' bread, toasted

## Method

Carefully clean the mollusks, removing the eyes and quill. Cut the cuttlefish into pieces; leave the tentacles of the octopus whole. Peel the shrimp, leaving the heads attached.
Clean, gut, scale, and fillet the fish carefully (or ask your fishmonger to do this for you). If they are large, cut them into pieces.
Sauté the chile and the garlic in the extra-virgin olive oil until the garlic turns pale gold. Discard the garlic and add the mollusks, letting them getting the flavors. Pour in the white wine and cook until evaporated.
Add the tomatoes. Season with salt and pepper. Cook over low heat for 15 minutes. Add the fish and shrimp.
Cook over low heat for 10 minutes more, without stirring to avoid breaking up the fish. Add the parsley halfway through and add a little fish stock or water, if needed to finish. Ladle the stew evenly into serving bowls, topping each serving with two slices of toast.

# Tuscan cantuccini semifreddo with Vin Santo di Carmignano custard

## Ingredients for 4 people
Preparation time: 1 h – Resting time: 12 h

**SEMIFREDDO**
4 egg yolks
1/2 cup (100 g) sugar
Scant 1/2 cup (100 g) milk
3 1/2 oz (100 g) nougat paste (can be purchased in specialist food stores among the ice-cream products)
3 1/2 oz (100 g) Tuscan cantuccini cookies, broken into small pieces
1 1/4 cups (300 g) whipping cream, whipped

**CARMIGNANO CUSTARD**
1 cup (250 g) milk
4 egg yolks
Generous 1/4 cup (60 g) sugar
Generous 1 tablespoon (20 g) Vin Santo di Carmignano

## Method

### SEMIFREDDO
Beat the egg yolks and sugar in a metal bowl. Bring the milk to a boil in a small saucepan over medium heat. Slowly whisk the hot milk into the egg mixture; transfer to the top of a double-boiler to cook. Remove the mixture from the heat when it is about to boil. Pour immediately into a mixer and beat until it becomes quite thick and smooth. Pour into a large bowl and whisk in the nougat paste (a little at a time to avoid lumps from forming) and the cookies. When the mixture has been well combined, slowly fold in the whipped cream with a wooden spoon. Pour the semifreddo into individual silicon molds and freeze for at least 12 hours.

### CUSTARD
Bring the milk to a boil. Use a whisk to beat the egg yolks and sugar in a bowl. Continue whisking, slowly mixing in the boiling milk. Pour the mixture into a saucepan. Cook, whisking constantly, until it reaches 185–195°F (85°–90°C). Remove from the heat; let the temperature drop to 160°F (70°C) and add the Vin Santo, mixing with a wooden spoon. Let cool before serving.

## Serving

When you are ready to serve, remove the semifreddo from the freezer and let stand several minutes at room temperature. Turn it out onto a plate and decorate with some crumbled cantuccini and the Vin Santo di Carmignano custard.

## Curiosity

Almond cookies, also called *cantucci*, are one of the most famous desserts in Tuscany. It is still tradition today to serve them, accompanied with Vin Santo, for special occasions or to send them around the world as a Christmas gift. They are ancient in origin. Some say that they are direct descendants of the melatelli, which were made in medieval times with wheat flour, water, and honey; eggs and almonds have been added to this mixture over the centuries. The recipe, then as now, was noted in the eighteenth-century cookbook by Amadio Baldanzi, but the distribution of these rustic cookies is owed to Antonio Mattei, nicknamed Mattonella, who opened a bakery for the preparation of pasta and desserts in the mid-nineteenth century on the main street in Prato.

# Luca Collami

## BALDIN RESTAURANT
### Sestri Ponente (Genoa)

Born together. In 1969 at the same time chef Luca Collami was born in Genoa, a couple opened the small *Baldin* restaurant in Sestri Ponente, a small district in Genoa. Neither knew of the other, but what would become his restaurant grew up with him. Then just before he reached legal age, they met. "The trattoria, which had the nickname of its owner, Teobaldo, I found purely by chance in 1989", said Luca. "As a boy I lived in Pegli, and the owners were my neighbors. At some point they needed help, so I began to work there. I was eighteen and a half, and I became their dependent, then less than a month later I decided with my parents – since the restaurant was working well – to enter in partnership, making the first payment. Six months later I made the second payment and twenty years later the restaurant was mine, together with my mother Maria."

Luca was not born into the art: "I was the first in my family to go into this work, but when I was just twelve I said: 'When I'm big I'm going to open a restaurant'..." And so it went. "I went to hotel school, then I did some apprenticeships in the summer, and I spent one and a half years in an important Genoa restaurant, but really very little to speak of. I would define myself 'self-taught'. I tried to deepen my passion, reading, studying, traveling, experimenting and above all comparing them with the experiences of my colleagues, often the most important people around me. In this sense my becoming part of the *Jeunes Restaurateurs d'Europe* helped me a lot."

The turning point came in'99, when he decided to completely restructure the restaurant, working with an architect friend and adding his name to the sign, below the historical name. "With the renovation of the restaurant something clicked inside me, and I have slowly grown to what I am today." He does not think of himself as 'anyone special', "but of course I enjoy my work, and I dedicate a lot of time, even when it's difficult, not so much to being in the kitchen, which I really enjoy, but to managing the restaurant from an administrative point of view..." He would like to be a chef full time, in short, because his talent is in cooking: "A new dish comes to me, instinctively. I prepare it and put it directly on the plate, no tests or proofs. Once cooked and tasted, at most I change the assembly or arrangement of the ingredients. Furthermore, the same plate is never the same: that 'inconsistency' is due to my continuous research to improve it."

It is not the type of cuisine, which is always "extravagant, although bound to tradition", as much as its presentation, which has undergone many changes over the last fifteen years: the chef prepares dishes that are refined and unique. He has accomplished this with the support of his wife Barbara, sommelier and head not just of the dining room but also the line of sweets and pastries.

"My cuisine is based on tradition, both in aromas and in the products, as well as in the flavors, which are quite strong, and therefore Ligurian and Mediterranean. For me regional cooking is sacred but, based on that, there is also creation and innovation that take place." After all, Genoan cuisine uses raw materials from the region, but in dishes that reflect the echoes of a trade past and contacts with distant peoples. Luca therefore interprets the ingredients of a dish to create a new dish, but with wise intuition and without going too far.

The menu selected for the book are dishes based on tradition. "As an appetizer I have chosen zucchini flowers stuffed with dried cod in a tomato mayonnaise and a garlic sauce, extra virgin olive oil from Liguria and salted anchovies." An appetizing reinterpretation of the classic stuffed vegetable of the Ligurian kitchen. "The first course is potato dumplings, whitefish cakes, black olives and marjoram." This is a variation of the classic potato dumplings, often served in Genoa with pesto; the scent is also different– marjoram is a typical Ligurian aroma – and the use of the black olives from the imperial city of Taggia. "Second course is our squid stuffed with porcini mushrooms: our region has some marvelous mushrooms." The method of cooking at low temperature makes a particularly fragrant and elegant dish. "For dessert we have Genoan cookies – a type of soft sponge cake – served with a mousse of hazelnuts and coffee."

# Zucchini flowers stuffed
with stockfish served
with a tomato, oil,
and anchovy mayonnaise

P.**104**

# Potato gnocchetti
with white fish, Taggiasca olives,
and marjoram

P.**106**

# Squid stuffed
with porcini mushrooms

P.**107**

# Genoa-style cookie
with coffee and gianduja mousse

P.**108**

# Zucchini flowers stuffed with stockfish served with a tomato, oil, and anchovy mayonnaise

### Ingredients for 4 people
Preparation time: 50'

1 1/3 lb (600 g) stockfish
Generous 1 tablespoon (20 g) capers
1 clove garlic
Generous 1 tablespoon (20 g) anchovies
8 tablespoons (80 g) Ligurian extra-virgin olive oil PDO
1 egg white
12 zucchini flowers
10 oz (300 g) cherry tomatoes

SAUCE
Cherry tomatoes and extra-virgin olive oil

### Method

Bring a saucepan with plenty of water to a boil over medium heat. Add the stockfish and let it soak for 10 minutes until ready. Remove from the water; remove the skin of the fish and remove the bones from the fish. Transfer to the food processor and add the capers, garlic, anchovies, and a scant 3 tablespoons (40 g) of oil to make a smooth and even cream.
When the fish has cooled, add the egg white, which has been beaten to stiff peaks.
Wash the zucchini flowers. Use a pastry bag to fill the flowers with the prepared mixture. Wrap them in aluminum foil and cook in a double boiler for 10 minutes.
Clean the tomatoes. Using a handheld immersion blender, emulsify them with 3 tablespoons of oil. Strain through a fine-mesh sieve to remove the seeds. Heat the remaining 2 tablespoons of oil.

### Serving

Arrange the zucchini flowers diagonally on the plate with the tomato mayonnaise. Drizzle with the hot oil.

# Potato gnocchetti with white fish, Taggiasca olives, and marjoram

### Ingredients for 4 people
Preparation time: 1 h

1 lb (500 g) potatoes
Salt
1 1/3 cups (200 g) flour
1 clove of garlic

1 white fish fillet
2 tablespoons Taggiasca olives
8 cherry tomatoes
Marjoram

### Method

Boil the potatoes with the skins on in plenty of salted water. Peel them when they are still hot and puree with a potato masher. Season with salt and add the flour.
Knead together quickly on a floured surface to make a soft dough in the shape of a sausage. The sizes suggested can be adjusted based on the quality of the potatoes and may change as needed. Test them by immersing a small piece of the mixture in boiling water. If the consistency of the dough isn't good enough, add more flour and test again.
Cut the dough into portions and use your hands to roll them out into cylinders about 1-inch (2.5-cm) thick. Cut crosswise into 3/4–1 1/4-inch (2–3-cm) gnocchi.
Press the gnocchi briefly under the prongs of a fork for decoration and to give them more shape. Arrange in a single layer on floured or parchment-lined baking sheets.
Bring plenty of salted water to a boil. Add the gnocchi. They will cook quickly; drain them as soon as they rise to the surface.
Sauté the chopped garlic in the oil in a frying pan. Add the fish, Taggiasca olives, and cherry tomatoes. Cook for a few minutes. Sauté the gnocchi in the sauce and add the marjoram.

# Squid stuffed with porcini mushrooms

### Ingredients for 4 people
Preparation time: 40'

12 squid
7oz (200 g) porcini mushrooms
1 zucchini
1/2 onion
1 clove garlic
1/3 cup (40 g) breadcrumbs

1 egg
Salt to taste
Pepper to taste
Scant 3 tablespoons (40 g) Ligurian
extra-virgin olive oil PDO
Parsley, to garnish

### Method

Clean the squid, removing the heads which will be used in the filling.
Set 3 whole squid aside per portion (12 altogether).
Make the filling: Chop up the squid and the leftover heads. Dice the porcini and chop up the zucchini, onion, and garlic. Mix all the ingredients together in a bowl. Add the breadcrumbs and egg. Season with salt and pepper.
Stuff the squid with the filling and secure them with toothpicks. Arrange them on a baking sheet and drizzle with a little oil. Bake at 325°F (160°C/gas mark 3) for 7 minutes.
Chop the parsley.
Serve the hot squid with a drizzling of extra-virgin olive oil and the parsley.

# Genoa-style cookie with coffee and gianduja mousse

### Ingredients for 4 people
Preparation time: 1 h – Resting: 3 h

GENOA-STYLE COOKIE BASE
6 whole eggs
2 egg yolks
1 cup (150 g) flour, sifted
Generous 3/4 cup (180 g) sugar
Scant 1/3 cup (40 g) starch
Scant 2 tablespoons (25 g) butter, plus
additional for molds

COFFEE OR GIANDUJA MOUSSE
Generous 3/4 cup (200 g) light cream
Scant 1/4 cup (50 g) glucose
1 1/4 cups (300 g) gianduja or 1/2 cup
(125 ml) of espresso coffee
1 1/4 cups (300 g) whipped cream

Chocolate, for serving

### Method

GENOA-STYLE COOKIE BASE
Heat the whole eggs and yolks in a saucepan, whisking until heated to 115-120°F (45-50°C). Transfer to a food processor, preferably an electric mixer, and beat with sugar. Fold in the flour, the starch, followed by the melted butter. Bake in the oven in buttered molds at 375°F (190°C/gas mark 5) for 35-40 minutes.

GIANDUJA MOUSSE
Mix the glucose with the light cream in a saucepan and let boil over medium heat. Blend the gianduja in a mixer, adding the hot cream mixture. When the mixture has cooled, fold in the whipped cream.

COFFEE MOUSSE
Follow the same method used to make the gianduja mousse, replacing the gianduja with 1/2 cup (125 ml) coffee.

### Serving

Use a round pastry cutter to cut the cookie base. Completely line the molds with the cake. Fill the lined molds with a little gianduja mousse, followed by the coffee mousse (the same method for gianduja ganache). Freeze for at least 3 hours. Decorate with chocolate before serving.

# Pino (Giuseppe) Cuttaia

## LA MADIA RESTAURANT
### Licata (Agrigento)

A restaurant like La *Madia* is unexpected in Licata, a busy seaside town in the Agrigentino. "In an unpretentious place like this, to find such professionalism is a surprise for our guests", says Pino Cuttaia, chef and co-owner of the restaurant with his wife Loredana, head of the dining room.

"The restaurant was founded in 2000 by me and my wife. Things were a little difficult at first, because the people here were not accustomed to a thought-out cuisine, a revisited regional cuisine." Even now Pino's dishes are not immediately accepted, "but we are more sure of ourselves and we also have the response of our clientele, who comes from other cities in the region as well as tourists who come this far, after finding the restaurant in the most important gourmet guides."

Pino's cuisine is based on fish, "*o*ne might define it a creation of the land, where land refers to this area where I was born 45 years ago. When I speak of a 'thought-out cuisine', I refer to the possibility of using the aromas, flavors, and colors of my memories." As far as local products, I mean "everything that Sicily has to offer: this fertile land has been dominated by many peoples throughout history, and everyone has left a special influence in terms of food and wine."

This tradition is enhanced by Pino to be able to offer its best features. "In an area like Licata, you must offer the dishes that people can also eat in their own homes, but prepared and presented creatively." His is a prized cuisine that researches, communicates and promotes the typical dishes of the area: the restaurant, which has two Michelin stars, is one of the benchmarks of the island's cuisine.

The chef of *La Madia* was first self-taught. "As a child I was fascinated by food: I saw the cook as a mysterious being who could transform matter..." By chance he found this to be his work. "I never went to cooking school. One New Year's Eve, when I was 13, a friend told me that if I was going to wash dishes in the restaurant where he worked, at midnight we could open the *champagne*. I had never had champagne, so I agreed. Since then I have not left the kitchen…" He has trained at different levels, the most important in the restaurant *Il Patio di Pollone* in Biella, Piedmont: "This is where I started to research everything, not just raw materials but also craftsmanship: since thought-out processes embrace various types of craft, from making bread and pastry to cutting meat, I tried little by little to make up for lost time."

For Pino "the most important thing is the quality of the raw materials." Knowledge of the products is fundamental for a chef: "The more you know about them, the more you will be able to convey." But technology also plays a role: "It helps to bring out what you want to convey to the client: emotions. To create flavors and beauty, without distorting the matter itself."

He lives his work as a state of mind. "Ours is a world in itself: in the kitchen you speak a language that others find difficult to understand, time is no longer time… Yet it has its own allure! When you are truly passionate about something and try to express a part of yourself, the work is more creative than one would ever think."

His menu for this book is an example of Sicily itself, the crosswords of various gastronomic heritage. The appetizer, *merluzzo all'affumicatura di pigna con patata schiacciata e condimento alla pizzaiola* (pinecone-smoked cod with mashed potatoes and sauce pizzaiola style), uses a typically regional fish and sauce. "It is simply revisiting a classic dish made of leftovers: the roasted meat left from lunch in the evening is moistened with a little tomato, olives and oregano."

The first course, *cannolo di melanzana perlina in pasta croccante, ripieno di ricotta e pomodorino dolce* (pearly eggplant cannolo in crisp pastry filled with ricotta and sweet tomatoes): "Is the same as the Messina eggplant, the only difference being that the ingredients are inverted: instead of putting the dough inside the eggplant I put it outside, leaving the flavors intact." The second course, '*spatola* (scabbard fish) with Sicilian caponata', "is a typical regional preparation and our classic caponata of vegetables, flavored with capers, pine nuts and olives and sautéed with honey and vinegar." For dessert, *cornucopia di cialda di cannolo con ricotta di pecora e marmellata di arance* (cornucopia of cannolo wafer with sheep ricotta and orange marmalade): "This is the classic Sicilian cannolo, but in a different shape and paired with a marmalade made of the most important citrus fruits cultivated in Sicily."

# Pine-smoked cod
with crushed potatoes and pizzaiola dressing
P.114

# Eggplant cannoli
with Ricotta wrapped in crispy pasta
and vine tomatoes
P.116

# Stuffed scabbard fish
with Sicilian caponata
P.118

# Cornucopia of cannoli wafers
with sheep's Ricotta
and orange marmalade
P.120

# Pine-smoked cod with crushed potatoes and pizzaiola dressing

## Ingredients for 4 people
Preparation time: 45' - Marinating: 2 h

1 cod fillet, weighing 1 lb (500 g)
Salt
Sugar, as needed
1 pine cone
3 potatoes

Scant 1/2 cup (100 ml) extra-virgin olive oil
2 tomatoes
Basil (optional)
1/2 cup (50 g) black olives in brine

## Method

Marinate the cod with the salt and sugar for 2 hours. Chop or break up pinecone into small pieces. Put pieces in a frying pan and place over medium heat. Heat well. When the pinecones are very hot, set them on fire and let burn for about 1 minute. Cover the pan to put out the fire. Place the smoking pinecones in the bottom of a roasting pan and arrange the fish on a wire rack placed inside the pan. Do not touch the pinecones.
Cover with another tray of the same size and seal with plastic wrap.
Wash and smoke the cod in the oven at a very low temperature with the smoking pine cone for about 30 minutes.
Boil potatoes a pot of salted water until cooked. Peel and dress them with oil and salt, mashing them with a fork.
Wash the tomatoes. Cut a cross into the bottom and blanch in boiling water for 1 minute. Let cool in ice water and dice them. Dress with oil and basil.

## Serving

Make 3 quenelles of the potato mixture and place them on the plate, crushing them slightly. Thinly slice the cod and arrange a slice on top of each quenelle. Top with 2 tablespoons of the seasoned diced tomatoes.

# Eggplant cannoli with Ricotta wrapped in crispy pasta and vine tomatoes

Ingredients for 4 people
Preparation time: 2 h

1 round eggplant, cut in half lenghtwise
Cornstarch, as needed, for frying eggplant
2 egg yolks, separated
Generous amount of oil, for frying
1/2 onion, chopped
3/4 oz (20 g) fresh basil
Generous 3/4 cup (200 g) cow's Ricotta cheese
Pinch of salt
Pinch of pepper
3/4 oz (20 g) grated Ragusano PDO cheese (about 3 tablespoons)
4 perlina baby eggplant
7 oz (200 g) capelli d'angelo pasta
1 teaspoon (5 g) ground saffron

TOMATO SAUCE
1/4 onion, chopped
7 oz (200 g) vine tomatoes
1 3/4 oz (50 g) basil
2 cloves garlic, unpeeled
Scant 1/4 cup (50 g) garlic honey
Generous 1 tablespoon (20 g) extra-virgin olive oil

BASIL OIL
1 small bunch of fresh basil
Generous 3/4 cup (200 ml) extra-virgin olive oil

TO GARNISH
1 3/4 oz (50 g) Ragusano PDO cheese, in shavings
Fresh basil leaves, for garnish

## Method

Thinly slice one eggplant half into 16 rounds. Dip each round in the cornstarch. Wrap them around an aluminum cannoli mold, using a dab of one egg yolk to seal. Fry the eggplant rolls in plenty of oil.

Cook 1/2 chopped onion, the basil leaves, and remaining eggplant, cut into cubes, in a saucepan until softened. Add the Ricotta (there's no need to strain it) and finish cooking by seasoning with salt and pepper to taste. Blend, adding the remaining egg yolk and grated cheese. Transfer mixture to a pastry bag and pipe filling into eggplant cannolis. Meanwhile, peel and fry the *perlina* eggplant, which have been cut in half and are still attached, making sure to leave the upper part whole. Let cool.

Parcook the *capelli d'angelo* pasta in boiling water with the saffron. Spread out on a work surface to cool. Insert a stuffed eggplant cannoli inside the perlina eggplant. Wrap the *capelli d'angelo* pasta around the eggplant cannoli, already been wrapped in the *perlina* eggplant.

Bake the cannoli in the oven at 400°F (200°C/gas mark 6) until the pasta is crispy and lightly browned (the time depends on the type of oven).

### TOMATO SAUCE

In a skillet, sauté the chopped onion and add the diced tomatoes and basil. Cook until the tomatoes soften and break down. Add the unpeeled garlic and honey. Cook over low heat for 20 minutes. Press through a fine-mesh strainer or food mill.

### BASIL OIL

In a blender or food processor, blend the basil leaves with the oil. Pass through a strainer to make a green-colored oil.

## Serving

Pour a generous spoonful of basil oil on the plate. Top with a crunchy eggplant cannoli; add the tomato sauce, the Ragusano shavings, and a few basil leaves to garnish.

# Stuffed scabbard fish with Sicilian caponata

## Ingredients for 4 people
Preparation time: 1 h

2 lb (1 kg) scabbard fish

### STUFFING
Generous 3/4 cup (100 g) breadcrumbs
1 small bunch of parsley, chopped
Juice and zest of 1/2 lemon

### SALMORIGLIO SAUCE
Scant 1/4 cup (50 g) extra-virgin olive oil
Scant 1/4 cup (50 g) water
2 teaspoons (10 g) lemon juice
Pinch of sea salt

### CAPONATA
3 1/2 oz (100 g) eggplant
1/2 onion
1 vine tomato
2 tablespoons (30 g) pitted green olives
2 teaspoons (10 g) pine nuts and honey
Scant 1 tablespoon (8 g) of capers
Scant 3/4 cup (100 g) celery chopped
Scant 1/4 cup (50 g) white wine vinegar
2 1/2 tablespoons (35 g) extra-virgin olive oil
Pinch of chile powder

## Method

Fillet the scabbard fish and remove the backbone. Scale and cut into 8 rectangles measuring 3–4 inches (8–10 cm) with a pastry cutter.

### STUFFING
Make the stuffing by mixing the breadcrumbs, parsley, and the grated lemon zest. Gradually add the lemon juice, mixing constantly.
Fill 2 fillets with the stuffing. Wrap in parchment paper. Steam for about 20 minutes, or until fish is just opaque.
Season with the sea salt.

### SALMORIGLIO SAUCE
Pour the oil, the lemon juice and the salt in a terrine. Warm the water separately. Gradually mix the warm water into the oil with a wooden spoon.

### CAPONATA
Peel the eggplant, onion, and tomato. Dice all the vegetables, keeping them separate. Chop the olives, pine nuts, and capers. Arrange the vegetables in layers in a saucepan (celery, then eggplant, onion, tomato, capers, and pine nuts). Cook them for about 10 minutes over high heat, then add the honey and finally the vinegar.
Increase heat to high and reduce cooking juices until thickened, then reduce heat and cook over low heat for another 10 minutes. Turn off the heat.

## Serving

Arrange the caponata on a plate and place the scabbard fish on top. Drizzle with a little salmoriglio sauce and garnish with a parsley leaf.

# Cornucopia of cannoli wafers with sheep's Ricotta and orange marmalade

## Ingredients for 4 people
Preparation time: 40' - Resting time for the pastry: 1 h

**FILLING**
Scant 1/2 cup (100 g) sheep's Ricotta cheese
2 tablespoons (30 g) superfine sugar
Generous 1 tablespoon (20 g) candied orange, diced

**PASTRY**
1/3 cup (50 g) all-purpose flour
2 tablespoons confectioners' sugar

2 tablespoons (10 g) cocoa
Generous 1 tablespoon (20 g) red wine vinegar
1 teaspoon (5 g) sugar
1 teaspoon (5 g) lard
Pinch of cinnamon
Oil, for frying

Confectioner's sugar, for serving
Orange marmalade, for serving

## Method

**FILLING**
Strain ricotta liquid to make cheese creamier. Beat the Ricotta and sugar in a bowl. Add the diced candied orange at the end. Keep the filling in a cool place until ready to use.

**PASTRY**
Make the wafer mixture by mixing together all the ingredients by hand on a work surface (or using an electric mixer) until a smooth dough is formed. Let rest for about 1 hour at room temperature if you are using it immediately. You can also make it the evening before, keeping it overnight in the refrigerator.
Roll out a fairly thin sheet of pastry (1.5 mm) using a rolling pin or a pasta machine, making sure that you sprinkle it with all-purpose flour if it begins to stick.
Cut the pastry using an oval cutter (about 4 inches in diameter) based on the size of the metal cannoli mold.
Cover the metal cannoli mold with the pastry (it doesn't have to be greased) and seal the edges by brushing it lightly with beaten egg yolk.
Heat the oil in a large pot to 350°F (180°C). Add the cannoli and fry until golden brown. Drain on paper towels and let cool. Carefully remove from the molds.

## Serving

Use a pastry bag to stuff the cannoli with the filling just before serving, so that they stay crunchy. Arrange the cannoli on the plate and dust with confectioners' sugar with a quenelle of orange marmalade on the side.

# Pier Luigi Di Diego

## IL DON GIOVANNI RESTAURANT
### Ferrara

Different from clay. From the time he was a child, Pier Luigi Di Diego, chef and co-owner with Marco Merighi of the *Il Don Giovanni* restaurant in Ferrara, handled fresh dough. Standing on his tiptoes, hand stretched out over the surface where his mother Carmela was working, he would take a small piece of dough to make a series of small breads. Not surprisingly, today he is known for his great touch as he stands in his restaurant every day rolling out the pasta.

The restaurant is located inside an 18th Century Palazzo, once the Board of Trade in downtown Ferrara, just in front of the 14th Century Castello Estense, the center of the historic district with its medieval streets and Renaissance district with its fine homes. But it was not always like this. The restaurant, opened in November 1998, was first located in Marrara, the last village in the Municipality of Ferrara on the road to Ravenna. The restaurant, an old renovated farm house, was named *Il Don Giovanni*. "We ask ourselves: what do we want from life? Beautiful women, beautiful music, good food and good wine. Who better than the character Don Giovanni, to embody these pleasures? We added the definite articles *il* (the) because it seemed rather pretentious to take the name of the great opera by Mozart...», chef Pier Luigi tells us. The restaurant, which moved to the city in 2003, was immediately accepted: though located in a secluded area of the Ferrara countryside, from the beginning it was found in the principal gastronomic guides, and four years later earned its Michelin star, the first in the history of the City of Ferrara.

"We use many regional products. Although my kitchen is traditional, it is not regional: I am not closed in by the walls of Ferrara. And I always try to understand the raw materials that are available, and not distort them. If anything, in certain cases I use the most modern form that we know of working and cooking." In any case, he tends to cook what he would like to eat. "That's the secret:

to be generous, and honest. I don't want to impress, that is the job of the tangible ingredients. I believe that people will trust you, if you work with transparency, simplicity, and linearity."

The typical dishes, which the Emilian city would never give up – *cappellacci di zucca* (pumpkin hats), *salama da sugo* (pork sausage) with mashed potatoes, macaroni pie, *tagliolina* cake with almonds or *tenerina* with chocolate – Pier Luigi offers them only when he can find the best raw materials available. "But without reinterpreting it, in fact trying to show their authentic flavor: for us tradition means experimentation consolidated over time until it is up to code." The typical pumpkin hats, for example, seasoned simply with butter and sage. "I want to taste the pumpkin: if it's good, then nothing else is necessary." For him cooking is "like riding a ray (half-line), you know when and how to start, but you never how and when it will end", 'simple and good' is his motto: "Every dish must be like a film with just one star and a few extras."

Born in 1967 in a family from Abruzzi, Pier Luigi has lived almost twenty years in the hinterland of Milan. After hotel school in Milan, at age fifteen he began to spend the summer and winter seasons in various tourism locales; at twenty he embarked on cruises, then back on land to start his experience in hotels: "I wanted to see and experience different forms of cooking so that I would find the one that was best for me." Finally in 1991 he arrived in Argenta, in the *Trigabolo* talent pool where he stayed until the restaurant closed. This experience was the cornerstone of his future: here he met Marco and together they first planned on having a restaurant together, precisely here in Ferrara where they wanted to live and cook.

The menu selected for this book is a 'thank you' to the land of Ferrara. The appetizer is a terrine of raw shrimp with a tomato *confit* with three pestos (basil, black olives and dried tomatoes): "A classic of our restaurant, but also a regional dish, because the Port of Garibaldi offers shrimp all year, except July and August." First course is the slightly spicy *spaghetti alla chitarra* with Goro clams and braised cabbage: a pasta with Abruzzi roots, with cabbage from his memory of Milan and the frank flavor of the Adriatic. Second course is a fricassee of Comacchio eel with chanterelle mushrooms and an emulsion of laurel, pecorino cheese and anchovies, starring the fish of the delta. And for dessert is a frangipane of Violina squash and fresh buffalo ricotta.

# Mantis shrimp terrine
with tomato confit and three pestos
P.**126**

# Slightly spicy spaghetti alla chitarra
with Goro clams
and stewed greens
P.**128**

# Fricassée of eel
and chanterelle mushrooms
with bay, pecorino, and anchovy emulsion
P.**130**

# Pumpkin and ricotta
frangipane
P.**132**

# Mantis shrimp terrine with tomato confit and three pestos

## Ingredients for 4 people
Preparation time: 20' – Tomato confit: 2h 20'

16 large mantis shrimp, or other shrimp
Drizzle of extra-virgin olive oil
Freshly ground salt, to taste
Freshly ground pepper, to taste
Several drops of red wine vinegar
Mixed fresh herbs
Basil leaves, as needed

### TOMATO CONFIT
4 ripe tomatoes
Generous 3/4 cup (200 ml) extra-virgin olive oil

10 g fresh thyme
2 cloves garlic, thinly sliced
Splash of red wine vinegar
Salt, to taste
Freshly ground black pepper, to taste
1 teaspoon (5 g) sugar

### SERVING
Taggiasca olive pesto, as needed
Basil pesto, as needed
Sun-dried tomato pesto, as needed
Basil leaves, for garnish

## Method

Shell the raw mantis shrimp; use scissors to butterfly them, cutting them halfway open along the length of the back Arrange them on a stone plate at 95°F (35°C). Drizzle with oil and season with salt and pepper. Add a few drops of vinegar and fresh herbs. Let marinate for 3 minutes.

### TOMATO CONFIT
Cut a cross in the bottom of each tomatoes; blanch the tomatoes for a few seconds in boiling water and peel them. Cut into quarters and remove the seeds. Arrange the peeled tomatoes on a baking sheet; toss with oil and thyme, placing a slice of garlic on top of each. Add the salt, pepper, and sugar. Let soften in the oven at 200°F (90°C) for 2 hours and 20 minutes.

Fill the molds in the following order: tomatoes, mantis shrimp, basil, tomatoes, basil, mantis shrimp, and basil again to finish.

## Serving

Turn out a mold in the center of each plate, drizzling with the three types of pestos and the cooking juices of the mantis shrimp. Garnish with fresh basil on top and the heads of the mantis shrimp.

# Slightly spicy spaghetti alla chitarra with Goro clams and stewed greens

## Ingredients for 4 people
Preparation time: 20'

1 1/3 lb (600 g) Goro clams, or other good-quality clams
Coarse salt, as needed
Extra-virgin olive oil
1 clove of Voghiera garlic or other garlic, crushed
7 oz (200 g) greens, cut into short lengths
Fresh green chile pepper, sliced, to taste
11 oz (320 g) spaghetti alla chitarra
Chopped parsley, for garnish

## Method

Purge the clams under cold running water with a handful of coarse salt for at least 30 minutes in the dark and covered. Choose them, letting them fall one by one into an empty container.
You can tell if the clams are empty or not by the noise they make as they fall.
Discard those leaking sand. Cook the clams, covered, in a frying pan with the oil, garlic, and a splash of water until they open (discard those that don't open). Shell the clams immediately and set clam meat aside. Strain and reserve the cooking water.
Make the sauce: In a large frying pan, sauté the clams with the oil, greens, and garlic over medium heat. Add the strained clam water and the clams. Simmer for 5 minutes. Add a few slices of fresh green chile pepper (cut using scissors so that the juices are not lost).
Cook the spaghetti in plenty of salted water until al dente. Drain and finish cooking in the pan with the sauce. Drizzle with a little oil and garnish with the chopped parsley.

# Fricassée of eel and chanterelle mushrooms with bay, pecorino, and anchovy emulsion

## Ingredients for 4 people
Preparation time: 40'

EMULSION
1 oz (30 g) aged pecorino
6 bay leaves
1 anchovy fillet in oil
Generous 3/4 cup (200 ml) extra-virgin olive oil
Salt and pepper to taste

MUSHROOMS AND EEL
7 oz (300 g) fresh chanterelle mushrooms
Salt , to taste
1 eel, weighing about 1 1/2-1 3/4 lb (700/800 g)

## Method

EMULSION
Chop all ingredients and place them in a blender. Blend for only a few seconds to avoid overheating the mixture.

MUSHROOMS
Clean and chop the mushrooms. Sauté them in a little oil in a frying pan for a few minutes with salt and some bay leaves. Keep warm.

EEL
Clean the eel and open it up (ask your fishmonger to do this for you). Cut into 4 pieces lengthwise. Roast in the oven at 400°F (210°C) for about 15 minutes. Fillet it, keeping the skin to be used as a garnish. Cut into small morsels.

## Serving

Mix the mushrooms, which have been cooked with the eel, in a steel terrine. Place a medium-sized cookie cutter in the center of the plate and fill with the eel and mushrooms, pressing down lightly with your fingertips.
Drizzle with a little sauce and garnish with the bay leaves and roasted eel skin.

# Pumpkin and ricotta frangipane

## Ingredients for 4 people
Preparation time: 1 h 20' – Resting time: 1 night

8 oz (250 g) Ferrarese Violina pumpkin, uncooked
3/4 cup (180 g) fresh Ricotta di Bufala

### FRANGIPANE
Scant 1/4 cup (50 g) cold hazelnut butter
2 whole eggs
3/4 cup (150 g) superfine sugar
1/3 cup (50 g) ground almonds
2 tablespoons (30 g) milk
2 tablespoons (30 g) fresh cream

### SHORTCRUST PASTRY
3 1/3 cups (500 g) flour
2 egg yolks
1 whole egg
Generous 3/4 cup (170 g) superfine sugar
1 1/4 cups (300 g) butter, at room temperature
1/4 teaspoon (2 g) yeast
Pinch of salt

Butter, for pan
Superfine sugar, for pan

## Method

Clean and peel the pumpkin. Cut into small to medium-sized cubes.
Melt a pat of butter in a large pot over low heat. Sprinkle the sugar into the bottom of the pot and gradually add the pumpkin, turning up the heat and brown for a few minutes. Set aside in a container.

### FRANGIPANE
Melt the hazelnut butter in a saucepan until it starts to color. Let cool slightly (but do not let it solidify). Beat the eggs and sugar in a steel bowl until frothy. Add the almonds and the remaining ingredients, followed by the melted butter. Cover and let rest in the refrigerator overnight.

### SHORTCRUST PASTRY
Sift the flour and make a hollow in the center.
Add all the ingredients to the hollow. Knead the mixture as quickly as possible (using a pastry cutter so that the mixture isn't overheated by your hands) to make a smooth pastry. Chill dough in the refrigerator for 3 hours before use.

## Serving

Butter a cake pan and sprinkle with superfine sugar, making sure that you tap the sides lightly to remove any excess sugar. Roll out the pastry to 1/8-inch (3-mm) thick and transfer to the prepared pan. Top with the pumpkin. Mix the frangipane with the Ricotta in a bowl until smooth. Pour the mixture into the cake pan. Bake at 350°F (180°C/gas mark 4) for about 15 minutes. The cake is done when a toothpick inserted in the center comes out clean. Let cool for a few minutes before turning cake out of the pan. Serve at room temperature or slightly warm.

# Paolo Donei

## MALGA PANNA RESTAURANT
### Moena (Trento)

From the veranda of the restaurant *Malga Panna* in Moena, a popular ski resort in Trentino, the view is breathtaking and completely silent. The 'fairy of the Dolomites' rests peacefully in a peaceful narrow river valley surrounded by the suggestive Latemar, Valacia and Costalunga mountains.

We also feel peaceful and welcome in this establishment, housed in an old and fully restored mountain hut at the foot of a beautiful wooded landscape. "In the family home, the mountain hut where they produced cream from the milk of cows grazing high on the mountain, there is now a restaurant that features that cream that has retained the name, the quality and genuine flavors" explains chef Paolo Donei, owner and co-operator of *Malga Panna* in cooperation with Michael Grossi, dining room maître and wine steward.

A family restaurant since the fifties, *Malga Panna* now offers a high level cuisine. This cuisine starts with tradition, of both the local Ladin people as well as the historical Trentino people, with elements of research and creativity, calibrated with a masterful technique and knowledge of raw materials. "For me, we have a relationship with the land that is very, very strong. We have a historic restaurant that has been going on for four generations: what we want is to give to the customer a journey back to the taste of our peasant origins... But without repeating the dishes. We want to bring out the flavors from traditions of the past and interpret them in a modern sense, using largely local products. The raw material is essential, it is eighty percent of the success of a dish..."

Today Paolo, who honors the territory with an open heart and without losing the traditional honesty of the mountaineers, has achieved significant professional recognition (he has been a Michelin star since 1993 and is a member of the *Jeunes Restaurateurs d'Europe* since 1997).

However it was not at all easy to convince his grandparents and parents to give a new face to the restaurant while presenting the recipes of the past in a more modern and lighter version. After learning the basics of cooking from the women in the house, Paolo attended hotel management school for a year, "But I did not really like the idea of continuing to study..." So, he dropped out of school to gain experience in the field. "From the age of 15 until I was 30 I interned in major restaurants to learn and improve my style, learning the deepest secrets of restaurant quality. First I worked in restaurants in Southern Tyrol, then in other regions such as the *Trigabolo* di Argenta inn the province of Ferrara. There I worked with Igles Corelli. I also worked abroad in Switzerland and in Germany. Meanwhile, between one stage and another, I continued to work in the family restaurant." At first he wanted to bring the cuisine he learned to his country, practicing with renowned chefs of influence, and for a brief period he even tried different experiments. But it didn't work: he understood that he had to return to his roots.

And it is his roots that are the protagonists of the courses chosen for this book. As an appetizer, a 'Rosé leg of venison with mixed dried fruit and ice cream mustard', a classic Trentino dish, combined with the flavors of its natural habitat including Golden apples. As a first course we have 'Barley with hop sprouts, smoked garlic cream and crayfish.' Barley is one of the most popular grains in the area; a dish that is typical of rural households is a simple barley soup. "The hop shoots are found in our meadows in the spring. The garlic is smoked with juniper, which provides that shade of smoke found the ancient barley soup, with its chunks of smoked pork. "

Next, as a second course, is: "Rabbit's leg with smoked potato salad and sprouts from radish to onion, and crispy bacon. The hare of our forests is of great quality; we combine it with smoked potatoes, typical of our land as well as bacon, and shoots to give it a grassy flavor."

Dessert is a 'compote of fruits and flowers' with "an elderflower mousse, served with a sauce of strawberries, a slush with violet petals served with fresh raspberries, a tiny *parfait* with *rosa canina* over a rhododendron honey jelly, served with mashed blackberries; a *crème brulée* with lavender and calendula, served with fresh red currants." A mine of flavors, fragrances and colors of the Moenese forest.

## Pink leg of kid
with mixed leaf salad, dried fruit
and mustard ice-cream
P.138

## Barley risotto
with hop sprouts,
crayfish,
and smoked garlic cream
P.140

## Leg of jack rabbit
with smoked potatoes, sprout salad,
and crispy speck
P.142

## An arrangement of fruit and flowers
P.144

# Pink leg of kid with mixed leaf salad, dried fruit and mustard ice-cream

## Ingredients for 4 people
Preparation time: 50'

### LEG OF KID
1 1/3 lb (600 g) leg of kid, cleaned
(ask your butcher to do this for you)
Salt, pepper
10 oz (300 g) whole dried spices, such as
cumin, juniper, pepper, mustard grains
Extra-virgin olive oil, for drizzling

### MUSTARD ICE CREAM
Scant 1/2 cup (100 g) extra-virgin olive oil
Scant 1 cup (225 g) mascarpone
1 tablespoon (15 g) plain yogurt
Scant 1 tablespoon (8 g) fresh chopped
chives
1/3 cup (80 g) tomato paste
Grainy mustard, such as *Moutarde de
Meaux*

### MIXED LEAF SALAD
2 Golden Delicious apples
2 bell peppers, 1 red, 1 yellow
3 oz (90 g) rye bread
2 tablespoons (30 g) veal demi-glace
1 1/4 cups (300 g) pumpkin seed oil
1/4 cup (60 g) apple vinegar
Extra-virgin olive oil, for sautéing
3 1/2 oz (100 g) mixed greens, such as
beet leaves, lovage, or sprouts
Plain yogurt, for serving
Olive oil, for serving

## Method

### LEG OF KID
Divide the leg of kid into parts weighing about 2 3/4-3 1/2 oz (80-100 g) each. Marinate it in salt, pepper, the dried spices, and a drizzle of olive oil for about 10 minutes. Place the meat in a vacuum pack and cook in a steam oven at a temperature of 140°F for 17-20 minutes.

### MUSTARD ICE CREAM
Meanwhile, mix the olive oil, sugar syrup, mascarpone, yogurt, chives, tomato paste, and mustard (all of which are cold). Season with salt to taste and churn in an ice-cream machine according to the manufacturer's instructions.

### MIXED LEAF SALAD
Dice the apples. Sauté the apples for a few minutes with the white wine and pepper. Cut the rye bread into cubes and toast in the oven. To dress the bell peppers, beat the reduced veal cooking juices with the pumpkin oil and apple vinegar. Sauté the bell peppers in a little oil in a frying pan. Add them to the dressing.

## Serving

Arrange the mixed salad on the plate with the apples, croutons, and dressing. Add a few drizzles of plain yogurt over the salad and place the kid on top, after having browned it all over. Add the mustard ice-cream and drizzle with a little olive oil.

# Barley risotto with hop sprouts, crayfish, and smoked garlic cream

Ingredients for 4 people
Preparation time: 40'

*STOCK
1 1/2 lb (700 g) beef
1 lb (500 g) veal
Salt
1 onion
1 carrot
1 celery stalk
1 bay leaf

SAUCE
1 3/4 lb (800 g) meat stock*
Generous 3/4 cup (200 g) mascarpone
2 oz (60 g) smoked garlic, unpeeled
Salt, pepper

BARLEY
1 3/4 oz (50 g) shallots, chopped
1 1/2 cups (300 g) pearl barley
Scant 1/4 cup (50 g) white wine
1 lb (500 g) hop sprouts
Generous 3/4 cup (200 g) extra-virgin olive oil
Salt, pepper
Scant 1/4 cup (50 g) butter
2 oz (60 g) Parmesan
14 oz (400 g) crayfish
3 1/2 oz (100 g) rolled pancetta
4 hop sprouts
1 clove of garlic

## Method

### STOCK
Put the meat in a large saucepan and cover with cold water.
Bring the water to a boil over medium heat, covered.
When the water comes to a boil, skim the froth, season with salt, and add the whole vegetables and the bay leaf.
Lower the heat, cover again, and simmer for about 2 1/2 hours.
Let cool and chill for at least 3 hours.
Before using the stock, remove the layer of fat that will have solidified on the surface.

### SAUCE
Bring a little stock to a boil with the mascarpone. Make small cuts in the unpeeled garlic and add to the stock. Let infuse. Season to taste and emulsify the sauce with the extra-virgin olive oil.

### BARLEY
Sweat the chopped shallot in a saucepan. Toast the barley for a few minutes. Add the white wine and let it evaporate. Continue cooking, adding the hot stock, mixing constantly. Meanwhile, blanch the hop sprouts. Sauté the sprouts in oil with the garlic and shallot. After the barley has been cooking for 40 minutes, add the prepared hop sprouts. Season to taste and add the butter and Parmesan at the end, like a risotto.

## Serving

Spoon the barley risotto into the center of a deep plate. Drizzle the foaming sauce around the barley and arrange the crayfish on top in the center, having just cooked them in a pan. Garnish with the pancetta, which has been dried in the oven, and the hop sprouts.

# Leg of jack rabbit with smoked potatoes, sprout salad, and crispy speck

### Ingredients for 4 people
Preparation time: 1 h 10'

1 lb (500 g) potatoes
Salted water
1 3/4 oz (50 g) larch shavings, or other aromatic smoking chips
14 oz (400 g) leg of jack rabbit
Extra-virgin olive oil
Fresh thyme branches
Fresh rosemary branches
Fresh sage leaves
Unpeeled garlic cloves
5 oz (150 g) speck (aged for 6 months)
3 1/2 oz (100 g) mixed sprouts, such as onion, radish, spelt, peas
Apple vinegar, to taste
Pumpkin oil, to taste
2 1/2 oz (100 g) game cooking juices
1/3 cup (80 g) butter
Wild thyme, or fresh thyme leaves, for serving

### Method

Cook the potatoes, skin on, in plenty of salted water. Meanwhile, toast the wood shavings dry in a pot. Once the potatoes have cooked, drain them and place them over the smoking shavings. Cover with a lid. Leave the potatoes to smoke for a few hours. If the aroma of the wood isn't sufficient, toast the shavings again.
Remove the fat and bone from the rabbit leg; clean the meat. Let marinate in olive oil, thyme, rosemary, sage, and garlic for 20 minutes. Brown the jack rabbit in very hot oil. Bake in the oven at 350°F (180°C/gas mark 4) for 5-6 minutes and let rest at 140°F (60°C) for 12 minutes.
While the meat is resting, cut the speck into thin sticks and brown in very hot oil. Drain on straw paper so that it stays crispy. Dress the sprout salad with apple vinegar, extra-virgin olive oil, pumpkin oil, salt, and pepper.

### Serving

Sauté the smoked potatoes in a pan with a pat of butter. Season with salt and pepper to taste. Arrange them on a plate. Cut the jack rabbit into four medallions and place on top of the potatoes. Drizzle the meat with the game cooking juices, whisk in butter and thyme (if possible, wild thyme that grows in the woods). Finish with the sprout salad and crispy speck.

# An arrangement of fruit and flowers

## Ingredients for 4 people
Preparation time: 4 h

### MLDERFLOWER MOUSSE
Generous 1/2 cup (125 g) sugar
Scant 1/4 cup (50 g) water
Scant 3 tablespoons (40 g)
lemon juice
4 sheets of gelatin
Generous 1 tablespoon (20 g)
soy lecithin
Generous 1 3/4 cups (450 g)
elderflower syrup
2 cups (500 g) whipped cream
1 tablespoon (15 g) candied
lemon
1 egg white

### DOG ROSE PARFAIT
1/4 cup (60 g) egg whites
2 tablespoons (30 g)
confectioners' sugar
4 egg yolks
1/2 cup (100 g) sugar
Scant 1 cup (140 g) dog rose puree
2 cups (500 g) whipped cream

### LAVENDER FLOWER CRÈME BRÛLÉE
1 1/4 cups (300 g) fresh cream
2 teaspoons (10 g) dried
lavender flowers
3 egg yolks
1/3 cup (70 g) sugar

### VIOLET GRANITA
1 1/4 cups (300 g) water
Scant 1/2 cup (90 g) sugar
Scant 3 tablespoons (40 g)
violet petal syrup

### ELDERFLOWER SYRUP
1 cup (250 g) water
Generous 3/4 cup (160 g) sugar
1 organic lemon
15 elderflowers

### SERVING
Scant 1/4 cup (40 g) brown sugar
Assortment of forest fruit, such
as strawberries, raspberries or
gooseberries

## Method

### ELDERFLOWER MOUSSE
To make the meringue, cook the sugar and water to a temperature of 250°F (121°C). Mix the sugar syrup into the beaten egg white; beat until it has cooled completely. Warm the lemon juice and add the gelatin, which has been soaked beforehand in water. Mix in the lecithin and elderflower syrup. Let the mixture cool. Mix it into the cream. Use a rubber spatula to spread out the meringue and chill in the refrigerator.

### DOG ROSE PARFAIT
Beat the egg whites with the confectioners' sugar until stiff peaks form. Beat the egg yolks with the sugar in the top of a double boiler. Mix in the rose puree and the whipped cream. Fold in the beaten whites. Divide the mixture into small molds and freeze for a few hours.

### LAVENDER FLOWER CRÈME BRÛLÉE
Bring the cream to a boil with the lavender flowers. Beat the egg yolks with the sugar and mix in the boiling cream. Strain the mixture and pour the cream into small ceramic molds. Cook in a steam oven at 195°F (90°C) for 30 minutes or in a static oven in a bain-marie for 25 minutes at 255°F (125°C).

### VIOLET GRANITA
Mix together the water, sugar, and violet syrup, all of which are cold. Pour the mixture into a wide, shallow container and place in the freezer. Use a whisk to break up the ice crystals every hour at least three times.

### ELDERFLOWER SYRUP
Boil the water with the sugar. Add the lemon, juiced and cut into tiny pieces, and the elderflowers and let marinate, in an airtight container, for 1 week.

## Serving
Sprinkle a small teaspoon of brown sugar over each crème brûlée and burn with a brûlée blowtorch. Decorate with currants and small lavender flowers. Spoon the granita into a small glass and decorate with fresh raspberries. Use a tablespoon to shape the elderflower mousse into quenelles and arrange them on a strawberry sauce. Remove the rose parfait from the freezer and decorate with a blackberry puree and small fresh fruits.

# Gennaro Esposito

## TORRE DEL SARACINO RESTAURANT
### Vico Equense (Naples)

Vico Equense, a charming town that dates back to the Etruscan age, hanging on a spur of rock over the Gulf of Naples, was celebrated in antiquity for its wines. Today it is known for the gastronomic delights of the restaurant *La Torre del Saracino,* founded in 1992 in the fishing village of Seiano. Destination of those who enjoy the pleasures of the table and a view like none other in the world, to celebrate the *otium* when the ancient Romans dedicated their numerous villas along this stretch of the Sorrento coast.

Reportedly the best restaurant in Campania in a renowned Italian food magazine and the owner of two Michelin stars, the restaurant owes its success not just to the talent of Gennaro Esposito, chef and co-owner with Vittoria Aiello: "I like to remember all the people who help me every day to produce quality, fellow workers who have followed me for years and who share with me many aspects of this work, allowing me to live it at its best." In addition to Vittoria who prepares the breads and sweets, starting and closing every lunch or dinner at the *Torre del Saracino*, thanks also go "to the stars of the dining room and kitchen: Ciro, Giovanni, Enzo, Salvatore, Fumiko, Giuseppe, Daniele and David."

The chef offers "a kitchen that is an expression of the different cultures of this land, through the use of the variety of local products." It is a porous kitchen, like the tuff of the land on which the restaurant stands, planned to use any product that Campania offers. Gennaro treats the raw materials of this land with grace. He gets excited: "When I look at a box of fish, a new world opens before me. I begin to think of how many dishes I could make… Every day, in our work, cooking is not a routine, but rather a pleasure."

"I have always had a great passion for cooking, because I had the good fortune to have a mother who was a very good cook. Working in the country, she always used quality products, and as a child I had the privilege of knowing and experiencing certain tastes." After first falling in love with the delicious dishes of mother Carmela, cooking became his "reason for living." The love with which he carries out his work and christens each dish creates a juxtaposition of flavors so well-paired they almost shine, as well as make everybody's mouth water. "I signed up in the hotel school and from there I began my training traveling through Italy and Europe. Each leg of the journey was important, and I even learnt what not to do..." The most significant were undoubtedly the lessons that I received from Gianfranco Vissani, "that gave me the respect, the love and sensitivity for the most important raw materials", and from Alain Ducasse in Montecarlo and in Paris, "where I learned the importance of the perfect organization of work and meticulous attention to detail." When there was an opportunity to open his own restaurant, he returned home. "Since I had already been working in kitchens for many years, I thought I would talk about it with Vittoria, another person with years of experience." And they capitalized on the opportunity. "When I came here, I recovered the identity of our land and tried to enable it in a noble way." And he has done so through a straightforward and effective planning. Since then, "mine has been a story of knowledge and awareness, above all through a continuous exchange with my experienced colleagues, thanks to the *Jeunes Restaurateurs d'Europe*, of which I am a member."

The menu in this book offers as appetizer a zucchini soup with prawns and poached egg: "Very evocative of tradition, but presented in a lighter version, close to our concept of cooking, both for the ingredients as well as the use of modern cooking methods." The first course is a *timballo di candele in piedi* (candele pasta) with Neapolitan sauce – a classic Neapolitan dish revised. "The ingredients are very traditional, such as the famous San Marzano tomatoes; only the way the dish is cooked has changed as well as the preparation of the filling to fit it within a meal." In the past it was a sumptuous dish, almost an exorcism of the atavistic hunger of Naples, well embodied by its famous mask of *Pulcinella*. "If the first course impresses you for the way it is put together, the second will excite with its freshness." This is a cod cooked in a broth with tomato leaves, saffron broth and citrus: "A simple dish, but with the great charm of the South." And to finish, a characteristic dessert: the Neapolitan *babà*, served with custard and wild strawberries.

## Zucchini soup
with shrimp and a poached egg
P.150

## Timbale of ziti pasta
served on Neapolitan ragù
P.152

## Salt cod cooked
in tomato leaves, saffron stock,
and citrus fruit
P.154

## Neapolitan Babà
with pastry cream
and wild strawberries
P.156

# Zucchini soup with shrimp and a poached egg

## Ingredients for 4 people
Preparation time: 20'

**VEGETABLE STOCK (1 LITER)**
1 potato
1 white onion
1 carrot
1 stalk celery
1 quart (1 liter) water
Small bunch of herbs (thyme, bay leaf, wild fennel)
1/4 teaspoon (2 g) coarse salt

**ZUCCHINI SOUP**
1 lb (500 g) whole, small zucchini, including leaves, stalks, sprouts, and flowers

1 tablespoon (15 g) chopped onion
Generous 2 tablespoons (35 g) extra-virgin olive oil
Generous 1 tablespoon (20 g) lard, diced
1 3/4 oz (50 g) new potatoes, peeled and diced
2 1/2 quarts (2.5 liters) vegetable stock
8 red shrimp, shelled
2 teaspoons (10 g) salt
Pepper
4 fresh eggs
Extra-virgin olive oil, for drizzling
Pinch *fleur de sel*, for garnish

## Method

### STOCK
Clean and peel the potato. Peel the onion. Clean the carrot and trim ends. Clean the celery. Pour the water into a large pot and add the vegetables and herbs. Bring to a boil and add a generous pinch of salt.
Lower the heat to its lowest setting and simmer, covered, for 45 minutes. Remove from the heat; strain the stock and let cool.

### SOUP
Clean the stalks, leaves, flowers, and sprouts well under plenty of running water. Blanch in boiling water and plunge immediately in ice water to stop the cooking. Drain, lightly squeezing zucchini parts dry; dice the zucchini.
Sauté the onion in the oil in a saucepan. Add the lard and potatoes and brown them. Add the all zucchini parts and vegetable stock. Cook over low heat for about 8 minutes. Heat the shrimp in a nonstick pan. Season with salt and pepper.

### POACHED EGGS
Break one egg at a time into salted, boiling water, using a slotted spoon to make sure that the egg yolk and white fall one on top of one another. This will ensure that the egg remains in once piece when cooked, as shown in the photo. Poach until set, 3 to 5 minutes.

## Serving

Ladle the soup into the center of a deep plate. Arrange 2 red shrimp in the center and place a poached egg on top. Garnish with a drizzling of oil and a pinch of *fleur de sel*.

# Timbale of ziti pasta served on Neapolitan ragù

## Ingredients for 4 people
Preparation time: 1 h - Cooking time: 5 h

14 oz (400 g) beef eye of round
1 small bunch of parsley
Scant 1/3 cup (50 g) pine nuts
3 cloves garlic, sliced
1 3/4 oz (50 g) Pecorino cheese, grated
Salt and pepper
10 oz (300 g) pork rinds
1 medium yellow onion, chopped
1 3/4 oz (50 g) beef suet
1 lb (500 g) pork ribs
5 oz (150 g) shin of beef
1/3 cup (80 g) extra-virgin olive oil
3 cups (750 ml) dry white wine

6 2/3 lb (3 kg) San Marzano tomato passata

FILLING
1 yellow onion
Scant 1/3 cup (70 g) extra-virgin olive oil
5 oz (150 g) ground meat (3 1/2 oz/100 g lean beef and 1 1/2 oz/50 g lean pork)
Generous 3 tablespoons (50 g) white wine
Generous 3/4 cup (200 g) tomato passata
3 1/2 oz (100 g) Mozzarella di Bufala Campana cheese, chopped

1/3 cup (80 g) cream
Scant 1/2 cup (50 g) semi-aged Caciocavallo cheese, grated
2 3/4 oz (80 g) Burrata cheese, chopped
Salt and pepper

TIMBALE
1 lb (500 g) ziti pasta
4 molds, buttered and sprinkled with breadcrumbs
Generous 3/4 cup (200 g) Ricotta cheese, cut into cubes
A drop of extra-virgin olive oil
Fresh basil leaves, for garnish

## Method

Fill the beef eye with some of the parsley, pine nuts, sliced garlic, grated Pecorino, salt, and pepper. Roll up meat and secure with kitchen string. Make more rolls using the pork rinds and the remaining filling ingredients. Sauté the onion, garlic, and suet in a pot (preferably copper or earthenware). Add the rolls, pork ribs, and shin of beef. Cook for 5 minutes. Add the white wine and let it evaporate. Add the tomato passata and season with a little salt. Cook over very high heat for about 5 hours. Season with salt to taste.
Sauté the chopped onion and garlic with the oil in a frying pan. Add the ground meat and brown over low heat. Add the white wine and let it evaporate. Pour in the tomato passata and cook over low heat for about 20 minutes. When the meat has cooled, add the Mozzarella di Bufala, cream, Caciocavallo, and Burrata. Season with salt and pepper.

TIMBALE
Cook the ziti pasta carefully in plenty of salted boiling water in a deep saucepan. Cook for 3 to 4 minutes. Drain well using two slotted spoons. Spread the pasta out on a work surface and let cool. Cut the ziti to the height of the mold. Fill the molds individually with the mixture using a pastry bag. Arrange the ziti vertically in the mold. Bake in the oven at 350°F (180°C/gas mark 4) for about 8 minutes. Butter a baking sheet and arrange the ricotta. Drizzle with a little olive oil. Bake in the oven at 350°F (180°C/gas mark 4) for about 4 minutes.

## Serving

Position a ladleful of hot ragù (meat sauce) in the center of the plate. Turn the timbale out on top of the sauce. Garnish with the ricotta and a few leaves of fresh basil.

# Salt cod cooked in tomato leaves, saffron stock, and citrus fruit

### Ingredients for 4 people
Preparation time: 50'

4 slices of salt cod, each weighing about 100 g
8 large tomato leaves
Scant 1/2 cup (100 g) extra-virgin olive oil
Freshly ground pepper
1 oz (30 g) seaweed
Scant 1/2 cup (100 g) tomato water*
1 tomato, cut into 4 slices and broiled
1 orange
1 lemon
Steamed vegetables, such as zucchini, carrots, and green beans, for serving, optional
Pinch *Fleur de sel,* for garnish
2 saffron strands

*\* The tomato water comes from separating the passata. For 100 g of water, you will need at least 1 kilogram of tomatoes (we like to use Cuore di Bue tomatoes).*

### Method

Wrap each slice of salt cod in 2 tomato leaves. Place in the vacuum packs used for sous vide cooking, adding 2 tablespoons of oil and a grating of pepper. Seal and cook at 160°F (70°C) for 30 minutes.
Dehydrate the seaweed, so that it becomes more delicate; cook in the oven at 175°F (80°C) for about an hour. Soak in the tomato water with the saffron at 160°F (70°C) for 10 minutes. The temperature is fundamental as it alters the flavor and aroma.

### Serving

Remove the seaweed and spoon a ladleful of the water in the center of a deep plate. Arrange a slice of broiled tomato with the salt cod on top. Grate the zest of the orange and lemon and sprinkle over the plate with a few crumbs of dehydrated seaweed.
Garnish with steamed vegetables, if desired. Finish with a pinch of *fleur de sel* and a drizzling of extra-virgin olive oil.

# Neapolitan Babà with pastry cream and wild strawberries

## Ingredients for 4 people
Preparation time: 45' - Leavening time: 2 h

### BABÀ
3 1/3 cups (500 g) manitoba flour (type 0)
2/3 cup (150 g) butter, softened
9 whole eggs
1/4 cup (50 g) sugar
Generous 1 tablespoon (20 g) brewer's yeast
2 teaspoons (10 g) table salt

### SYRUP
2 cups (500 g) water

1 1/4 cups (250 g) sugar
Orange and lemon zests
1 vanilla pod

### PASTRY CREAM
2 cups (500 ml) milk
Orange and lemon zests
3/4 cup (150 g) sugar
6 egg yolks
4 tablespoons (60 g) all-purpose flour

## Method

### BABÀ
Combine the flour, scant 1/2 cup (100 g) butter, 8 eggs, sugar, salt, and the yeast in an electric stand mixer or a food processor. Mix until ingredients form a dough. Knead in the remaining egg and butter by hand, adding a little at a time to form a voluminous and elastic dough. Let rise for about 1 hour, or until doubled in volume. Beat the dough again in a stand mixer or food processor. Use a pastry bag to pipe the dough into buttered molds. Let rise for another hour. Bake baba in the oven at 400°F (200°C/gas mark 6).

### SYRUP
Bring the water to a boil with the sugar, orange and lemon zests, and vanilla pod in a small saucepan. Let cool until lukewarm.

### PASTRY CREAM
Bring the milk to a boil with the citrus zests. Beat together the sugar, egg yolks, and flour in an electric mixer. Slowly whisk in the boiling milk; transfer mixture to the top of a double boiler and cook gently, stirring constantly to ensure that the eggs don't curdle.

## Serving

Soak the baba in the syrup before serving. Arrange the babà on a plate, served with the pastry cream and the wild strawberries.

# Alfio Fascendini

## VECCHIO RISTORO RESTAURANT DA ALFIO E KATIA
### Aosta

t may sound like a fairy tale, but it is a true story with a happy ending. When Alfio Fascendini was just 15 years old, he left his home in Val Chiavenna to wash pots in a restaurant, with a cardboard suitcase and a dream of becoming a chef. He came from a humble peasant family, the second of seven children. It was hard to leave his loved ones and face the prospect of sacrifice, but his dream could not wait. With strong determination, cheerful and positive, he moved forward. "It's been thirty five years since I left home", he says, "together with Katia, a very special person with whom I have been married for over twenty years. I certainly have been amply rewarded."

His pride is the restaurant *Vecchio Ristoro* that he runs with his wife who is in charge of the dining room, located in the historic center of Aosta, a charming place with a cozy and delightful thousand-year history, as indicated by the name that satisfies both the soul and the palate. "From an early age I was charmed by the work done in hotels: I often fantasized about an uncle who worked in a hotel in Germany... I have also always had a great love for the products, the curiosity to understand them and continually discover new ones." After attending hotel school in Sondrio, Valtellina, in 1978 he began to work in Valmalenco. He then worked at seaside locations, such as Sardinia, Calabria, and Puglia. In 1985 he worked at the *Hotel Gallia* in Milan, then the *Grand Hotel Brun*, and finally went to Aosta with his wife, who was also from Valtellina, in the spring of '89. He started at the famous *Cavallo Bianco* restaurant of the brothers Paolo and Franco Vai, which was awarded two Michelin stars. He worked there, in the kitchen of a landmark Italian restaurant, until '91 when the restaurant was closed. This marked the beginning of his professional transformation: I was given the opportunity to focus on what I had learned in previous years and to understand how that could help me bring out my personality." After his years at the *Hotel Europe* in the heart of Aosta, in '95 he took over the *Vecchio Ristoro* and decided to stay in the land of the Aosta Valley. After two years of work, mastering this culinary tradition, he earned a Michelin star.

"My cooking is very traditional, but with slight changes, improved, personalized but without straying excessively from the original. I am quite inflexible, being a mountaineer, so I never change the ingredients: I think that is dangerous territory..." He may revisit tradition, then break down the dishes into their component parts. As Alfio says, "Tradition must always be treated with respect: it is history and continuity, and it means looking back to be able to go forward. And for a chef it is crucial to possess a depth of traditional culture." All menus in this book are regional. The starter is a leek pie with a lard Arnad mousse and a sauce of rye bread flavored with honey: "In the Aosta Valley there is a tradition of making toasted black bread with butter smeared on - in this recipe I eliminated that. - Other ingredients are honey, which is harvested in different parts of the region, and varies in each region of the valley, as well as slices of lard. I have not moved away from this traditional dish so much: I made a pie with leeks and I maintained the main components of lard with rye bread and honey."

The first course is a Bavarian *Fontina* cheese served with a warm soup of whipped barley cream with carrots. "Here, in winter, barley or spelt soups are very popular." The second course, however, is a fillet of beef reminder the classic Val d'Aosta *carbonade*. "It's served on polenta with a *carbonade* sauce and creamy onions." Finally, for dessert, a frozen yarrow parfait with a sauce of honey, chestnuts and yarrow: "Yarrow is an herb, slightly bitter but pleasant, which is frequently used here to make herbal teas in summer evenings." A dessert not to be missed, like all those by Alfio. Suffice it to say that a New York couple who tours Europe every year, always stops in Aosta, to enjoy peach *zuccotto* with *amaretto* custard filling, served with raspberry sauce. "This for me is the essence of a successful chef, whose efforts extend far beyond just profit..."

# Leek timbale

with lard d'Arnad mousse

P.162

# Creamy pearl

barley risotto in carrot sauce,
served with fontina bavarian cream

P.164

# Fillet of beef

served on polenta toasts
with carbonade sauce

P.166

# Yarrow semifreddo

with chestnut honey
and mountain juniper sauce

P.168

# Leek timbale with lard d'Arnad mousse

### Ingredients for 4 people
Preparation time: 50' – Resting time: 20'

**SHORTCRUST PASTRY**
1 3/4 cups (250 g) all-purpose flour
4 tablespoons (60 g) butter
1 egg
Salt to taste
Water, as needed

**LARD MOUSSE**
7 oz (200 g) lard d'Arnad, or other
good-quality lard
Scant 1/4 cup (50 g) whipped cream
Scant 1/4 cup (50 g) stiffly beaten
egg white

**TIMBALE**
7 oz (200 g) shortcrust pastry
5 oz (150 g) stewed leeks
2 eggs
2 Scant 1/2 cup (100 g) cream
Salt, pepper and nutmeg

**RYE BREAD SAUCE**
Generous 3/4 cup (200 g) water
Scant 1/4 cup (50 g) milk
Scant 1/4 cup (50 g) flower-
scented honey
3 1/2 oz (100 g) rye bread

### Method

**SHORTCRUST PASTRY**
Knead together all the ingredients listed above on a wooden surface and
let the pastry rest for a few hours in a cool place.

**TIMBALE**
Roll out the shortcrust pastry to 1/4 inch (1/2 cm) thick and cut out four
discs with a pastry cutter. Use the discs to line 4 timbale molds. Arrange
the stewed leeks in the molds, dividing them evenly.
Meanwhile, beat the eggs with a whisk. Add the cream and season with
salt, pepper, and nutmeg. Pour the mixture into the molds and bake in
the oven for 15 minutes at 425°F (220°C/gas mark 7).

**MOUSSE**
Dice the lard and blend it in a food processor until a smooth, thick puree
is obtained. Mix together the whipped cream and stiffly beaten egg white
and add the lard puree. Chill for 20 minutes.

**RYE BREAD SAUCE**
Place a saucepan over medium heat and bring the water, milk, and honey
to a boil. Add the bread, cut into cubes, and blend with a hand-held
immersion blender. Strain through a sieve and keep warm.

### Serving

Turn out the timbales and arrange them in the center of each serving
plate. Use a pastry bag to pipe a rosette of the mousse on the top of each
timbale. Garnish with fried leek and serve with the rye bread sauce.

# Creamy pearl barley risotto in carrot sauce, served with fontina bavarian cream

### Ingredients for 4 people
Preparation time: 45' – Soaking: 12 h – Resting time: 2 h

**STOCK**
1 1/2 lb (700 g) beef
1 lb (500 g) veal
Salt
1 onion
1 carrot
1 celery stalk
1 bay leaf

**FONDUE**
5 oz (150 g) fontina cheese
1 cup milk, plus additional for soaking cheese
1 1/2 oz (40 g) butter
1/3 cup (40 g) all-purpose flour

**BAVARIAN CREAM**
Generous 3/4 cup (200 ml) fondue
2 sheets of gelatin

Scant 1/4 cup (50 ml) cream, whipped
1 1/2 oz (50 g) egg whites, beaten to stiff peaks

**CARROT SAUCE**
10 oz (300 g) carrots
1 potato, approximately 3 1/2 oz (100 g)
Salted water
Generous 1 tablespoon (20 ml) extra-virgin olive oil

**BARLEY**
2 cups (500 ml) vegetable stock
12 1/2 oz (360 g) dried barley, soaked in cold water for 12 hours
Raw, julienned carrots, for serving
1/2 cup (80 g) toasted hazelnuts, for serving

## Method

### STOCK

Put the meat in a large saucepan and cover with cold water.
Bring the water to a boil over medium heat, covered.
When the water comes to a boil, skim the froth, season with salt, and add the whole vegetables and the bay leaf.
Lower the heat, cover again, and simmer for about 2 1/2 hours.
Let cool and chill for at least 3 hours.
Before using the stock, remove the layer of fat that will have solidified on the surface.

### FONDUE

Cut the Fontina into small cubes and soak in a little milk.
Melt the butter in a small saucepan and add the flour to make a roux. In a separate saucepan, bring the milk to a boil; slowly pour it into the roux and bring mixture to a boil. Add the Fontina and stir until melted (You can add a drop of white wine, which will help you to dilute the cheese). Remove from heat and cover with plastic wrap once fully melted.

### FONTINA BAVARIAN CREAM

Pour the fondue into the top of a double boiler and let melt. Add the gelatin, which has been softened beforehand in cold water, drained, and squeezed out. Dissolve the gelatin and lower the temperature of the fondue to 105°F (40°C). Fold in the whipped cream and egg whites until well combined. Pour the mixture into individual molds. Chill for at least two hours before serving. (You can also prepare these the day before).

### CARROT SAUCE

Peel the carrots and potato, cut them into large pieces, and cook in salted water until tender. Transfer the vegetables to a food processor with one-part of the cooking water. Add the extra-virgin olive oil and blend until a smooth, even cream forms. Pour into a saucepan and keep warm.

### BARLEY

Bring the vegetable stock to a boil; add the barley. Cook until tender and drain. Add the barley to the carrot sauce and boil for 4 minutes, stirring with a wooden spoon (like a risotto). When the carrot sauce and barley are thick and there is plenty of liquid, cover the saucepan for 1 minute before serving.

## Serving

Place each Bavarian cream mold in the center of a deep, chilled plate. Garnish with raw carrot sticks and pour the barley mixture around the cream. Sprinkle with hazelnuts and serve.

# Fillet of beef served on polenta toasts with carbonade sauce

### Ingredients for 4 people
Preparation time: 2 h 30' – Marinating: 1 day

SAUCE
4 cups red wine
1 lb (500 g) beef cuttings
1/2 cup (50 g) smoked pancetta
2 medium onions, finely chopped
1 celery stalk, finely chopped
15 black peppercorns
10 whole cloves
3/4 teaspoon (2 g) ground cinnamon
10 juniper berries
1 bay leaf
2 tablespoons all-purpose flour
2 cups water

BEEF
3 beef fillets, each weighing 4 oz (120 g)
Extra-virgin olive oil, for frying

### Method

SAUCE
Place all the ingredients in a stainless steel or other nonreactive bowl and chill for 24 hours to marinate.
Drain the marinade, reserving the liquid. Sauté the drained vegetables and beef cuttings in a deep frying pan. Sprinkle with 2 tablespoons of flour and add the wine from the marinade. Add 2 cups (500 ml) of water and simmer for 2 hours.
Strain mixture into a bowl; you should have a sauce that is fairly thick and shiny. Keep warm while you prepare the beef.

BEEF
Fry the 4 fillets in extra-virgin olive oil in a frying pan until cooked. Remove from heat and let rest in warm pan for 5 minutes.

### Serving

Arrange 4 round polenta toasts, which have been sautéed in butter, in the center of the plates. Place the fillets on top and drizzle with the sauce. Serve at once.

# Yarrow semifreddo with chestnut honey and mountain juniper sauce

### Ingredients for 4 people
Preparation time: 40' – Cooling: 8 h

YARROW SYRUP
1/2 cup (125 g) water
Scant 2/3 cup (125 g) sugar
2 teaspoons (10 g) lemon juice
2 tablespoons (30 g) dried yarrow

*PARFAIT*
12 egg yolks
1/3 cup (50 g) confectioners' sugar
2 cups (500 g) cream, whipped
2 teaspoons (10 g) glucose

CHESTNUT HONEY AND MOUNTAIN JUNIPER SAUCE
Generous 3/4 cup (200 ml) chestnut honey
10 juniper berries, crushed
Scant 1 teaspoon (4 g) gelatin

### Method

YARROW SYRUP
Boil all the ingredients together for several minutes; strain syrup into a pot.

*PARFAIT*
Beat the egg yolks with the confectioners' sugar. Slowly beat in the the syrup, which has been heated to 230°F (112°C), and mix until the mixture has cooked. Fold in the whipped cream and pour the mixture into individual molds. Freeze for at least 8 hours before serving.

HONEY SAUCE
Boil the chestnut honey; whisk in juniper berries and gelatin until gelatin is completely dissolved. Let cool.

### Serving

Remove the semifreddo from the mold and arrange in the center of the plate.
Decorate with yarrow, fresh mint, and caramelized sugar. Glaze with the honey sauce.

# Claudio Filoni

## LA PURITATE RESTAURANT
### Gallipoli (Lecce)

The philosophy of the *La Puritate* restaurant in Gallipoli, located on the splendid Ionic coast in the Province of Lecce, is like the interior of the Baroque churches of Salento, abandoning the pictorial overabundance that characterize this style in the rest of Italy and becoming more simplistic. The restaurant, considered by many as the best on the Salento Peninsula, offers frank and straightforward dishes with no cessions to fad.

"Mine is a simple kitchen, fast and flavorful", states chef Claudio Filoni, who works at *La Puritate* six months every year, from June to November, when work increases and an extra hand is needed to help the children of the owners, Daniela Fedele. "The raw materials cannot be changed by the addition of spices or flavors; it must be processed as little as possible and prepared as quickly as possible." A clear and concise mandate, which the restaurant has successfully honored for over ten years. Opened in 1997 by Paolo Fedele with the assistance of father Ernesto, both dining room managers, the restaurant is backed by more than one generation of restaurateurs. From a simple inn at the beginning of the 20th Century, the first of its kind in Gallipoli, to the *trattoria* after World War II with an adjoining grocery store.

The restaurant today, named *La Puritate* for its location next to the historic Church of Santa Maria della Purità, offers a monographic kitchen that still offers a thousand pleasures: "We serve fish almost exclusively." And they do not neglect any of the great wealth offered by the Ionian Sea to the table: hake, tattler, squid, cuttlefish, skipjack, monkfish, mackerel, lobster, crab, mullet, swordfish, tuna…

"We use very few vegetables. Our fish is so fresh that the client is satisfied with just that and does not feel the need for a side dish." And although the Salentino table offers, especially in the hinterland, other delicious vegetables and dairy products and legumes of great renown, Claudio does not attempt any combination. The fish, "brought directly to our restaurant by a fisherman every morning, when he arrives in his boat", it must be served 'by itself', with no gastronomic dressing. "My philosophy is that we should taste the fish for what it is, without either preparing it or eating it with strong seasonings."

The menu, with specialties of the house and classic examples of the local cuisine, does not often change. Its universal nature is not misled by creative experiments. "But when we have a fish other than those mentioned – we work with the fish of the day – the waiter informs the client of this." Recipes from the past are not changed in any way, shape or form. "Tradition remains untouched, there is no change, as it should be." Like the rooster with the crown that appears in the Gallipoli coat of arms with the Latin inscription that reads *fideliter excubat*, or 'watch over carefully', so is the cooking of Claudio, with his gastronomic past.

Claudio was born in Milan of parents from Galatina, a wonderful Salentino city. "In 1983 I worked in a restaurant in Germany for about a year, then I came back to Italy and together with my brother Enzo Fusari, a great chef and teacher in a famous hotel school in Milano, I opened a restaurant on the Isle of Elba. He taught me all the tricks of the trade: he was an excellent teacher. Then about twenty years ago while I was on vacation in this area, I fell in love with a girl from Galatina, we got married and I decided to come and live here. I started to work in different restaurants in the Lecce area; I traveled the entire coast from Santa Maria di Leuca to San Giovanna until in 2004 I found here, in the *Puritate*, the perfect setting."

The menu selected for the book naturally revolves around Ionian fish. As appetizer we have 'marinated fresh tuna', "served with a drizzle of our extra virgin olive oil, which is essential on the fish", the first course, 'linguine with bonito fish' covered with cubed tomatoes, and the second course is 'Angler fish medallions with lemon', "lightly floured and browned in oil – without bruising in the pan – and served with lemon juice, a knob of butter, a scattering of parsley, salt and pepper." As *dessert*, is a *torta pasticciotto*, "a typical sweet, made of a very crisp pastry, stuffed with lemon custard: the perfect ending of a meal based on fish." The sweet, created by a pastry chef of Galatina in the mid-18th Century, is a Salento custom, often eaten for breakfast, freshly baked, almost boiling.

# Fresh marinated mackerel

P.**174**

# Linguine with bonito fish

P.**176**

# Angler fish medallions with lemon
al limone

P.**178**

# *Torta pasticciotto*

P.**180**

# Fresh marinated mackerel

### Ingredients for 4 people
Preparation time: 30'

2 lb (1 kg) mackerel
6 lemons
Pinch of salt
Pinch of pepper
Parsley
1 quart (1 liter) extra-virgin olive oil

### Method

Clean the mackerel, removing the insides. Use a sharp knife to cut into two fillets. Use some small pliers to remove the bones remaining in the central part of the fillet.
Place a saucepan full of water over medium heat. Add the juice of the lemons and the lemons themselves. Season with salt and pepper. When the water comes to a boil, add the fish and cook for about 8 minutes.

### Serving

Drain the fish and arrange in a dish. Sprinkle with the chopped parsley and drizzle with the extra-virgin olive oil.

# Linguine with bonito fish

## Ingredients for 4 people
Preparation time: 25'

7 oz (200 g) bonito fish
1 clove garlic
tablespoons extra-virgin olive oil
Salt, to taste
Pepper, to taste
5 oz (150 g) peeled and chopped tomatoes
7 oz (200 g) linguine pasta

## Method

Sauté the bonito fish, cut into small strips, with the garlic in
a little oil in a pan for a couple of minutes. Season with salt
and pepper. Add the chopped tomatoes.
Meanwhile, cook the linguine in plenty of salted water until
*al dente*.

## Serving

Drain the pasta. Transfer to the pan with the sauce.
Cook for a few minutes over low heat and serve.

# Angler fish medallions with lemon

## Ingredients for 4 people
Preparation time: 20'

7 oz (200 g) angler fish or monkfish, cleaned and cut into slices
4 tablespoons extra-virgin olive oil
Salt, for seasoning
Pepper, for seasoning
Flour to dust
4 tablespoons lemon juice
1 pat of butter
Parsley

## Method

Skin the angler fish and cut into 1 1/4-inch (3-cm) thick slices.
Warm a little oil in a frying pan over medium heat. Season the fish
with salt and pepper. Dip them in the flour, shaking off the excess.
Fry the fish for 5 minutes in the heated oil in the pan.
Strain off the cooking oil. Drizzle the fish with the lemon juice and
add a pat of butter. Sprinkle with the parsley and season with salt
and pepper. Serve at once.

# Torta pasticciotto

## Ingredients for 4 people
Preparation time: 1 h

PASTRY CREAM
1 cup (250 ml) milk
1/2 vanilla pod
Zest of 1/2 lemon
1 cup (250 g) egg yolks
3/4 cup (150 g) sugar
Scant 3 tablespoons (40 g) flour, sifted
1 cup (250 ml) cream

SHORTCRUST PASTRY
4 cups (600 g) flour
Generous 3/4 cup (200 g) lard, diced
Scant 1/2 cup (100 g) butter, softened
1 1/2 cups (300 g) sugar
2 whole eggs
2 egg yolks
Grated lemon

## Method

PASTRY CREAM
Bring the milk to a boil in a saucepan with the vanilla and lemon zest. Beat the egg
yolks and sugar in a metal bowl. Add the flour and mix well. Slowly whisk in the boiling
milk. Return the mixture to the heat in the saucepan used to boil the milk. Bring to a
boil for 2 minutes. Pour the custard into a metal bowl and let cool.

SHORTCRUST PASTRY
Mix the flour with the diced lard and softened butter on a work surface. Add the sugar,
egg yolks, and grated lemon. Knead the mixture quickly.
Oil a cake pan. Roll out half the pastry and use it to line the pan. Pour the pastry cream
into the cake pan. Roll out the remaining pastry and cover the pastry cream. Brush with
beaten egg whites. Bake in the oven at 350°F (180°C/gas mark 4) for about 1 hour.

## Serving

Serve very hot.

# Giuliana Germiniani

## CAPRICCIO RESTAURANT
### Manerba del Garda (Brescia)

Giuliana Germiniani, started from the bottom of the menu. Chef and co-owner, along with her young daughter Francesca Tassi of the *Capriccio* restaurant in Montinelle, a hamlet of Manerba on the Brescia side of Lake Garda. She has moved forward, with great humility and mastery. Her desserts made her famous, and then she conquered the seconds, firsts, and finally appetizers. Requited love, joyful and faithful, which blossomed into a state- of- the- art cuisine.

The Michelin-starred restaurant is in an elegant house surrounded by greenery with an impressive, wide summer veranda and an elegant dining room. Wide windows look out on myriads of flowers grown by Giuliana against the sweet outline of hills of olive groves and vineyards, between lush green fields and the tranquil blue waters of the lake. Everything, from the bread made fresh daily and available in different versions, to desserts made with constant enthusiasm and originality, "aims to show that we think of our customer first and foremost as a guest to 'be cherished', to provide him/her with a serene experience to be remembered with pleasure", says Giuliana.

The *Capriccio* was founded in 1967 by Maria Veggio and Martino Germiniasi, Giuliana's parents, who decided to open a restaurant – with her in the kitchen and him in the dining room –, open from Easter until the end of September and just a few kilometers from their current home. As it often happens, Giuliana and her future husband, Giancarlo Tassi, who was then working at a car dealership, helped in the restaurant. "Seeing that Giancarlo was very good in the dining room, after the restaurant lease expired my father suggested they look for another place, this time to buy, where we could move the venue. So we started this adventure together. The new *Capriccio* was inaugurated in 1985, when we got married, and marked the beginning of a close-knit team."

As a girl Giuliana did not think of becoming a chef. "After finishing with high school specializing in modern languages, I was supposed to go abroad to improve my languages, but my mother told me: Help out this season, and leave in October. I accepted... and as it turned out, I never moved on from the restaurant." In the new *Capriccio*, Giuliana was in the dining room with her husband for eight years until she realized that the desserts were not up to the restaurant's standards. "At that point, a kitchen boy told me, very politely: if you don't like them, you make them yourself. I accepted the challenge and started taking courses at confectioners' level to learn how to create the best desserts. Eventually, I liked art of pastry so much that, in mid- service, I would go into the kitchen to prepare dessert. So my mother asked me to permanently enter the kitchen to learn everything she could teach me so that someday I could take her place. So I did, and I slowly got a passion for savory dishes. And now the kitchen is my life." A passion but with talent: her dishes are well thought out, consistent, balanced and never dull, able to combine flavor and lightness.

"Although my kitchen is Mediterranean because we offer seafood, we love to complete our menu with traditional local dishes with both meat and fish from the lake." Many of the dishes are from Garda. Here innovation, which must never be lacking, plays into the recipes with cooking techniques such as vacuum-packed and using low temperatures as well as presentation. "For me this is very important because my philosophy is that a person first sees a dish and then tastes it to decide if it is good or not."

The menu chosen for this book is completely regional, with courses that allow you to breathe the fresh air and sunny fragrance of the Garda Riviera. The starter is a variation on fish from the lake, a true harmony of flavors: a terrine of whitefish and vegetables, *cous-cous* with carp tartar (a delicious fish that lives in Lake Garda), lake-water shrimp marinated in sweet passion fruit sorbet with fennel and fried bleak. The first course is fresh *ravioli*, stuffed with creamed corn and *Bagòss* cheese, typical of the nearby village of Bagolino, black Valtenesi truffles and a poached egg. As a second course, perch fillet with a thin golden crust of bread and thyme, crispy prawns with chanterelles mushrooms in two firings and their concentrated juice. And for dessert, a seven-grain tart with elderflower cream, marinated peaches and their juice.

## A variety of lake fish:
whitefish and vegetable terrine, couscous
with carp tartare, crayfish marinated in passion fruit
with fennel sorbet, and fried bleak

P.186

## Ravioli filled with polenta cream
and Bagòss cheese, served with Valtenesi black truffle

P.190

## Browned perch fillets
in a light thyme breadcrumb with crispy tiger shrimp
and two types of chanterelles and their reduction

P.192

## Mixed grain tart
with elderflower cream and peach puree

P.194

# A variety of lake fish: whitefish and vegetable terrine, couscous with carp tartare, crayfish marinated in passion fruit with fennel sorbet, and fried bleak

Ingredients for 4 people
Preparation time: 2 h – Cooking time for couscous: 2h 30'

### WHITEFISH TERRINE
3 1/3 lb (1.5 kg) whitefish
2 1/4 lb (1 kg) perch and pike
2 cups (500 g) butter
Scant 1/2 cup (100 g) Lugana white wine
2 cups (500 g) cream
1 carrot
1 zucchini
1 freshly squeezed orange
2 small bunches of mixed herbs, chopped
5 oz (150 g) tomato confit*

### COUSCOUS WITH CARP
5 cups (500 g) couscous
Scant 1/2 cup (100 ml) oil
Generous 3/4 cup (200 ml) Garda extra-virgin olive oil
Pinch of salt
2 carp, each weighing 1 lb (500 g)
shallot
Pinch of pepper nad few capers
1 small bunch of marjoram

### FRIED BLEAK
2 1/4 lb (1 kg) bleak
1 2/3 cups (250 g) all-purpose flour
1 1/4 cups (300 ml) extra-virgin olive oil
Pinch of salt

### FENNEL SORBET
1 1/4 cups (300 ml) water
3/4 cup (150 g) sugar
1/4 cup (50 g) glucose
2 cups (500 ml) pureed fennel
1 tablespoon extra-virgin olive oil
Pinch of pepper
Pinch of salt

### CRAYFISH
12 crayfish
1 small bunch of herbs
1 1/4 cups (300 ml) passion fruit juice
Pinch of pepper
Pinch of salt

## Method

### WHITEFISH TERRINE

Clean and fillet the whitefish, perch, and pike (or ask your fishmonger to do it for you. Brown the fish in the butter in a large pan over medium heat. Add the white wine and cook, letting it evaporate for a few minutes. Lower the heat and add the cream. Cook until thickened and it has reduced by one-third.

Clean the carrot and zucchini. Only keep the green part of the zucchini and dice both vegetables. Sauté the vegetables in oil over high heat. Let cool to room temperature.

Meanwhile, mix the fish mixture in a bowl with the cold butter (2 cups) and orange juice. Puree in a blender until a smooth cream has been obtained. Divide mixture into three parts: one part flavored with the herbs, the second part with the sautéed carrot and zucchini, and leave the remaining part plain.

Layer the different mixtures in a terrine mold, starting with the plain cream, alternating with the tomato confit and then the herb and vegetable mixtures to finish. Let rest in the refrigerator for at least 1 hour.

*Tomato confit: bring a pot of water to a boil. Cut a cross in the bottom of the tomato, so that the skin can be removed easily afterwards. Blanch the ripe tomatoes for a few seconds in the water.

Remove and let cool in ice water. Drain and remove the skin. Cut tomatoes into quarters, removing the seeds. Arrange on a baking sheet and season with table salt, sugar, and julienned lemon zest. Bake in the oven at 225°F (100°C) for about 2 hours.

### COUSCOUS WITH CARP

Cook the couscous.: fill a pot with water and bring to a boil. Place the couscous in a sieve over the pot, steaming it for about 45 minutes. Remove and mix in 3 tablespoons of water and oil. Return to the steam and cook for about 45 minutes. Remove from the steam, adding 2 more tablespoons of oil and break up the grains rubbing it through your hands so that the grains have separated completely. Return to the steam for 30 minutes and add the remaining 2 tablespoons of oil. Add a few chopped capers, if desired, or season with salt. Let cool. Drizzle with a little Garda extra-virgin olive oil and mix well. Mold the couscous in a pastry cutter, filling it halfway.

Clean the carp and fillet it (or ask your fishmonger to do this for you). Dice it with a sharp knife, making a tartare. Finely chop the shallot. Drizzle the fish tartare with extra-virgin olive oil, a pinch of salt and pepper, and a little shallot. Fill the rest of the pastry cutter with the fish mixture.

Garnish with a few marjoram leaves.

### FRIED BLEAK

Leave the bleak whole without removing anything.

Dry with kitchen paper. Place the flour on a plate and dip the bleak in it, covering them completely, shaking off the excess.

Heat the extra-virgin olive oil into a deep frying pan. Add the bleak, a few at a time, into the boiling oil. Let them brown, turning them carefully, for 3 minutes. (The cooking time varies according to their size.) For them to be cooked well, the flour must be browned and crispy. Make sure you don't cook them too long, or the flavor will alter.

Drain with a slotted spoon on several layers of kitchen paper. Season with salt and repeat the method to cook the remaining fish.

### FENNEL SORBET

Combine the water, sugar, and glucose over the heat until the sugar has dissolved. Add the pureed fennel and strain through a fine-mesh sieve. Add the sorbet powder. Let rest for 1 hour, before churning in an ice cream maker according to the manufacturer's instructions. If you don't own an ice-cream machine, place sorbet in the freezer in a metal container. Season with salt and pepper. Mix the sorbet well every 30 minutes, 5 or 6 times.

### CRAYFISH

Clean the crayfish, removing the black vein along the back (or ask your fishmonger to do this for you). Steam the crayfish with the herbs in a pan or a pressure cooker. Remove the shells and marinate in the passion fruit juice.

Serve with the fennel sorbet.

# Ravioli filled with polenta cream and Bagòss cheese, served with Valtenesi black truffle

## Ingredients for 4 people
Preparation time: 2 h

POLENTA CREAM
2 cups (500 g) water and a pinch of salt
2/3 cup (100 g) *farina di Storo* (or polenta flour)

PASTA
1 1/3 cups (200 g) flour
2 whole eggs
Pinch of salt

FILLING
1 3/4 oz (50 g) summer Bagoss cheese, aged for 36 months
4 eggs

SERVING
Scant 1/4 cup (50 g) butter, melted
1 sprig of marjoram
4 whole eggs
Shavings of Bagoss
Valtenesi black truffle

## Method

POLENTA CREAM
Bring 2 cups (500 ml) of water and salt to a boil in a pot. Sift in the polenta and cook for 30 minutes, stirring constantly.

PASTA
Sift the flour onto a wooden surface and shape into a mound. Make a well in the center. Pour the eggs into the hollow, add the salt, and knead until the dough is smooth and even. Wrap in plastic wrap and let rest for 30 minutes.
Use a long rolling pin to roll out the pasta into very thin sheets. Lay out the pasta on a baking sheet and cover with a cloth. Cut it into rounds with a 3-inch (8-cm) diameter pastry cutter. Fill with the polenta cream and grated Bagoss and close with another round.
Cook the pasta in salted boiling water for a few minutes.

## Serving

Arrange 4 ravioli per portion on plates. Drizzle with the butter flavored with the marjoram.
Arrange a poached egg yolk in the center, which has been cooked in boiling water for 2-3 minutes.
Garnish with the shavings of Bagoss and plenty of truffle.

# Browned perch fillets in a light thyme breadcrumb with crispy tiger shrimp and two types of chanterelles and their reduction

Ingredients for 4 people
Preparation time: 40' + 12 hours for the reduction

### REDUCTION
1 clove garlic, central green part removed
1 Tropea red onion, coarsely chopped
1 bay leaf
Chanterelles
Basil
12 tiger shrimp
1 3/4 lb (800 g) perch
Salt, pepper

Majoram and thyme leaves
Scant 1/2 cup (100 g) butter, melted
bread crumbs

### MUSHROOMS
10 oz (300 g) chanterelles
3 tablespoons polenta flour
1 1/4 cups (300 ml) extra-virgin olive oil
pine nuts

## Method

### REDUCTION
Cook all the ingredients for the reduction over low heat. Add 8 shrimp heads and let them stew.
Add 3 cups (750 ml) of water and cook over low heat for about 30 minutes. Pass through a vegetable mill and strain well.
Cook strained mixture for about 15 minutes over medium heat, adding water if needed. Strain through a fine-mesh sieve and let rest overnight in the refrigerator. Gently reheat in a saucepan before serving.

### PERCH
Clean the perch, scaling and filleting it, and removing the central bones (or ask your fishmonger to do this for you). Cut the perch into fillets. Season the perch with salt and pepper and add a few marjoram leaves. Pair them up, coating with the thyme and bread crumbs, after having brushed the fish with the melted butter.
Place the buttered fish in a very hot frying pan to cook.

### MUSHROOMS
Clean the mushrooms and remove the caps. Sauté half of them in a little oil with the thyme and marjoram. Add the chopped parsley and pine nuts at the end. Dip the remaining mushrooms in the polenta flour and sauté them in a frying pan.
Remove the mushrooms and set aside. Change the oil and sauté the shrimp until opaque.

## Serving

Spoon the warm reduction into the bottom of the plate. Arrange two perch fillets in the center of each plate with the shrimp on one side and the mushrooms on the opposite side. Drizzle with extra-virgin olive oil.

# Mixed grain tart with elderflower cream and peach puree

## Ingredients for 4 people
Preparation time: 1 h – Sorbet infusion: 1 h

### SWEET SHORTCRUST PASTRY
1 2/3 cups (250 g) bread flour
3/4 cup (125 g) mixed grain flour
1 cup (250 g) butter
Generous 1/2 cup (125 g) sugar
3 egg yolks
Pinch of salt
vanilla pod, seeds scraped

### ELDERFLOWER CREAM
7 oz (200 g) dried elderflowers*
vanilla pod, split and scraped
2 cups (500 g) milk
Scant 2 1/2 cups (600 g) cream

6 egg yolks
1/2 cup (100 g) sugar
1 sheet of gelatin
white chocolate

### PEACH PUREE
1 1/4 cups (300 g) peach puree
Generous 1/4 cup (60 g) brown sugar
1 teaspoon (5 g) pectin

### ELDERFLOWER SORBET
Dried elderflowers*
2 cups (500 g) water at 90°F (32°C)
Syrup for sorbets

*Available from herbalist's shops

## Method

### SWEET SHORTCRUST PASTRY
Sift the flours onto a wooden surface and make a hollow. Place all the ingredients in the center and knead together quickly. Let rest for 30 minutes in the refrigerator. Roll the pastry out and use it to line tart molds. Bake at 300°F (150°C/gas mark 2) until golden all over.

### ELDERFLOWER CREAM
Add the elderflowers and vanilla to the milk. Let infuse overnight. Strain and add the cream, egg yolks, and sugar. Simmer over low heat, stirring constantly, until the mixture forms a custard.
Add the gelatin, which has previously been softened in cold water. Add the white chocolate and mix well.

### PEACH SAUCE
Cook all the ingredients together over low heat.

### ELDERFLOWER SORBET
Add the elderflowers to the water and let infuse for 1 hour.
Prepare the sorbet by churning it in an ice cream maker according to the manufacturer's instructions. If you don't own an ice-cream machine, pour the liquid into a wide, shallow metal pan and place in the freezer. Stir again after 30 minutes. Return to the freezer and repeat the operation twice more. Just before serving, break up the sorbet, puree briefly in a blender and return the mixture to the freezer for 10 minutes. Serve.

# Herbert Hintner

## ZUR ROSE RESTAURANT
### S. Michele Appiano (Bolzano)

itteleuropa can talk to the Mediterranean. This is the motto of the cuisine of Herbert Hintner, chef and co-owner together with his wife, Margot, of the *Zur Rose* restaurant of San Michele Appiano, in the province of Bolzano. Although he was born fifty six years ago in the Casies Valley, in the heart of the Dolomites, he is German-speaking, forged his creativity in Austria's *Hotel Klosterbräu* in Seefeld and works in the beautiful garden of South Tyrol, Chef Herbert believes that at the table mountain food is perfect, when combined with elements from the hills, the plains and the sea.

Despite (or perhaps because of) this dialectic spirit, Herbert has strong ties to the territory of South Tyrol. Beginning with the restaurant, located in a building from the 12$^{th}$ Century, first restored in 1773, it was purchased and renovated by the parents of Margot, who had a tavern there, over sixty years ago. Then in 1982, Herbert married the young daughter of the Rabensteiners, who he fell in love with on the benches of the *istituto alberghiero* (Hotel School) in Bolzano. Assisted by his wife, who looks after the dining room and makes recommendations on selection of wines, he started changing the cuisine philosophy of his in-laws. He never lacked experience: he made his debut in the kitchen at age fourteen as an apprentice chef at the Hotel Central in Alta Badia, and then, after finishing his studies, he became the classic apprentice in South Tyrol, as well as abroad. In 1985 the Hintners took over the restaurant and took the courage to revolutionize all the dishes offered. "When wine and food critic Luigi Veronelli mentioned the restaurant in his guide and a local newspaper reviews the restaurant with just a few lines, such as 'here you eat well' we were able to make the leap and put ourselves in this age group of haute cuisine where we are today." In '95, the restaurant received a Michelin Star, plus a whole range of hats, forks and spoons from other food guides, which helped to give it an undeniable visibility outside of the region.

From 1997 to 2003, Herbert was president of the *Jeunes Restaurateurs d'Europe*, where he remains today as an honorary member. It may be precisely because of this that experienced international chefs call him "not a closed traditionalist, but rather open to other cultures." He still believes that "only by embracing my own gastronomic tradition can I respect others." For him the future is here: "People will always want to try local products and the foods offered in the area and, while doing that, they will think about what they are eating... Also, if you cook like that, you also convey a message and people become curious about certain tastes and how they came about..."

Herbert's motto is "Reject global and consume only foods grown where we live and use the freshest product after it's been pulled out of the earth; you'll live better." Not only that, but "For me the ethical aspect of the food is very important. To awaken a good taste requires intelligence and the simplicity of nature, including the culinary arts." Consistent with this he offers a "cuisine that is closely connected to the territory – aimed at freshness, using the products of the surrounding area and season and the gastronomic history to reinterpret the dishes." And he is a minimalist: "A few ingredients in the pot, but held together by a good, always well thought-out concept."

The menu designed for this book expresses his love for his roots. The starter is a *tartare* of oxtail from the Valle di Casies with potatoes and thyme *vinaigrette*: potatoes, queen of the mountain cuisine, a traditional South Tyrolean meat and an aromatic herb from the Mediterranean that can grow up to 1500 meters in height. This is followed by ravioli of pasta of dried pears served with grey cheese. "I like that my dishes feel the true taste of their origin, which is only possible if I put together a product that is cooked and raw: in this case, the traditional meal of dried pears and the typical *Graukäse*, present both in the ravioli and in the sauce." Second course is a veal shank with roasted vegetable ratatouille. A simple dish, but full of flavor, including herbs, lovage or even mountain celery. Finally, a *Schmarren*, a traditional South Tyrolean sweet of Austrian origin, with caramelized apples and sour cream ice cream, "a sophisticated version of a typical sweet." Brought to life, like a postcard from South Tyrol: an old image, but with a contemporary message on the back.

## Oxtail tartare
with potatoes and thyme vinaigrette

P.**200**

## Dried pear ravioli
with *formaggio grigio*

P.**202**

## Roasted veal shank
with *ratatouille*

P.**204**

## Schmarren
with caramelized apples and ice-cream

P.**206**

# Oxtail tartare with potatoes and thyme vinaigrette

## Ingredients for 4 people
Preparation time: 1 h 30' - Resting: 1 day

### TARTARE
14 oz (400 g) oxtail braised in red wine
14 oz (400 g) potatoes, diced
5 tablespoons (50 g) shallots, finely
chopped
5 sprigs of thyme
1/4 cup (50 g) balsamic vinegar
3/4 cup (150 g) extra-virgin olive oil
1/4 cup (50 g) olive oil for frying
2 teaspoons (10 g) butter
salt and pepper

### BRAISED OXTAIL
1 lb (2 kg) oxtail
1/2 cup (60 g) carrots, coarsely chopped

1/2 cup (60 g) onions, coarsely chopped
1/2 cup (60 g) celery, coarsely chopped
2 shallots, chopped
2 cloves garlic
5 juniper berries
salt and pepper
2 tablespoons tomato paste
3 1/2 oz (100 ml) Madeira wine
2 quarts (2 liters) red wine
Herbs (2 bay leaves, 2 sprigs of thyme,
a small bunch of parsley)

### GARNISH
3 1/2 oz (100 g) mixed salad (lollo, corn
salad, lamb's lettuce, curly endives)

## Method

Clean and wash the oxtail. Season with salt and pepper. Brown the oxtail in the oil in a large pot over high heat. Drain any fat from the pan. Add the carrots, onions, and celery, chopped coarsely, and sweat for a few minutes. Add the peppercorns, juniper berries, garlic, chopped shallots, and tomato paste. Add the Madeira wine and let it evaporate. Pour in the red wine.
Bake the meat, covered, in a preheated oven at 350°F (180°C/gas mark 4) for 2-3 hours. Halfway through cooking, add the herbs and season with salt. When the meat is very tender, remove meat from the bones (discard bones) and pick out any cartilage. Place the meat in a nonstick mold, pressing it down as much as possible, using a weight if needed. Let cool completely.
Brown the shallots in a small saucepan. Make a vinaigrette by beating the vinegar with the thyme, salt, and pepper. Slowly whisk in the extra-virgin olive oil until a sauce forms. Add the browned shallots before serving.
Sauté the potatoes in the oil in a frying pan for 7 minutes. Season with freshly ground salt and pepper. Add the oxtail tartare, made by cutting half the meat into small cubes the same size as the potatoes, a pat of butter, and toss to combine. Continue sautéing for 3 minutes more.

## Serving

Cut the other half of the meat very thinly. Arrange the slices like petals on a plate. Place round molds 2 inches (5 cm) in diameter on top and fill with a mixture of oxtail and potatoes. Carefully remove the molds and garnish with a little mixed salad. Drizzle with the vinaigrette.

# Dried pear ravioli with *formaggio grigio*

## Ingredients for 4 people
Preparation time: 30' - Resting: 1 h

### PASTA
1/2 cup (50 g) all-purpose flour
2 1/2 tablespoons (30 g) durum wheat semolina
1 3/4 oz (50 g) ground dried pears (*kloaznmehl*)
1 whole egg

### FILLING
7 oz (200 g) boiled and peeled potatoes
3 1/2 oz (100 g) *formaggio grigio*
salt and pepper
1 3/4 oz (50 g) butter
chopped chives

## Method

### PASTA
Sift the flour and semolina onto a wooden surface and mix in the ground dried pears.
Shape into a mound. Make a well in the center. Break the egg into the hollow and
knead until the dough is smooth and even. Let rest for 1 hour in a cool place.

### FILLING
Press potatoes through a strainer or food mill. Season with salt and pepper.
Add half of the formaggio grigio and mix well.

## Serving

Roll out the pasta using a pasta machine to a thickness of 1/4 inch (2 mm). Cut into
rounds 2 1/2 to 3-inch (7 cm) in diameter, add the filling, and fold over rounds and
press edegs to seal, making half-moon shapes. Cook the ravioli in plenty of salted
water for about 3-4 minutes. Melt the butter in a small frying pan. Shape the remaining
formaggio grigio into 4 small balls and cover them in chopped chives.
Arrange some ravioli on each plate and drizzle with the melted butter. Place a
formaggio grigio ball in the center of each dish.

# Roasted veal shank with *ratatouille*

## Ingredients for 4 people
Preparation time: 4 h

### SHANK
1 boned veal shank
1 carrot, diced
1 medium onion, diced
5 cloves garlic, diced
1 sprig of rosemary
3 sprigs of thyme
20 bay leaves
5 sprigs of marjoram
1 sprig of lovage
5 bay leaves

1 celery stalk, diced
2 quarts (2 liters) vegetable stock
salt and pepper
extra-virgin olive oil

### RATATOUILLE
3 1/2 oz (100 g) zucchini
3 1/2 oz (100 g) peeled tomatoes
3 1/2 oz (100 g) eggplant
3 1/2 oz (100 g) peeled bell peppers
1 tablespoon herbs (thyme, basil, parsley),
finely chopped

## Method

### SHANK
Bone the veal shank and separate the large part from the small part (or ask your butcher to do this for you). Season with salt and pepper.
Brown the meat on both sides in extra-virgin olive oil. Dice the carrot, onion, garlic, and celery. Spread them out in a roasting pan and place the meat on top.
Bake in a preheated oven at 325°F (160°C) for about 30 minutes.
Add the herbs, pour in the vegetable stock, and continue to bake at 250°F (120°C) for another 3 hours, basting the meat with the cooking juices from time to time.
Remove from the pan and transfer to a bowl, keeping it hot.
Strain the cooking juices through a fine-mesh sieve (removing the fat) and return to the heat. Let it reduce until a fairly thick consistency forms.

### RATATOUILLE
Dice all the vegetables. Sauté them in the olive oil in a frying pan over medium heat for about 10 minutes. Season with salt and pepper and add the chopped herbs.

## Serving

Arrange the ratatouille in the center of the plate using a metal mold.
Slice the shank and arrange on top of the ratatouille, drizzling with the cooking juices.

# *Schmarren* with caramelized apples and ice-cream

Ingredients for 4 people
Preparation time: 40'

ICE-CREAM
2 cups (500 g) sour cream
3/4 cup (100 g) confectioners' sugar
2 tablespoons (15 g) powdered milk
3 tablespoons (50 g) lemon juice

SCHMARREN
1 1/4 cups (300 g) milk
2 tablespoons (30 g) butter
1/4 cup (70 g) Ricotta cheese
2 egg yolks
1 1/2 tablespoons (20 g) vanilla sugar
3/4 cup (100 g) flour
1/2 lb. (200 g) apples
5 1/2 tablespoons (70 g) sugar
1 tablespoon (15 g) butter
1 tablespoon (10 g) golden raisins
3 egg whites
pinch salt

Method

ICE-CREAM
Mix all the ingredients together in a bowl. Churn in an ice-cream maker according to the manufacturer's instructions.

SCHMARREN
Bring the milk to a boil with the butter. Transfer to a food processor, gradually adding the Ricotta, egg yolks, vanilla sugar, and flour.
Continue blending for 5 minutes (if necessary, strain the mixture through a fine-mesh sieve); refrigerate.
Peel the apples and slice them thinly. Mix them with the sugar and cook in the butter in a pan over medium heat for 4 minutes. Remove from the heat and add the raisins.
Beat the egg whites with the salt until stiff peaks form. Fold one-third into the batter (prepared in the food processor), mixing well. Add the remaining two-thirds, folding them in carefully.
Arrange the apples and sultanas evenly in a nonstick pan. Pour the batter over the top. Bake in a preheated oven at 300–325°F (150–160°C) for 10–15 minutes.

# Maria Lombardi

## VECCHIA TRATTORIA DA TONINO RESTAURANT
### Campobasso

"Mine is a mamma's kitchen", affirms Maria Lombardi, chef and co-owner of *Vecchia Trattoria da Tonino* in Campobasso, together with her husband Aldo Casilli, who is the head of the dining room. It could not be defined better: "I have no desire – she says – for a cerebral kitchen: I think that the food should speak to the heart, not the mind. Mother is emotion… I don't want to impress, but to give pleasure through an unexpected smell, a forgotten flavor." Maria offers a regional cuisine, philological and rich in taste with traditional recipes from Molise that have been reworked without changing the spirit, strictly local raw materials that have been carefully chosen and portions similar to what you would have at home, elegantly presented according to the design of the main dish. And, an important detail, "at a reasonable price."

The restaurant is located right in the heart of the capital of Molise, in a beautiful palace from the late 19th Century. In 1954 it was the rotisserie of Tonino Casilli, Maria's father in law. "It wasn't a typical rotisserie: even then you could buy some excellent wines or the best Parma prosciutto." In short, the locale was already dedicated to quality. In 1992 Tonino's son, Aldo, converted it into a fine restaurant, a difficult task but destined for success: from accolades in the specialized press who considered it a *gourmand* point of reference for the region (it was awarded a Michelin star in 1994) to public opinion.

"Mine is a simple cuisine in terms of both ingredients and execution, but with a careful study of raw materials. The same Molise kitchen, with a poor basis, is made up of only a few ingredients; what makes the difference is the quality of its raw materials. I feel it is almost a duty to go into the area and use its best products, exactly when they are in season." It is a family cuisine, maybe even in Maria's history. There are no hotel schools in her resume, but a high school degree the Classics and a Bachelor's Degree in Humanities from the University of Naples. After this, she toured Italy, but not to 'go shopping' for famous chefs, rather following her husband who due to his business had to move from North to South. When they decided to take over the delicatessen of Aldo's parents and to dedicate themselves to the restaurant, Maria, the mother of two children, moved from the family stove to those of the *Vecchia Trattoria da Tonino*.

In Maria's mind, cooking is an integral part of her personality. "I have always been curious about different cuisines, and I have always enjoyed reading and gradually going deeper in my readings. You could say that I have learned with both my eyes and with my hands: I have seen and experienced so much. Of course I missed some comparisons with structured environments, but when I began to cook as a profession I applied what I was already doing at home, enriching my knowledge and putting it into play, making each dish with care." Even today she continues to cook as well as read, indeed: "I continue to read with passion and interest, perhaps fewer recipe books and more volumes dedicated to the history of eating habits."

Maria is not part of the world circuit of Italian cooking, she is much more: she cooks with love. This starts with the selection of raw materials. Vegetables – "the products that I clearly prefer" – she purchases from a local supplier of trust, as well as legumes, like from Capracotta and beans from Paolina, a district of Riccia. The other raw materials are delivered to her kitchen by small local producers of Molise, assuring the excellent quality of the products.

The menu chosen for the book opens with 'small flans of ricotta cheese from sheep's milk with dried sausage preserved in oil and turnip greens', which often contain, in addition to a typical regional cheese, brawn, capocollo, sausages and *ventricina* (cold cuts) – and a vegetable widely used in local cuisine. First course is a traditional dish, reinterpreted: 'linguine with cod sauce, walnut sauce and fried bread crumbs'. Second course is a 'fillet of veal with cheese and a *Tintilia* wine reduction'. An extremely robust red wine is used here, "obtained from an ancient vine that arrived in Molise in the wake of the Spaniards."

For dessert, 'false peaches filled with a custard cream', a typical sweet of Molise originally from the convent, prepared for weddings, baptisms, communications or confirmations. This versions uses an old regional liqueur, Milk Cream based on sheep's milk and saffron, which dates back to the 18th Century.

# Sheep Ricotta
and cured sausage flan
with a sauce of turnip greens

P.212

# Linguine with salt cod sauce,
served with walnut sauce and fried breadcrumbs

P.214

# Tenderloin of veal
with Caciocavallo
and native Tintilia red wine reduction

P.216

# Peach-like pastries filled
with lemon cream

P.218

# Sheep Ricotta and cured sausage flan
# with a sauce of turnip greens

## Ingredients for 4 people
Preparation time: 50'

**BATTER**
2 cups (500 ml) sparkling mineral water, iced
1 1/3 cups (200 g) flour

**SAUCE**
1 lb (500 g) turnip greens
Salt
Water
Extra-virgin olive oil

**RICOTTA FLANS**
1 1/4 cups (300 g) sheep Ricotta
Salt
Pepper
Generous 1/3 cup (50 g) Pecorino Dolce, grated
3 1/2 oz (100 g) Mozzarella appassita
(Scamorza appassita)
1/2 cup (50 g) cured sausage in oil, diced
1 small bunch of parsley, chopped
3 eggs, separated

## Method

**BATTER**
Blend the very cold sparkling mineral water with the flour in a bowl. Let rest in the refrigerator until ready to use.

**SAUCE**
Clean and wash the turnip greens. Set aside 6 perfect leaves, which will be used as garnish.
Boil in plenty of salted water; drain greens (reserving some of the cooking liquid) and let cool in ice water to maintain the brilliant color. Drain and puree in a blender with extra-virgin olive oil. Adjust the thickness of the sauce by adding some cooking water if needed. Season with salt.

**RICOTTA FLAN**
Strain the Ricotta through a fine-mesh sieve. Season with salt and pepper. Add the grated Pecorino, the diced Mozzarella and sausage, a pinch of parsley, and egg yolks. Mix well.
Beat the egg whites to stiff peaks and fold into the mixture.
Pour the mixture evenly into 6 buttered molds. Bake in a bain-marie in the oven at 300°F (150°C/gas mark 2) for about 30 minutes.

## Serving

Serve the flans on a spoonful of turnip greens sauce.
Garnish with fried turnip greens, which have been dipped in the batter.

# Linguine with salt cod sauce, served with walnut sauce and fried breadcrumbs

### Ingredients for 4 people
Preparation time: 1h 20'

1 lb (500 g) desalted salt cod fillet*
1 stalk celery
1 carrot
onion
1 clove garlic
2 spicy chile peppers
2 tablespoons (30 ml) extra-virgin olive oil
4 anchovy fillets in oil
1/4 cup (60 ml) dry white wine
3 1/3 lb (1.5 kg) peeled tomatoes
1 small bunch of parsley
1 sprig oregano
3 1/2 oz (100 g) day-old bread, crumbled
Salt

Pepper

*If you buy salt-cured cod, soak it in water for 2-3 days, changing the water regularly

WALNUT SAUCE
1 cup (100 g) walnuts
1 3/4 oz (50 g) day-old bread, softened in milk
clove garlic
1 small bunch of parsley
Salt
Pepper
Scant 1/2 cup (100 ml) extra-virgin olive oil
14 oz (400 g) linguine pasta

## Method

Bone and skin the salt cod fillet. Clean, wash, and chop the celery, carrot, and onion. Peel the garlic.
Sauté the chopped vegetables in the oil with 1 chile pepper, the anchovy fillets, and the bones and skin of the salt cod in a large pot. Add the wine and cook until evaporated.
Add the tomatoes and cook over medium heat for 40 minutes. Add half the chopped parsley, the remaining seeded chile pepper, and a sprinkling of oregano. Let cool and puree using a food mill.
Transfer the sauce to a large pot. Add the salt cod fillet, cut into cubes, and cook over low heat for a few minutes until the ingredients are well mixed.
Toast the breadcrumbs in the oil in a nonstick pan and sprinkle with oregano. Season with salt and pepper.

### WALNUT SAUCE
Chop the walnuts in a food processor with the bread softened in the milk and squeezed dry. Add the garlic, parsley, salt, and pepper. Gradually add the oil at the end.
Cook the pasta in plenty of salted water. Drain and add to the salt cod sauce.

## Serving

Add the walnut sauce and the remaining parsley and cook over high heat for a few minutes, tossing. Divide evenly among the plates, sprinkle with the toasted breadcrumbs, and serve.

# Tenderloin of veal with Caciocavallo and native Tintilia red wine reduction

### Ingredients for 4 people
Preparation time: 20'

Generous 3/4 cup (200 ml) Tintilia
1/2 teaspoon honey
1 sprig of sage
1 sprig of rosemary
1 sprig of thyme
1 bay leaf
1 veal tenderloin, weighing 7 oz (200 g)
Scant 3 tablespoons (40 g) butter
Generous 1 tablespoon (20 ml) extra-virgin olive oil
Generous 1 tablespoon (20 ml) brandy
Salt
Pepper
1 tablespoon light cream
Generous 1 tablespoon (20 ml) grated Caciocavallo cheese

Roasted rosemary potatoes, for serving
Sauteed porcini mushrooms, for serving

### Method

REDUCTION
Pour the wine in a saucepan with 1/2 tablespoon of honey and herbs. Bring to a boil and cook over low heat until reduced by half.

TENDERLOIN
Brown the tenderloin on both sides in the pat of butter and the oil, keeping it rare. Add the brandy and let it evaporate. Season with salt and pepper.
Place the tenderloin on one corner of a hot plate. Deglaze the cooking juices with about 1/4 cup (50 g) of the wine reduction. Add a spoonful of cream.
Return the tenderloin to the pan, top with the Caciocavallo, and keep warm covered with a lid. The cheese will have melted and the cooking juice will be creamy after a couple of minutes.

### Serving

Serve with roasted potatoes cooked with rosemary and sautéed porcini mushrooms.

# Peach-like pastries filled with lemon cream

## Ingredients for 4 people
Preparation time: 1 h

### PASTRY
1 cube of brewer's yeast (25 g)
Scant 1/2 cup (100 ml) milk, gently heated
7 tablespoons extra-virgin olive oil
3 1/3 cups (500 g) all-purpose flour
3 eggs
1/2 cup (100 g) sugar

### LEMON CREAM
2 cups (500 ml) milk
1 organic lemon, zested

4 egg yolks
1/2 cup (100 g) sugar
4 tablespoons (60 g) all-purpose flour

### TO DECORATE
*Crema Milk* (a liqueur from Molise made from sheep's milk and saffron)
Sugar syrup
Alchermes
Sugar
Bay leaves, for garnish

## Method

### PASTRY
Dissolve the yeast in the warm milk and oil. Sift the flour onto a wooden surface and make a well in the center. Add the eggs, sugar, and yeast mixture. Knead the ingredients to make a smooth, elastic dough.
Shape into balls the size of walnuts, flattening them at the bottom. Arrange them on a buttered and floured baking sheet. Let rise for about 2 hours, or until they have doubled in volume.
Bake in the preheated oven at 350°F (180°C/gas mark 4) for about 20 minutes.

### PASTRY CREAM
Bring the milk to a boil with the lemon zest in a small saucepan over medium heat. Strain it. Use a whisk to beat the egg yolks and sugar in a metal bowl. Whisk in the flour, followed by the milk (add slowly to avoid curdling the eggs).
Cook over low heat for about 10 minutes, stirring constantly.
Make a hole in the flat part of the pastry balls and soak them in 1 tablespoon of Crema Milk and 1 tablespoon of sugar syrup. Fill with the pastry cream.

## Serving

Stick 2 balls together (on the flat side) to form peach-like cakes. Brush with the Crema Milk and Alchermes and dip in the sugar. Finish with a bay leaf.

# Agata Parisella

## AGATA E ROMEO RESTAURANT
### Rome

When the restaurant closes, at about two in the morning, she looks up towards Santa Maria Maggiore and thinks about how incredibly beautiful it is. But perhaps she never thinks of her cuisine that way. Of all the great basilicas of the capital city, this is where the different architectural styles combine with the greatest grace and elegance. And it is here that Agata Parisella, chef and co-owner of the *Agata e Romeo* restaurant in Rome, together with her husband Romeo Carraccio combines the most authentic Roman traditions with simplicity and harmony, to meet new requirements for a creative combination and presentation.

"I am closely linked to the region and to the traditions of Roman and Lazio cuisine – she says – and although there have been many changes in the restaurant industry and there will be many more in the future, I will never abandon our typical dishes." The menu offers many of the most characteristics of this culinary culture, typical recipes that express the sincere, rustic and lively soul of Rome. But here Agata often combines traditional dishes with raw materials from other regions. "When I make fettucine with chicken giblets – inner organs – for example, a dish that is typical of our city, I add a sprinkling of Reggiano Parmesan…"

The *Agata e Romeo* restaurant is located in the Esquiline district, in an historical building that has changed its organizational structure over time. In the thirties it was an inn owned by Agata's grandfather. It was the last stop for all the cars that carried barrels of wine before they took the Appian Way to return to Castelli Romani, "It was an inn where only wine was sold, frequented by the so called 'fagottari', people who brought their food from home in a backpack." Over the years he began to serve bread and pork as well as the wine of Castelli Romani and it slowly evolved to become a true inn and trattoria under Agata's parents. "*Da Gabriele* was one of the typical restaurants that were popular in Rome in the fifties and sixties, it was open seven days a week, with dishes typical of Roman cuisine.

My mother was in the kitchen, my father in the front, and we kids when we got out of school were here to lend a hand."

Agata and Romeo took over the restaurant in 1974. "Although I have been involved in the restaurant business since I came into the world, I've also done higher studies that were not related to cooking. When I finished my father wanted to send me to the *istituto alberghiero* in Stresa, but I balked: I will never do your job because it's too tiring!." Still, you cannot escape fate... "When I was around twenty, of five children, I was the only one who offered to continue with our parents' business." It was a choice that also involved her future husband, whom she met in the university: "He left his medical studies to take care of the dining room and tavern of the restaurant." And today he is one of the most sought-after sommelier in Italy with an award-winning wine cellar.

After the knowledge inherited from her family – "I was strongly influenced by my grandmother and from my mother" –, Agata has traveled extensively, beginning when she was 22, and also had internships abroad to learn of other culinary cultures. After that, she has stayed in her own restaurant, and together with her husband has slowly transformed the trattoria with home cooking into one of the pillars of Capitoline restaurants, frequented by an international clientele. There are so many pluses. Agata, a Micheline star, is part of a small group of chefs who are called on to prepare receptions for heads of state and foreign governments visiting Italy; she also takes her talent abroad, where she is often invited to cook. A member of the *Jeunes Restaurateurs d'Europe*, she is a true ambassador of Italian cuisine in the world.

"My kitchen is regional, where almost everything we cook is from Latium, with products included, according to the season, in a menu that has cyclical changes." In addition to cheeses, meat and fish, we use legumes such as beans, peas and chickpeas, and vegetables such as Roman artichokes and *puntarelle* (chicory), the tips of the endive salad.

The menu chosen for this book comes from the heart of a lover of Rome. The appetizer is a tart with anchovies and white endive, a traditional dish on the Capitoline table. The first course is pasta and broccoli in *brodo d'arzilla* (skate broth), followed by *coda di bue alla vaccinara* an (oxtail terrine). Finally for dessert is the millefeuille Agata, her specialty, "Prepared with traditional ingredients, but served in a different way."

# Anchovy and curly
### endive tartlet
P.**224**

# Pasta e broccoli
### served with skate stock
P.**226**

# Oxtail vaccinara
P.**228**

# Agata's millefeuille
P.**230**

# Anchovy and curly endive tartlet

## Ingredients for 4 people
Preparation time: 35'

2 lb (1 kg) fresh anchovies
2 lb (1 kg) yellow-white curly endives
Salt, pepper and lemon juice
Fennel seeds
Cherry tomatoes
Ligurian extra-virgin olive oil
Breadcrumbs
Curly parsley
Pepper, to taste
Wild fennel, for garnish
Tomato wedges, for garnish
Parsley sprigs, for garnish
Basil leaves, for garnish

## Method

Remove all the bones from the anchovies. Cut the endives into thin
strips. Let marinate in the salt and fennel seeds for about 1 hour.
Oil the disposable individual molds. Cover them completely with the
raw anchovy fillets, letting them partly stick out.
Cut the cherry tomatoes into quarters and place in a small bowl,
setting 4 aside. Drizzle with the oil and season with salt and pepper.
Fill with the marinated endives and press down. Top with a few pieces
of anchovies and the seasoned tomatoes. Top the tartlet by placing
the anchovies that are sticking out in the center. Drizzle with the oil,
some breadcrumbs, and a crushed tomato in the center, which will
help to keep the tartlet moist. Bake in a bain-marie in the oven at
350°F (180°C/gas mark 4) for 10 minutes.
Make a sauce by beating together the oil, lemon juice, and fennel
seeds. Season with salt and pepper to taste.

## Serving

Serve the hot tartlet with the sauce. Garnish with raw wild fennel,
a few cherry tomato wedges, a sprig of parsley, and a basil leaf.

# Pasta and broccoli served with skate stock

## Ingredients for 4 people
Preparation time: 1 h

2 lb (1 kg) whole *arzilla* (skate)
Salt
1 onion
1 stalk celery
2 cloves garlic
Parsley
Garlic
Chile pepper
1 anchovy fillet
Generous 3 tablespoons (50 g) extra-virgin olive oil
Generous 3/4 cup (200 g) peeled and chopped tomatoes
White wine
10 oz (300 g) Romanesco broccoli
7 oz (200 g) Ave Maria pasta or broken-up spaghetti
Grated Parmesan (optional)

## Method

Clean and wash the *arzilla* (and place in a fish kettle with cold water. Add the salt, onion, celery, and a whole clove of garlic. Cook for about 30 minutes. Drain and remove the head and the cartilaginous part. Return the removed parts to the cooking pan and cook for another 20 minutes. Strain stock into a bowl.
Sauté the chopped parsley, garlic, a little chile, and anchovy fillet in the oil in a frying pan. Add the peeled and chopped tomatoes. Add the white wine and cook for 20 minutes.
Separate the broccoli into florets and cut the larger ones into quarters. Blanch in salted boiling water for 3 minutes; drain. Add the florets to the pan with the anchovy. Cook, adding the stock. Add the pasta halfway through the cooking time.
Pour mixture into a soup tureen and serve with a sprinkling of Parmesan, if desired. The *arzilla* fish can be dressed with oil and lemon, chopped garlic, and parsley and served as a main course. According to tradition, it was added to the soup, thereby making it a nice filling meal.

# Oxtail vaccinara

## Ingredients for 4 people
Preparation time: 1 h – Minimum cooking time: 3 h

### CELERY ROOT PUREE
14 oz (400 g) peeled, boiled, and diced celery root
3/4 cup (180 g) butter, softened and cut into pieces
Salt
White pepper

### OXTAIL
2 lb (1 kg) oxtail and cheeks
onion
2 cloves garlic
1 celery stalk
chile pepper
carrot
White wine
1 1/2 lb (700 g) peeled tomatoes
Salt, to taste
Generous 1 tablespoon (20 g) golden raisins
Generous 1 tablespoon (20 g) pine nuts
Generous tablespoon bittersweet cocoa
Tablespoon tomato paste

## Method

### CELERY ROOT PUREE
Cover a potato masher with a cloth and use it to puree the celery root . Mash the vegetable several times, pressing down lightly, so that as much water as possible is removed. It is important to remove the majority of the juice contained in the celery to make a firm, dry puree. You could gather the juice that the celery gives out and use it in other recipes. Transfer the celery puree into the bowl of a food processor. Season with salt and pepper. Blend until a smooth and creamy mixture forms.
The consistency of the puree depends on how watery the vegetables are. The more juice you're able to extract, the firmer and drier the mixture becomes.

### OXTAIL
Ask your butcher to cut the oxtail into its various vertebra and the cheeks into even pieces. Wash well. Chop the onion, garlic, celery stalk, and parsley. Sauté the chopped mixture in the oil in a large pot. Add the oxtail and cheek pieces and brown them. Add the white wine and let it evaporate. Add the peeled tomatoes. If they don't cover the meat completely, add hot water. Cover and bring to a boil. Lower the heat and simmer.
The cooking time is very lengthy and depends on the size of the oxtail pieces. It will vary from 3 to 6 hours. 30 minutes before the end of the cooking time, add the remaining celery, cut into small sticks. Season with salt and add the raisins, pine nuts, the cocoa dissolved in water and the tomato concentrate. When cooked, bone the oxtail and arrange the meat in a terrine mold. Let rest.

## Serving

Serve the oxtail cut into slices with the celery root puree cooked with shallots, oil, and cream. Blend, served with julienned celery hearts.

# Agata's millefeuille

## Ingredients for 4 people
Preparation time: 1 h 15'

### PUFF PASTRY
3 1/3 cups (500 g) all-purpose flour
2 cups (500 g) butter
Pinch of salt
Water, as needed

### CUSTARD
5 egg yolks
3/4 cup (150 g) sugar
Generous 1/3 cup (60 g) sifted all-purpose

flour
2 cups (500 ml) milk
1 vanilla pod, split
2 cups (500 ml) whipping cream

### DECORATIONS
confectioners' sugar, as needed
3 1/2 oz (100 g) extra bittersweet chocolate, chopped
1/2 cup (50 g) slivered almonds

## Method

### PUFF PASTRY
Make the initial dough on a wooden surface: mix 2 1/2 cups (375 g) of all-purpose flour, a pinch of salt, and enough water to make a soft dough. Knead it. Let rest under a cotton cloth while you make the second dough.
Make a ball of dough with 3/4 cup (125 g) of flour and all the butter. Let rest under a cloth. Roll out the first dough and the second into a rectangle and place the second dough over the first. Fold into three. Repeat (rolling out and folding into three) this method six times every 15 minutes, making sure that you always keep the dough under a cloth in the lowest part of the refrigerator. The puff pastry will then be ready to roll out to 1/3-inch (1-cm) thick. Bake in the oven at 350°F (180°C/gas mark 4) for 15-20 minutes. When ready, sprinkle the pastry with plenty of confectioners' sugar. Caramelize in the oven at 400°F (200°C/gas mark 6) for about 5 minutes. Cut into large pieces when it has cooled.

### PASTRY CREAM
Beat the egg yolks with the sugar and flour in a copper pot. Whisk without beating. Meanwhile, in a separate small saucepan, bring the milk to a boil with the vanilla pod. Slowly whisk in the egg yolks and cook gently for 5-6 minutes, heating the mixture to 175-180°F (80-85°C). Let cool, preferably in a blast chiller. Whip the cream and fold into the custard.

### DECORATIONS
Melt the chocolate in a double boiler. Form 10 leaves in small cones of parchment paper. Freeze for 5 minutes.
Toast the slivered almonds at 350°F (180°C/gas mark 4) until golden brown, about 5 minutes.

## Serving

Place a generous spoonful of the pastry cream in the center of the plate with a few pieces of puff pastry, the slivered almonds, and a sprinkling of confectioners' sugar. Finish with a chocolate leaf.

# Marco Parizzi

## PARIZZI RESTAURANT
### Parma

The cooking of Marco Parizzi, owner and chef of the *Parizzi* restaurant, is in the spirit of the great sculptor Benedetto Antelami. As the great medieval sculptor and architect embraced the solid Romanesque tradition, raising it to subtle Gothic flexibility, and in fact does so just a few steps from the restaurant in the splendid Battistero of the Piazza Duomo, so does Marco keep his feet firmly on the ground to achieve elegance.

Connected to robust local flavors, he lightens them and then finds them again. "Being from Parma, I have a stamp for taste that is quite strong, as are most of our products", he says. "My cuisine is always marked, in fact defined, with a pinch of salt that tends to be more, rather than less." Even when working with fish, the dishes have a vigorous structure, in perfect parallel with the strong essence of the Po plains. But the dishes that result are light, "offering a sensation of strong taste with herbs and spices." He does not however substitute one ingredient with another, such as oil with butter, as a simple bow to fashion: "Substitutions should be made only if they make sense: tortelli with herbs and Parmesan need butter…"

The restaurant, which is located in the historic district inside a palazzo from the 16th Century on the Via Emilia, the ancient Roman road that crosses the region, has a long history that is tied to Parma. Three generations have served here: a host, a restaurateur, and a chef: "It doesn't matter if we served only a ladle of broth, two slices of meat or a glass of wine: we put our heart and souls into it, and were happy to do it."

In 1946 Marco's grandfather, Pietro Parizzi, and his wife Luigina opened an inn in another part of the city, then moved here to 71 on Via Repubblica in 1956. A delicatessen, home cooking for take-out, a few tables to play a game of cards or for a drink. In '67 Marco's father, Ugo, who took over management of the restaurant, met Graziella and together they decided to design what would become the *Parizzi* restaurant, one of the first in the city: "My father organized it in a modern way, hiring a staff with a chef and some assistants along with the inevitable *rezdore* (as women who cook are called in Parma), and waiters in suits and bow ties for the dining room." In 1980, with the arrival of his Michelin star, Ugo started a renovation of the restaurant, making it more refined and with fewer tables, beginning a turn to an *elite* clientele.

Marco began working in the restaurant as a child: "When I was eleven I was already helping my parents as a waiter, when I was done with school. Finally at nineteen I began to work more regular hours." His training began in the kitchen: after accounting school, cooking for him was a world to discover. "After four and a half years of apprenticeship with chef Gino Giulianotti, I preferred to choose people who could start me in a less classic cooking: I hired chefs like Davide Oldani and especially my most important teacher, Patrik Massera, who stayed here for two years, from '94 to '96." At the end of an intense and fruitful apprenticeship, Marco took command of the kitchen and also became a member of the *Jeunes Restaurateurs d'Europe*. His wife Cristina became sommelier and head of the dining room, and the restructured restaurant became part of the prestigious association of 'Le Soste', which includes the elite of the Italian culinary scene.

"I have never forced myself to do research. My cooking, built on the great raw materials of the region, is a slower movement: it's not avant-garde, it's now. I can use an old technique for a new dish, or rethink an old dish with a new technique." Ideal for a city that looks to the future but with culinary traditions that are still alive and deeply rooted.

In the menu chosen for this book, "that bond with the land is evident in all the courses." As appetizer, 'smoke pork tenderloin with old vinegar, Fragno lack truffles and shavings of Parmesan cheese', where the meat of the great protagonist from Bassa, used for more than just delicious sausages. Then 'slices of Parmesan with a veal ragout and candied tomatoes', where he could not forget the prince of vegetables and the glorious cheese tradition of Parmesan cuisine; then a 'skewer of beef stew with fried polenta', a typical dish but presented differently: sheets of crusty polenta alternated with small medallions of stewed beef and closed with a skewer. As a dessert finally a *Zuppa inglese alla parmigiana* (*Italian trifle*), a version of the sweet that uses Alchermes.

# Salad of smoked pork fillet
with black truffle and aged vinegar

P.236

# Parmigiano Reggiano crowns

P.238

# Parma-style skewer
of beef stew

P.240

# Italian trifle

P.242

# Salad of smoked pork fillet with black truffle and aged vinegar

### Ingredients for 4 people
Preparation time: 30' - Smoking: 40'

Food-grade beech wood chips
2 quarts (2 liters) water
7 oz (200 g) sea salt
3 1/2 oz (100 g) mixed spices (black pepper, cinnamon, cloves, juniper)
2 pork fillets
12 asparagus

7 oz (200 g) spinach
Generous 1 tablespoon (20 g) lard
3 tablespoons (50 g) extra-virgin olive oil
3 1/2 oz (100 g) mixed herbs
1/3 oz (10 g) Parmesan cheese
4 quail's egg
vinegar and truffle

### Method

Bring the water to a boil with the salt and spices. Let cool. Add the pork fillets and let marinate for 4 hours. Cold-smoke it (see directions below).
Blanch the asparagus in a pot of salted boiling water, leaving them crunchy. Transfer immediately to a bowl of ice water to preserve the brilliant green color.
Clean and wash the spinach. Sauté the spinach with the lard in a frying pan over medium heat. Add the asparagus and a vinaigrette of the aged vinegar, which is made by first dissolving the vinegar with the salt and then emulsifying it with extra-virgin olive oil. Cut the fillet into thin slices. Arrange the spinach on the plate, followed by the mixed herbs, asparagus, fillet, Parmesan, truffle, and the egg (previously hard-boiled), cut in half.
Drizzle with the remaining vinaigrette (optional).

#### COLD SMOKING

Create a smoking chamber (an oven that's turned off works well).
Arrange the beech chips in a roasting pan and heat until it becomes red-hot. Season with herbs, such as rosemary, bay leaves, and lavender. Cover with a tight-fitting lid and position at the bottom of the oven. Place a baking tray containing ice on the upper shelves and above that a tray with holes containing the items to be smoked: meat, fish, oil, and salt all seasoned in the bowls and anything else you would like to smoke.

# Parmigiano Reggiano crowns

## Ingredients for 4 people
Preparation time: 30'

### TOMATO CONFIT
6 oz (180 g) tomatoes
1 1/4 cups (300 ml) extra-virgin olive oil
1 teaspoon (5 g) thyme
Garlic, thinly sliced
Generous 1 tablespoon (20 g) salt
Pepper
Generous 1 tablespoon (20 g) sugar

### PASTA
3 1/3 cups (500 g) flour
5 large eggs

### FILLING
5 oz (150 g) Parmesan cheese
5 oz (150 g) Provolone cheese

Generous 3 tablespoons (50 g) fresh light cream
Generous 3 tablespoons (50 g) meat stock
Grated zest of 1/2 lemon
Nutmeg

### SAUCE
5 oz (150 g) veal, cut into cubes
2 tablespoons clarified butter
Generous 3 tablespoons (50 g) tomato confit
1 teaspoon (5 g) thyme
Generous 3 tablespoons (50 g) veal cooking juices
Generous 3 tablespoons (50 g) stock

## Method

### TOMATO CONFIT
Make a cross in the base of the tomatoes; blanch the tomatoes for a few seconds in boiling water and peel them. Cut into quarters and remove the seeds. Arrange the tomatoes on a baking sheet with oil and thyme, placing a slice of garlic on top of each. Add the salt, pepper, and sugar. Let soften in the oven at 200°F (90°C) for 2 hours and 20 minutes.

### PASTA
Sift the flour onto a wooden surface and shape into a mound. Make a well in the center. Pour the eggs into the hollow. Knead until the dough is smooth and even. Let rest for 1 hour in a cool place.

### FILLING
Mix all the filling ingredients in a bowl, including the grated Parmesan and Provolone cheeses, until smooth.

### SAUCE
Brown the veal in the clarified butter. Add the tomato confit, thyme, veal cooking juices, and the stock.

## Serving

Roll out the sheet of pasta in a pasta machine and place small amounts of the filling on the pasta. Seal well and cut using a round pastry cutter.
Cook the pasta in plenty of boiling water. Serve hot with the sauce.

# Parma-style skewer of beef stew

## Ingredients for 4 people
Preparation time: 3 h 30'

10 carrots
4 onions
1 stalk celery
1 head of garlic
Extra-virgin olive oil
1 shoulder of beef*
3 1/4 cups (500 g) flour
3 quarts (3 liters) full-bodied red wine
5 cloves
1 cinnamon stick
1 teaspoon (5 g) peppercorns

*\* Cut of meat from the front quarters of the cow, which is found between the fesone di spalla (shoulder clod - at the back) and the girello di spalla (shoulder round - in front).*

POLENTA
Generous 1 3/4 cups (450 g) salted water
2/3 cup (100 g) *polenta taragna* (a mixture of cornmeal and buckwheat)
Butter, for molds

## Method

Chop the vegetables and brown them in extra-virgin olive oil in a large pot. Sprinkle the meat with the flour. Brown the meat in a frying pan. Season with salt. Add the meat to the vegetables and pour in the red wine. Add the spices. Cover and bake at 300°F (140°C) for 3 hours.
Remove the meat. Let cool in the refrigerator. Strain the sauce and reduce in a saucepan until fairly thick.
Bring the salted water to a boil. Add the polenta, mixing constantly. Cook over low heat for about 40 minutes. Add a pat of butter and pour into molds (the shape of the molds is optional).
Slice the meat to a thickness of 3/4-inch (2 cm) and cut slices into 12 rounds with a diameter of 5 cm using a round pastry cutter. Spoon a little sauce over the meat and heat them just before serving.
Remove the polenta from the molds and fry.

## Serving

Assemble the skewer as shown in the photo, taking care that the meat doesn't break and alternating it with the polenta.
Sheets of polenta can also be made to garnish the dish. Spread out the polenta dampened with a drop of water on a sheet of parchment paper. Bake at 175°F (80°C) for 2 hours, or until it has dried out completely.
Serve hot with plenty of sauce.

# Italian trifle

Ingredients for 4 people
Preparation time: 1 h 30'

LADYFINGERS
2/3 cup (150 g) egg yolks
2 tablespoons (30 g) sugar
8 (210 g) egg whites
1 1/4 cups (180 g) sifted flour

OLD-FASHIONED PASTRY CREAM
1 cup (250 ml) milk
1/2 vanilla bean
Zest of 1/2 lemon
10 (250 g) egg yolks
3/4 cup (150 g) sugar
Scant 3 tablespoons (40 g)
sifted flour
1 cup (250 ml) cream

CHOCOLATE CUSTARD
2 cups (500 ml) milk
Scant 1/2 cup (100 g) egg yolks
3/4 cup (150 g) sugar
2/3 cup (100 g) cocoa
3 1/2 oz (100 g) chocolate

DIP
Scant 1/2 cup (100 g) water
1/2 cup (100 g) sugar
1 2/3 cups (400 g) Alchermes liqueur
1 vanilla pod
Liqueur-soaked cherries and fresh fruit
Whipped cream, to decorate
Broken chocolate, to decorate

## Method

LADYFINGERS
Beat the egg yolks with the sugar in a bowl. In a separate bowl, beat the egg whites with the sugar. Fold in the egg yolk mixture and the flour. Make a 1/8-inch (0.5-cm) layer on a baking sheet that has been buttered and floured. Bake at 350ºF (180ºC/gas mark 4) for 10 minutes. Remove from the oven and cut into 3/4 x 2 3/4-inch (2 x 7-cm) rectangles.

OLD-FASHIONED PASTRY CREAM
Bring the milk to a boil with the vanilla bean and lemon zest. Beat the egg yolks and sugar together in a bowl. Add the sieved flour and mix. Pour in the hot milk. Pour the mixture back into the pan that contained the milk and bring to a boil for 2 minutes. Pour the custard into a bowl and let cool.

CHOCOLATE CUSTARD
Follow the same instructions given to make the old-fashioned pastry cream. Beat the egg yolks and sugar together in a bowl. Add the boiling milk and return to a boil. Add the cocoa and chocolate and mix until it has melted completely. Pour the custard into a bowl and let cool.

DIP
Bring the water to a boil with the sugar. Let cool and stir in the Alchermes.

## Serving

Make a layer of soaked (in the dip) ladyfingers, then an initial layer of one custard, another of ladyfingers, another one of chocolate custard, and another one of ladyfingers to finish. Cut into squares. Decorate with liqueur-soaked cherries, fresh fruit or whipped cream and pieces of chocolate. Serve cold.

# Giancarlo Perbellini

## PERBELLINI RESTAURANT
### Isola Rizza (Verona)

t is not true that "there is no world beyond the walls of Verona", as claimed by the protagonist of Shakespeare's 'Romeo and Juliet', the famous work set in the fascinating city on the Adige. In lower Verona we find a place where the great Venetian cuisine - both aristocratic and popular - finds its full expression: the *Perbellini* restaurant.

Located 24 kilometers from Verona in the agricultural/industrial area of Isola Rizza, which has few other attractions, it is located next to the family business. Although not in an extraordinary location, the name itself on the sign, "*Perbellini Premiata Offelleria*" from *offella*, a sweet invented by Perbellini in 1891 and still their flagship pastry, is enough to seduce those who arrive at the restaurant. "The restaurant is definitely a result of madness", admits Giancarlo Perbellini, chef and owner (assisted by his wife Paola in the dining room). "Despite its location, inside the kitchen I was able to make it look the way I wanted, and after more than twenty years, it is just what I strived for."

Giancarlo has taken to a family activity; restaurants have been in the Perbellini family DNA since 1952. "My grandfather and his brother had a café-restaurant with a guest house and a bakery. In '89, when I decided to follow this career, I followed my grandfather's steps, who has always been the cook in the family." A grandson of the art, then? "Yes, because my father was always a baker. It was while I was attending hotel school that he chose for me the places of work that would help to form my craft and show me the way, so I would be able to open my own restaurant." That training first brought him back to his hometown, to the *Dodici Apostoli*, then one of the most famous restaurants in Italy; and then on to the *Marconi*, a local restaurant which has since closed. After completing his studies, he moved on to *San Domenico* in Imola, which was at the time the *state of the art* of the new haute cuisine.

He moved from one quality restaurant to another; in France he worked from the *Taillevent* to the *Ambroisie*, from there to the *Terrasse* of Juan les Pins and then to the *Château d'Esclimont*. In England he worked with a chef from the school of Angelo Paracucchi, "one of the greatest Italian chefs who for thirty years had set the bar for quality of raw materials." Back in Italy, he worked a while as a *sous* chef (assistant chef) at the *Concorde* in Villa Poma in the province of Mantua, and then he decided to open his own restaurant. He quickly earned his first Michelin star in '96, and then a second in 2002.

Giancarlo defines his cuisine as "*classic-modern.*" His dishes are not an Olympic abstraction, but a smart mixture of history and nature: "My cuisine tends to relate to the season, and sometimes it even ties with traditional recipes."

This innovation compared to traditional cuisine may affect taste, but also the technique used in its preparation and cooking. "We always try to offer dishes that are not flights of fancy, but food with basic common sense. Sometimes we offer creative dishes such as smoked caviar and frozen eggnog or, at times, traditional dishes with a new twist. Some things cannot change: pork cheek, for example, is baked in the oven, the same method that was used to cook it twenty years ago..." Culinary history is today's reality, and must be held secure to prevent it from fading or vanish.

Although he loves his Verona for its special charisma, the recipes chosen for the book are a tribute to the Veneto region, featuring many of the regional products that he uses in his kitchen. As a starter, is cod and potatoes in puff pastry with a fresh salad, made using 'pulled cod Venetian-style'. "It is dedicated to the long history of the Venetian plain with a fish that, while not native to this region, has become an integral part of each province, which has its own version of cod, always combined with fresh or roasted polenta.*"*

First course is a black risotto with cuttlefish, basil and tomato *confit*, "a Venetian classic with a modern interpretation;" and second is one of the most typical dishes of the region, *polenta e osei* (little bird), "in yesterday's version with swallows, a saddle of bacon and flavored with sage, cooked in the oven at a low temperature for an hour and a half and in a today's version, with foamy polenta combined with the birds roasted on a spit."

For dessert we have *fogazzin con la polenta*, a traditional cake of rural Veneto, made of polenta from the day before, raisins and anise liqueur. "A plate of leftovers, but very pleasant, and that can be enjoyed either warm or cold."

# Salt cod
and potato millefeuille on a bed of salad

P.248

# Squid ink
and basil risotto with tomato confit

P.250

# Polenta and birds, today and yesteryear

P.254

# *Polenta fogazzin*

P.256

# Salt cod and potato millefeuille on a bed of salad

## Ingredients for 4 people
Preparation time: 1 h

3 medium potatoes
Scant 1/2 cup (100 ml) extra-virgin olive oil
Scant 1/2 cup (100 ml) milk
1 bay leaf
1 clove garlic
Salt, to taste
Pepper, to taste
10 oz (300 g) fresh salt cod (*gabilo*)
Scant 2 tablespoons (25 g) butter
1/2 lemon, squeezed
Chives, as many as needed
2 tomatoes
Scant 1/2 cup (100 ml) balsamic vinegar
1 1/2 oz (40 g) salad greens
Chervil, as much as needed

## Method

Peel the potatoes and cut them very thinly on a mandolin. Arrange them on an oiled baking sheet in a rose-shaped pattern. Drizzle with oil. Bake in the oven at 250°F (110°C) until golden and crisp.

Bring the milk to a boil in a pot with the bay leaf and garlic. Season with salt and pepper to taste.

Add the salt cod, having removed the skin and bones. Let cook at 200°F (90°C).

Drain cod and beat with a whisk, gradually adding the olive oil, butter, lemon juice, and finely chopped chives.

Cut a cross in the bottom of each tomato; blanch the tomatoes, remove the seeds and skins. Cut into evenly sized cubes.

Dissolve a pinch of salt in the vinegar in a small bowl. Gradually pour in the oil and emulsify to make a vinaigrette.

Clean and wash the salad greens, drying it well.

## Serving

Layer the potatoes with the salt cod, forming three layers. Warm in the oven and serve on a little salad dressed with the balsamic vinaigrette. Garnish with the diced tomatoes and a sprig of chervil.

# Squid ink and basil risotto with tomato confit

Ingredients for 4 people
Preparation time: 55'

STOCK
1 1/2 lb (700 g) beef
1 lb (500 g) veal
1 onion
1 carrot
1 celery stalk
1 bay leaf
Salt

*SHELLFISH BISQUE OR FISH SOUP
1 1/2 lb (700 g) shellfish
1/3 cup (50 g) flour
1 tablespoon extra-virgin olive oil
Generous 3/4 cup (200 ml) brandy
2 tablespoons tomato paste
2 tablespoons water
Salt, to taste
Pepper to taste
2/3 cup (150 g) butter
1 oz (30 g) mixed herbs (sage, rosemary, etc)
3 quarts (3 liters) water

RISOTTO
7 oz (200 g) black squid
4 shallots
1 clove garlic
White wine
1 quart (1 liter) fish soup or shellfish bisque*
Scant 1/4 cup (50 g) tomato passata
2 quarts (2 liters) stock
2 1/2 cups (300 g) Carnaroli rice
Butter
Grated Parmesan
Salt
Tomato confit
1 basil leaf
Basil-infused oil
Extra-virgin olive oil
1 lemon

## Method

### STOCK

Put the meat in a large saucepan and cover with cold water.

Bring the water to a boil over medium heat, covering it with a lid.

When the water comes to a boil, skim the froth, season with salt, and add the whole vegetables and the bay leaf.

Lower the heat, cover again, and simmer for about 2 1/2 hours.

Strain, let cool and chill for at least 3 hours.

Before using the stock, remove the layer of fat that will have solidified on the surface.

### SHELLFISH BISQUE

Toast the flour in a frying pan over high heat for about 3 minutes so that it loses its humidity and becomes slightly brown. Set aside.

Brown the vegetables in the oil in a large pot over high heat. Add the shellfish and mix well. Break them up with a spoon and continue mixing for 5 minutes. Add the toasted flour, mixing well.

Pour in half the brandy, add the tomato paste and water, and season with salt and pepper.

Mix well and let the liquid reduce to half the original volume over high heat. This will take 1 hour. When reduced, add the remaining brandy, mix for 1 minute, and remove from the heat. Add the butter, melting it, and continue mixing.

Place a strainer in the pot and pour the bisque, breaking up and mashing the contents up well so that all of it is strained.

### RISOTTO

Clean the squid, removing the quill and taking care to keep the ink sacs intact.

Sauté the chopped shallots and garlic until pale gold. Let it braise.

Add 3 1/2 oz (100 g) of squid and let them brown. Drizzle with the white wine. Pour in the fish soup or fumet, the squid ink, and tomato passata. Season with salt and pepper. Cook and puree in a blender when ready.

Toast the rice without any oil in a large skillet. Drizzle with the white wine and then add the squid ink mixture. Continue cooking, slowly adding the fish soup or shellfish bisque and the stock. Stir constantly.

Add the butter at the end and a sprinkling of grated Parmesan. Season with salt to taste.

Serve the risotto, garnishing it with the tomato confit, a basil leaf, basil-infused oil, the remaining squid (finely cut into a julienne and lightly cooked in the fumet, drizzled with extra-virgin olive oil and chives) and the grated lemon zest (optional).

### TOMATO CONFIT

Bring a pot of water to a boil. Cut a cross in the bottom of each tomato (this will make it easier to remove the skin afterwards) and blanch the ripe tomatoes in the water for a few seconds.

Remove and let cool in ice water. Drain and remove the skin, cut tomatoes into four, removing the seeds. Arrange on a baking tray and sprinkle with table salt, sugar, and very finely cut lemon zest. Bake in the oven at 225°F (100°C) for about 2 hours.

## Polenta and birds, today

### Ingredients for 4 people
Preparation time: 1 h 30'

1 tablespoon coarse salt
1 2/3 cups (250 g) polenta flour
10 oz (300 g) pork
2 carrots
2 onions
2 celery stalk
7 oz (200 g) smoked bacon

4 egg whites
4 warblers or larks, cleaned
Salt, to taste
Pepper, to taste
1 pat of butter
1 oz (30 g) foie gras
2 teaspoons (10 g) hazelnut paste

### Method

Bring a liter of water to a boil. Dissolve a tablespoon of coarse salt in it and sift in the polenta flour, mixing with a whisk to make a smooth polenta. Continue cooking for about 45 minutes, stirring constantly. Meanwhile, cut the pork into pieces, as well as 1 carrot, 1 onion, and 1 stalk of celery. Cover with water and bring to a boil, keeping the surface free from impurities using a slotted spoon and making sure that the liquid remains at a simmer. Blend the polenta and keep it in a whipped cream siphon properly charged. Strain the pork stock through a fine-mesh sieve and wait until it cools. Clarify: pass the bacon through a meat grinder with 1 carrot, 1 onion, and 1 stalk of celery. Mix it all together with the egg whites, which have been beaten to stiff peaks. Pour the mixture into the stock, letting it simmer for 3 hours. It will collect any impurities from the stock. When the clarification has been completed, you will be able to pour the consommé through a fine-mesh strainer covered with gauze. Clean the birds, setting the internal parts, such as the liver, heart, and lungs, aside. Cook the birds on a spit arranged horizontally on the cooking axle. Season with salt and pepper and let them turn until cooked.
Let the consommé reduce in a large pot and bind it together with a pat of butter.
Pass the interiors of the birds and the fois gras through a strainer. Mix together with the hazelnut paste to form a puree. Plate, arranging the polenta mousse in the center with the fois gras puree on top. Drizzle with the hot bacon consommé and arrange the roasted birds on top.

# and yesteryear

### Ingredients for 4 people
Preparation time: 1 h 30'

8 warblers (or larks or thrushes), cleaned
8 slices of marinated pancetta
8 sage leaves
1/4 cup (60 g) butter
1 cup (150 g) polenta flour
Salt
1 clove garlic

### Method

Clean the birds on the outside, removing the feathers, but leaving the interiors intact.
Wrap in the slices of pancetta with the sage leaves. Bake at a low temperature of
about 200°F (90-95°C), for 1 1/2 hours.
Meanwhile, make the polenta, bringing the salted water to a boil and mixing in the
flour. Cook for 45-50 minutes.
Serve the birds on the soft polenta with their cooking juices.

# Polenta fogazzin

## Ingredients for 4 people
Preparation time: 1 h 20'

Generous 2 cups (250 g) polenta flour
1 tablespoon coarse salt
Scant 1/3 cup (70 g) melted butter
5 oz (150 g) eggs
Generous 1/3 cup (80 g) sugar
1 teaspoon (5 g) all-purpose flour
10 oz (300 g) sultanas, soaked
1 tablespoon (15 g) anisette
Pinch of vanilla
breadcrumbs

## Method

### POLENTA
Bring 1 liter of water to a boil. Add a tablespoon of coarse salt and sift in the polenta flour, mixing with a whisk to make a smooth polenta. Continue cooking for about 45 minutes.

### FOGAZZIN
Pass the polenta through a vegetable mill. Add the melted butter, followed by the eggs and sugar mixed with the flour and the remaining ingredients.
Butter the mold and sprinkle with breadcrumbs. Bake in the oven at 325°F (160°C) for 18 minutes.

# Luigi Pomata

## LUIGI POMATA RESTAURANT
### Cagliari

"This land is like no other place. Sardinia has its own identity: an enchanting space and places to travel, no end, no beginning, nothing that can be defined. It is like freedom itself*", wrote English writer D. H. Lawrence in his travel diary in 1921. A freedom that Luigi Pomata, chef and *owner* of the *Luigi Pomata* restaurant in Cagliari, has known how to get the most from with passion and insight.

Heir to a family tradition of cooks and restaurateurs from Carloforte, the only city on the island of San Pietro, founded in the 18th Century by a colony of Ligurian fishermen from Tabarka, a small island off the coast of Tunisia, he has not stopped at his father Nicolo's restaurant. "My father grew up an artist, because my grandfather Luigi worked as a chef in the restaurant of the Hotel Riviera in Carloforte. He opened his own restaurant, which he still manages, in 1968" – says Luigi. "I graduated from the naval institute, and then from hotel management." In 1999 he joined his father in the family restaurant, taking advantage of the winter months to continue his studies in Italy and abroad. "I've been traveling now for about ten years, working in very important places in Milan, London, and New York; I have been second chef in restaurants with three Michelin stars, like the Marco Pierre White's *Oak Room* in London or *Le Cirque* and Sirio Maccioni's *Osteria del circo* in New York as well as others. Even though I don't use all of the techniques that I have learned, I have a great cultural heritage. This is a constantly evolving work, where training is truly non-stop: it is never done, you even learn from the dishwasher and from the last chef's assistant hired at the restaurant."

In July 2006, Luigi decided to open his own restaurant in Cagliari, the capital city that blooms like a turquoise flower in the south of Sardinia. Located in the historic district, ninety nine per cent of its offerings are fish: "Especially raw, in line with Italian seafood cuisine." Luigi's kitchen honors the region, both in the use of materials from the area as well as in reusing local dishes, relearned with new and lighter flavor combinations. A quick cuisine "an impromptu cuisine, which is based on products that I find and I like when I go to the market." Taking care of the cooking in both family restaurants, I have to have two different menus: "In Carloforte my clients are tourists on vacation; in Cagliari my clients are the people who work and want to go out for a good meal without spending a fortune." In the restaurant that bears his name "the prime materials are of the highest quality and cooked fresh: we create our dishes in 38 square meters of space." All the dishes are "complemented" by "a wide range of drinks by the glass, local beers and a beautiful selection of Italian and French bubblies."

According to Luigi, a member of the *Jeunes Restaurateurs d'Europe* (Young Restauranteurs of Europe), "nobody creates new things in the kitchen: innovation is set to work on traditional recipes and local products. It is important not to overpower the raw material or use more than two or three ingredients per dish. I want the flavors of every single product to stand out for itself. My philosophy is a minimalistic cuisine: for me the raw material are not the fois gras or the caviar, but local tomatoes and simple salads."

The menu for this book is completely traditional, and it comes from the local cuisine. The appetizer, called '*cappunadda* new', is a revisit of the typical *capponata di tonno*, a tabarkin speciality from Carloforte: "You break six or seven crackers softened in water, set them in a bowl and then add tuna, some sliced tomatoes and white onion slices, all seasoned with oil, vinegar, pepper and salt. Then garnish with basil or marjoram." The first course is *fregola*– the small sized durum wheat pasta typical of Sardinia, similar to *pasta grattata*, (grated pasta) toasted in a wood oven to dry it and give it that wood flavor – cooked like a risotto with clams and lemon, a typical dish of the local cuisine; and second course is lamb with artichokes, saffron and eggs, which uses a meat from the pastoral tradition of inland Sardinia, a well-known vegetable typical of the area with a classic aroma. In the fall it is rather common to find among the freshly ploughed fields in the hills of Southern Sardinia entire fields colored with the bright purple of crocus flowers. Finally dessert is a parfait of *Pardulas*, a sweet characteristic of the Easter season, offered to family guests: a small cake made of cheese or ricotta flavored with orange or lemon.

# New cappunadda
P.262

# Fregola
with clams and lemon
P.264

# Lamb
with artichokes,
saffron, and egg
P.266

# *Pardulas* semifreddo
P.268

# New cappunadda

## Ingredients for 4 people
Preparation time: 30'

### TUNA
14 oz (400 g) fresh tuna scraps
7 oz (200 g) sea salt
1/4 cup (50 g) brown sugar
2 teaspoons (10 g)
Black pepper
1 bunch of mixed herbs (thyme, mint, marjoram)

### GALETTE PASTRY
1 cup (150 g) flour
Generous 3/4 cup (200 ml) water
1 tablespoon extra-virgin olive oil
Salt and pepper, to taste

### GALE
6 red tomatoes
1 white onion
1/2 cup (100 ml) water
1 tablespoon vinegar
1 bunch of fresh basil
Salt, pepper, marjoram to taste

## Method

### TUNA
Wash the tuna scraps and dry them. Make the marinade with salt, brown sugar, flavored pepper and the mixed herb leaves. Place the tuna in the marinade and refrigerate, covered with plastic wrap, for 3 hours.

### GALETTE PASTRY
Mix the flour with the water, oil, and salt to make a thick dough. Roll out the dough to 1/8 inch (1/2 cm) thick and cut into 2 3/4-inch (7 cm) squares. Prick with a fork and brush with oil. Season with salt. Bake on a baking sheet at 400°F (200°C/gas mark 6) for 7–10 minutes until golden and crisp. Let cool.

### TOMATO-ONION SALAD
Cut a cross in the bottom of the tomatoes and blanch in boiling water for 30 seconds. Peel and cut into quarters. Remove the seeds, reserving them. Slice tomato. Finely julienne the onion and soak in a scant 1/2 cup (100 ml) water and 1 tablespoon of vinegar for about 20 minutes. Remove from the liquid and squeeze them dry. Sweat the onion in the oil in a frying pan for about 5 minutes. Wash the basil leaves and dry them (reserve some leaves for garnish). Puree in a blender with the water and reserved tomato seeds and a few tablespoons of oil to make a thick pesto. Add salt and pepper. Rinse and dry the tuna. Combine in a bowl with the tomatoes, the onion, and marjoram leaves. Add the oil, but no salt as it's already been salted. Mix well.

### TUNA CAPPUNADDA
*Cappunadda* is a cold dish that's usually made in the summer. It's easy to make this specialty from Carloforte. 6 or 7 galettes are left to soak in water, making sure that they don't absorb too much water. They're then broken into different pieces and arranged in a large salad bowl. 6 or 7 tomatoes, cut into wedges, and a white onion, sliced, are added. It's dressed with oil, vinegar, salt and pepper.

## Serving

Spread out the basil sauce on the plate. Place a gallette on top of the basil sauce. Arrange some of the tuna-tomato mixture on top; repeat 3 times. Finish with basil.

# Fregola with clams and lemon

## Ingredients for 4 people
Preparation time: 30'

2 lb (1 kg) *arselle* (live clams), or other clams
2 tablespoons (30 ml) extra-virgin olive oil
1 clove garlic
1 bunch of parsley
1 large floury potato
1 cup (150 g) *fregola**

1 quart (1 liter) vegetable stock
Salt
1 red chile pepper, thinly sliced
1 lemon, not too yellow

## *Fregola

A typical dish, *fregola* or *frugla* is a small-sized durum wheat pasta (with the appearance of a grated pasta). There are three different types based on size: small, medium, and large.
The real homemade *fregola* involves toasting in a wood-burning oven to give a smoky taste, while drying the pasta out at the same time. It's usually cooked in meat or fish stock.

## Method

Wash the clams and place them in a container, covered with salted water, for a couple of hours to help remove any sandy residue.
Put the oil, 1 unpeeled clove of garlic, and a bunch of parsley in a wide pot. Cook the clams, covered, until they open up.
Transfer clams to a plate and strain the remaining cooking water, reserving it.
Remove the clams from their shells.
Boil the potato, remove the peel, and mash with the strained clam liquid.
Cook the fregola like a risotto, adding the stock a little at a time, for about 9–12 minutes.
Add the clams, chopped parsley, the thinly sliced chile pepper, and lemon zest at the end.

## Serving

Spoon the creamy cooking liquid in the bottom of the plate and top with the fregola.

# Lamb with artichokes, saffron, and egg

## Ingredients for 4 people
Preparation time: 50'

2 lb (1 kg) leg of lamb
1 sprig of mint, chopped
1 sprig of thyme. chopped
1 lemon, zested
1 bunch of parsley
1 onion, chopped
Extra-virgin olive oil, as needed
2 cups (500 ml) dry white wine
1 sachet of saffron
10 oz (300 g) artichokes, dark green
outer leaves removed and purple heart
removed
2 eggs
Salt and pepper to taste

## Method

Butterfly the leg of lamb and remove the bones and fat (or ask your butcher to do this for you), tenderizing it. Sprinkle with the chopped mint, thyme, and lemon zest. Roll it up and secure as tightly as possible with kitchen string.
Sauté the parsley and onion in the oil in a large pot. Add the leg of lamb and wine. Add the saffron and cook over high heat for 10 minutes.
Cover the pot and bake in a ventilated oven at 275°F (130°C) for about 40 minutes. After 20 minutes, add the cleaned artichokes (to clean, remove the dark green outer leaves and scoop out the bristly, purple center), cut into wedges. At the end of the cooking time, remove the leg of lamb and let rest on a cloth. Remove the artichokes and keep warm.
Off the stove, add the eggs to the cooking liquid and mix well. Season with salt and pepper to taste.

## Serving

Arrange the slices of lamb on the plate with the artichokes and finish with the sauce.

# *Pardulas* semifreddo

### Ingredients for 4 people
Preparation time: 40' - Resting: 5 h

**PASTRY**
1 1/3 cups (200 g) flour
1 egg white
2 teaspoons (10 g) lard

**SEMIFREDDO**
Scant 2/3 cup (130 g) sugar
Generous 2 tablespoons (36 g) water
Scant 1/2 cup (100 g) egg yolks
Generous 3/4 cup (200 g) Ricotta cheese

1 sachet saffron
1 orange
1/4 oz (7 g) gelatin (1 sheet)
2 quarts (2 liters) semi-whipped cream
Confectioners' sugar

**SAUCE**
Mixed berries
1 pinch of sugar

## Method

**SEMIFREDDO**
In a saucepan, cook the sugar in the water, stirring occasionally, to 250°F (121°C).
Beat the egg yolks in a stand mixer. Gradually add the sugar syrup and beat until the mixture cools.
Add the semifreddo, strained Ricotta, saffron, and orange zest to the mixture.
Add the softened (in cold water) gelatin and lighten it all with the cream.
Spoon the mixture into the molds and let cool in a chiller.

**PASTRY**
Mix the flour with the egg white, lard, and a pinch of salt to make a smooth dough.
Roll it out. Cut into rounds that are about 4 inches (10 cm) in diameter.
Place the pastry rounds into molds. Bake in a ventilated oven at 400°F (200°C/gas mark 6) for 10 minutes.

## Serving

Place 1 tablespoon of filling in the center of each round.
Arrange the molds on a baking sheet and freeze for about 5 hours.
Serve with a fruit or chocolate sauce and sprinkle with the confectioners' sugar.

# Antonella Ricci

## AL FORNELLO DA RICCI RESTAURANT
### Ceglie Messapica (Brindisi)

The kitchen of the *Al Fornello da Ricci* restaurant in Ceglie Messapica, an ancient hilltop stronghold in Altosalento, is quite state of the art, spacious and bright, which still guards the 'stove' that made the restaurant famous and full of constant activity, like a statue of a goddess is held in a Greek temple. "*Il fornello* (the stove)" – says Antonella Ricci, chef and co-owner of the restaurant with her husband Vinod Sookar who has joined her in the kitchen for eleven years with her sister Rosella, head waiter and chef-assistant – "is a type of cooking typical of our area: it's structured like a regular oven, but it works on charcoal and with vertical spits. Under the oven is a small tank, which collects fats that we empty daily. It is made completely of stone and is used to cook only meat. At one time, in Puglia, all the butchers had this stove where they would directly cook whatever the customer purchased."

The Ricci family *Fornello* has been serving the public for over forty years. "The restaurant was opened in 1967 by my grandma Rosa, who decided to put on her apron to work. She opened the restaurant with her son Angelo and daughter in law Dora. Then there were very few dishes offered that changed according to the season: homemade pickles, orecchiette and roasted meat." As time passed the restaurant passed to Angelo, then to Antonella who is part of the *Jeunes Resturateurs d'Europe*; and now to her, her husband, and to Rossella. Over the years, the simple *trattoria* has transformed into the fine restaurant that it is today. "A very important stage in the history of the restaurant was the visit of the great wine and food critic Luigi Veronelli at the end of the eightie, who gave the 'goat leg with potatoes roasted in the ashes' the Veronelli 'sun'. Then the Michelin star 15 years ago marked the restaurant's superb quality, research and hospitality."

The kitchen of Antonella "seeks – and I stress the word seeks – to bring the heart and mind together." On the one hand there is the genuine excitement of the typical flavors of Puglia; on the other, the modern and thoughtful way of how to use them. "My kitchen is in pure symbiosis with the land. I use all the products that are available in Puglia. Whoever visits our restaurant is told – and this is important – that the fish is preserved, such as the cod and salted anchovies. The fish is not fresh: the restaurant has been roasting meats with the fornello, and we have opted to continue in that same direction." However the restaurant is found in the hinterland of Puglia, as far from the Adriatic as well as the Ionian coast. «It is not that I am obsessive about local raw materials, but I am convinced that people who come to eat here want to sample what the area has to offer." In short, the truly *avant-garde* does not follow trends, but the specialties of its own history.

Antonella, born to the trade through her mother – "my grandfather Antonio was a chef in Brindisi: cooking runs in my family..." – has a diploma from the *istituto alberghiero* in Brindisi and served various internships in Italy and in France. She also has a degree in Economics and Banking from the University of Lecce, "a bet with myself, to prove that I could be a scholar like my sister." As a child she helped out in her parents' restaurant, and after she graduated in 1995, she started cooking full time. Since 1997 Vinod himself, famous exotic chef from the Mauritius islands, has given her new suggestions. "In addition to the presentation of various dishes, he influenced my inventive use of spices, which I began to use in some marinades, fruit salads, and desserts dishes."

The recipes chosen for this book "are all tied to the region and represent the generosity and variety of the marvelous products of Puglia." As appetizer, 'zucchini flower stuffed with goat cheese and dressed with tomatoes shaken with basil', with Brindisi DOP extra virgin olive oil. The first course is '*millefeuille* with black olives and braised veal with creamed beans', "which uses a native variety of olives, very small and very black." Second course is leg of rabbit, stuffed with Ceglie almond mousse and a spicy fruit salad, "which also features Canestrato semi-aged cheese from Puglia made from whole sheep milk from *Gentile di Puglia* sheep, similar to Pecorino." For dessert, 'upside down tart with figs and goat's milk cheese ice cream and crunchy almonds'.

## Zucchini flowers stuffed
with goat's ricotta with a basil
and fiaschetti tomato pure

P.**274**

## Black olive and veal stew millefeuille
with basil-flavored *piattelli* bean puree

P.**276**

## Rabbit thighs stuffed
with cegliese almond mousse
and spicy fruity salad

P.**278**

## Upside-down fig tartlet
with goat's milk ice-cream
and almond brittle

P.**280**

   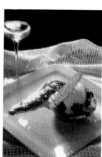

# Zucchini flowers stuffed with goat's ricotta with a basil and fiaschetti tomato puree

## Ingredients for 4 people
Preparation time: 40' - Resting: 1 h

### TOMATO PUREE
10 medium vine-ripened tomatoes, cored and chopped
Generous 3/4 cup (200 ml) Brindisi PDO extra-virgin olive oil, or other good-quality olive oil
2 teaspoons (10 g) sugar
1 bunch basil
Pinch of salt
Pinch of chile powder

### ZUCCHINI BLOSSOMS
4 zucchini flowers
1/3 cup (80 g) goat's milk Ricotta cheese
2 small mint leaves
Pinch of salt
Pinch of nutmeg
Pinch of pepper
1 egg
1 1/4 cups (150 g) breadcrumbs
Slivered almonds
Olive oil for frying

## Method

### TOMATO PUREE
In a food processor or blender, puree the tomatoes . oil, sugar, basil leaves, salt, and chile powder.

Remove the pistil from the flowers and wash well. Let blossoms dry, on a paper towel-lined baking sheet, in the refrigerator for at least 1 hour. Mix the Ricotta, mint, salt, and nutmeg in a bowl. Fill the flowers with the Ricotta mixture. Dip them first in the beaten egg, followed by the breadcrumbs mixed with slivered almonds. Fry the flowers in a deep pan. Drain on a paper towel-lined plate.

## Serving

Arrange a generous spoonful of tomato puree in the bottom of a plate and place the stuffed flowers on top.

# Black olive and veal stew millefeuille with basil-flavored *piattelli* bean puree

## Ingredients for 4 people
Preparation time: 45' - Resting: 2 h

5 whole eggs
1 2/3 cups (250 g) flour
2 cups (500 g) milk
1 Salt
Scant 1/3 cup (20 g) black olives
Melted butter
2 zucchini
4 walnut halves
5 ice cubes
2 teaspoons (10 g) extra-virgin olive oil,
plus additional, for serving
1 bunch basil, plus additional leaves, for
serving
5 oz (150 g) diced veal stew meat
1 1/2 oz (40 g) smoked Scamorza cheese
3/4 oz (20 g) Parmigiano Reggiano

Scant 3 tablespoons (40 g) piattelli bean
puree (see recipe, below)
Pepper to taste
4 nonstick molds, about 2 inches (6 cm)
in diameter

### *PIATTELLI* BEAN PUREE
5 oz (150 g) white beans, shelled
1/2 potato
1/2 carrot
1/2 onion
1/2 stalk celery
Salt
2/3 cup (150 ml) milk
Scant 2 tablespoons (25 g) butter, diced
2 to 3 tablespoons light cream
4 oz (120 g) fried toast

## Method

### *PIATTELLI* BEAN PUREE
Place the beans in a saucepan with cold water, potato, carrot, onion, celery, and salt. Boil
until vegetables are tender. Drain, reserving 2 cups (500 ml) of the cooking liquid, Force
all drained vegetables through a food mill. Stir milk and reserved cooking liquid into the
puree. Return to the heat and cook for 20 minutes. Mix in the diced butter and a few
tablespoons of light cream. Whisk the eggs and flour in a large bowl. Gradually whisk
in the milk and season with salt. Blend the olives in a food processor with a little water.
Stir it into the milk mixture. Cover mixture and refrigerate for 2 hours. Strain through a
fine-mesh strainer. Make into thin crepes: Pour the mixture in a nonstick frying pan with
a melted pat of butter and heated, evenly covering the bottom of the pan. Blanch the
zucchini in boiling water for 1 minute. Let cool in ice water. In a food processor, blend
three-quarters of the zucchini with the walnuts, ice, oil, basil, and a pinch of salt to make
a green puree. Cut the remaining zucchini into small cubes. Cut the crepes into 2-inch
(5-cm) squares. Place a layer of crepes in the nonstick molds and alternate with the meat,
Scamorza, and Parmesan up to the brim. Bake in the oven at 350°F (180°C/gas mark 4)
for 12 minutes.

## Serving

Turn out onto a plate. Serve on the bean puree, pesto, and zucchini cubes. Drizzle
with a little extra-virgin olive oil and garnish with a few basil leaves.

# Rabbit thighs stuffed with cegliese almond mousse and spicy fruity salad

Ingredients for 4 people
Preparation time: 45' - *Demi glace*: 5 h

### STUFFED RABBIT THIGHS
4 rabbit thighs
Handful of herbs (thyme, rosemary, sage, parsley)
1 teaspoon (5 g) garlic
3/4 cup (120 g) blanched almonds
1 3/4 oz (50 g) semi-aged Canestrato*
Pugliese cheese
5 oz (150 g) caul fat or 4 bamboo skewers
Generous 1 tablespoon (20 g) extra-virgin
olive oil, to brown
Scant 1/4 cup (50 g) rabbit demi-glace* (made
using the thigh bones)
Pinch of salt
* Canestrato is a cheese made from whole
milk, similar to Pecorino.

### DEMI GLACE*
Rabbit bones and thighs
Scant 2 tablespoons (25 g) lard
2 carrots, 1 stalk of celery, 1 onion
1 1/4 cups (300 g) peeled ripe tomatoes
1 clove garlic and 1 small bunch of parsley

2 tablespoons (30 g) olive oil
2 teaspoons coarse salt. Pepper
Scant 1/2 cup (100 g) dry white wine
Generous 2 tablespoons (35 g) all-purpose flour
2 quarts (2 liters) water
Scant tablespoon (10 g) dried mushrooms

### SALAD
3 1/2 oz (100 g) mixed salad greens
2 strawberries, julienned
3/4 oz (20 g) pineapple, peeled, cored, and
julienned
3/4 oz (20 g) peaches, peeled, pitted, and
julienned
3/4 oz (20 g) kiwi fruit, peeled and julienned
4 melon balls

### VINAIGRETTE
1 tablespoon (15 g) extra-virgin olive oil
1 1/2 teaspoons (8 g) cider vinegar
1 teaspoon (5 g) sugar
1/4 teaspoon (2 g) chile powder
Pinch of salt

## Method

Bone the thighs, taking care to leave the shank intact. Make the demi-glace with the bones.

### DEMI-GLACE (2 CUPS/500 ML)

Soften the mushrooms in 1 cup (250 ml) of water. Dice the lard. Peel the carrots and clean the celery stalk. Chop up the carrots, celery, onion, the tomatoes, garlic, sage, and parsley.

Drizzle a little oil in a heat-proof casserole. Add the lard and the rabbit bones. Mix over medium heat and season with salt and pepper. Add the chopped vegetables. Bake in the oven at 350°F (170°C) for 20–30 minutes.

Return the dish to the heat. Add the white wine and flour and mix well.

Pour in the water and mix. Return to the oven.

Continue cooking for another 3 hours; return the dish to the heat and add the mushrooms, which have been drained and squeezed dry.

After another 30 minutes, remove the bones; strain sauce.

Return the sauce to the heat. Simmer for an additional 1 1/2 hours to thicken. At the end of the cooking time, turn off the heat and let cool.

Wash and chop the herbs and garlic. Blend the almonds, Canestrato cheese, vegetables, garlic, and a drop of oil. Stuff the thighs with the mousse, sealing them with with the caul fat or a bamboo skewer. Heat the oil in a frying pan and brown the thighs. Transfer to a baking sheet. Bake in the oven at 350°F (170°C) for 15–18 minutes, or until cooked through.

Mix the salad , julienned fruit, and melon in a large bowl. Whisk together the vinaigrette ingredients.

## Serving

Slice the thighs and serve with the hot demi-glace on top and the salad dressed with the vinaigrette on the side.

# Upside-down fig tartlet with goat's milk ice-cream and almond brittle

## Ingredients for 4 people
Preparation time: 1 h 30'

### ICE-CREAM
2 cups (500 g) goat's milk
3/4 cup (150 g) sugar
1 Vanilla bean, split open
2 tablespoons (30 g) powdered milk
1 egg yolk
Scant 1/2 cup (100 g) cream

### ALMOND BRITTLE
Scant 3/4 cup (100 g) blanched almonds
1/2 cup (100 g) superfine sugar
1 lemon
Oil

### SHORTCRUST PASTRY
1 cup (150 g) all-purpose flour
Scant 1/2 cup (100 g) margarine
Scant 3 tablespoons (40 g) water
1 teaspoon (5 g) salt
4 individual aluminum molds
Scant 3 tablespoons (40 g) fig preserves
4 oz (120 g) figs, washed , patted dry, and sliced
1/3 cup (80 g) goat's milk ice-cream
1 tablespoon (15 g) almond brittle, broken into pieces

## Method

### ICE-CREAM
Heat the goat's milk to 195°F (90°C) in a saucepan over medium heat with the sugar and vanilla. Remove from the heat and add the powdered milk and egg yolk. Mix in the cream and beat well.

### ALMOND BRITTLE
Coarsely chop almonds (or leave them whole). Spread out on a very clean baking sheet. Bake in a 350°F (175°C) preheated oven, toasting them lightly. Meanwhile, caramelize the sugar. Add a few drops of lemon juice and the toasted almonds. Mix well and pour the brittle onto a lightly oiled marble work surface.. Use a lightly oiled lemon to spread out the brittle to the desired height. Before it hardens completely, use a large knife to cut the brittle to the preferred size. Let cool.

### SHORTCRUST PASTRY
Mix the flour, margarine, water, and salt a bowl. Let rest in the refrigerator for 1 hour. Use a rolling pin to roll out the pastry to 1/3-inch (1-cm) thick. Cut pastry into rounds and line each mold with pastry round. Spread the fig preserves on the bottom of the pastry and arrange the fig slices on top. Bake in the oven at 350°F (180°C/gas mark 4) for 15 minutes.

## Serving

Serve warm with the ice-cream and almond brittle.

# Emanuele Scarello

## AGLI AMICI TRATTORIA RESTAURANT
### Godia (Udine)

He never gives up outspoken traditional flavors, but always enriches them with a rich, motivated and stylish essence. This is the cuisine of Emanuele Scarello, chef and owner with his sister Michela, of the *Agli Amici trattoria* restaurant in Godia, a small hamlet on the outskirts of Udine in the heart of Friuli-Venezia Giulia.

A culinary philosophy celebrates the long history of the restaurant, which was founded by his family in 1887. "My sister and I have been running the restaurant since 1999, but we are aware of what was done by the four generations that came before us", says Emanuele. At first it just sold foods and things in general, managed by his great- great grandfather Umberto, and a *trattoria* that was run by his great-grandmother Emilia. After this, it was run by Emanuele's grandfather and grandmother, and later by his parents, who in '93 renovated the whole building, adding on until it reached the size and appearance of today.

Papa Tino and mamma Ivonne still work in the restaurant, one in the kitchen and the other in the dining room with their daughter Michela, who is a wine steward. All four are surrounded by excellent collaborators: "We are like a soccer team. I am the striker and I have to score goals, however, there must be a goalkeeper, a defender, a midfielder... Everybody must play well and all are very important."

At first, their parents discouraged him and Michela, encouraging them to undertake other work. "For a while we listened to them, but then we realized that the desire for food was in our DNAs as it was in theirs, so much so that we have followed the family business and, after experiencing other things, we came back." Indeed for them it is not a restaurant, but "our home, that we open to guests." The restaurant overlooks the central square of a small agricultural village in a suburb miraculously spared from factories and chimneys. It is simple, but elegant, and now it is part of the prestigious association of 'Le Soste'.

"When I graduated from hotel school, I was convinced that I could begin working immediately in the restaurant. But that was not true. My parents sent me off to experience the world and to learn. I was fortunate: I received the right incentives to continue and to want to push forward." He worked in some of the best places in Europe as well as Italy, but it was right around the corner where he found his two mentors, "After my parents, of course" who made haute cuisine what it is today: Giorgio Trentin and Vinicio Dovier, owner and chef respectively of the *Boschetti* restaurant in Tricesimo. "At the time, I was 16 years old and the restaurant had two Michelin stars..." Emanuele, however, did not adhere to any one discipline: "I have my own definite identity that is tied to my land. If you ride a wave that is not your own, it makes little sense..."

He defines his cuisine defines 'contemporary', enhanced with two Michelin star. "Although I always keep my feet firmly on the ground in the land where I was born and use everything that it can offer, I also like to look for opportunities beyond that." He is open to dialogue and exchanges with other chefs and open to the new frontiers of taste.

He doesn't serve the traditional dishes in strictly traditional form. "At the restaurant I am looking for something that tickles me and entertains me, something that makes me savor the traditional taste, but without duplicating it. I love and believe in tradition, but I look at it with new eyes." But he always does it with sincerity and transparency: "In my restaurant what the guest eats my family should also eat." And humility: "Even if our work is in the spotlight now, we are still people who put a pan on the fire..."

For the appetizer course for the menu in this book, he chose the warm sea bass *tartare* with *horseradish*. First course is a *panade* with tripe and *popcorn* cod. "I started with a *panade*, which is a traditional bread soup that is prepared slowly on a spolert, a typical wood-burning stove. The soup is made of chicken broth or beef broth, with a raw egg yolk and pork with fennel. I use the fish stock as I like to serve it with cod tripe and a '*popcorn style*' crispy breaded cod." The second course is a cheek of corned veal served with cream of celeriac and *picecui* mustard, the Friulian rosehips. Dessert is *Zamò & Nonino Sweet*, a "tribute to two people who have done so much for the food and wine of Friuli: Giannola Nonino of the historic family of brandy distillers and wine producer Tullio Zamò. "

# Warm tartare of sea bass,
### *musetto*, and horseradish
P.**286**

# Bread soup
### with salt cod tripe and popcorn
P.**290**

# Salted veal cheeks
### with celery root puree
P.**292**

# Zamò & Nonino
### dessert
P.**294**

# Warm tartare of sea bass, *musetto*, and horseradish

### Ingredients for 4 people
Preparation time: 20' – Cooking time for *musetto*: 2 h – Oil butter: 48 h

TARTARE
3 1/2 oz (100 g) musetto* (previously cooked and diced)
1 wild sea bass, weighing about 1 lb (500 g)
Salt, for seasoning
Freshly ground black pepper, for seasoning
Chives, chopped
Fresh horseradish, grated
Radish sprouts
Extra-virgin olive oil

* The best-known Friulian sausage, *musetto* is a ground seasoned pork mixture Stuffed into sausage casings. *Musetto* is made from lean pork snout meat (where its name comes from), the tastiest and most delicious part of the whole pig, mixed with a bit of firm lard.

OIL BUTTER
1 cup (250 g) Carso extra-virgin olive oil, or other good-quality olive oil

### Method

OIL BUTTER
Pour the oil into a container and keep it in the freezer for 24 hours. Chill in the refrigerator for 1 day.

TARTARE
Simmer the *musetto* in its casing very slowly over low heat for about 1 1/2–2 hours. Cut into small cubes.
Transfer the *musetto* cubes to a large pot and heat them through.
Cut the sea bass flesh into small cubes and season with salt and pepper. Toss with the chives and fresh horseradish.
Mix the sea bass with the musetto and warm (but take care not to cook the eel) over low heat.

### Serving

Arrange the tartare in the center of the plate using a pastry cutter; top with the radish sprouts. Finish with a quenelle of oil butter.

# Bread soup with salt cod tripe and popcorn

### Ingredients for 4 people
Preparation time: 1 h – Cooking time for soup: 3 h – Drying the tripe: 24 h

FUMET
Fish trimmings
Vegetables (such as carrot, celery, and
mushroom stalks)
Onion
Garlic
Herbs (bay and parsley)
Salt
White wine
Peppercorn

SOUP
1 3/4 oz (50 g) shallot
2 salt-cured anchovy fillets
Garlic-infused extra-virgin olive oil
1 sprig of thyme
4oz (125 g) dry white bread
5 cups (1.2 kg) fish fumet
Salt, to taste
Freshly ground black pepper, to taste
Dill

*SPICY TOMATO SAUCE
4 tablespoons extra-virgin olive oil
2 onions, chopped
3 cloves garlic, chopped
1/2 cup (125 g) tomato passata
2 lb (1 kg) tomatoes, cut into cubes
1/2 cup (125 ml) red wine
1 tablespoon traditional balsamic vinegar
1 teaspoon brown sugar
1 tablespoon (15 g) parsley, chopped
1 chile pepper

SALT COD TRIPE
14 oz (400 g) salt cod tripe
1 2/3 cups (400 g) spicy tomato sauce*

POPCORN
14 oz (400 g) salt cod tripe
Salt, for seasoning

## Method

### FUMET

This concentrated fish stock is made by cooking fish trimmings with vegetables, salt, and herbs for a long time. Gut the fish (medum and large-sized fish are preferable as they are rich in collagen) and cut the fish bones into pieces. Add the bones, head, tails, and flesh to a saucepan with the carrot, celery, onions, mushroom stalks, garlic, bay leaf, and parsley. Cover the mixture with water and white wine and cook for at least 1 hour, Skim the foam occasionally. Add the peppercorns at the end. Let rest for at least 15 minutes before straining.

### BREAD SOUP

Chop the shallot. Rinse the anchovies and cook over low heat in a little garlic-infused oil. Add the thyme, which will be removed at the end, and bread. Mix well and add enough of the fumet until it all ingredients are covered.
Cook over low heat (if possible, use a flame tamer to help evenly distribute the heat of the burner) for 3 hours until the bread starts to stick to the bottom of the pan. Season with salt and pepper to taste and add the chopped dill.

### SPICY TOMATO SAUCE

Heat the oil in a large pot. Add the onions, garlic, and chile pepper. Cook over medium heat for 5 minutes. Add the tomato passata and cook for 3 minutes, mixing occasionally. Pour in 2 cups (500 ml) of water with the tomatoes, wine, vinegar, and sugar. Bring to a boil, stirring often. Lower the heat and simmer for 25 minutes, until the mixture thickens.
Finish with the remaining parsley 2 minutes before removing from the heat.

### SALT COD WITH TOMATO SAUCE

Use a knife to remove the skin from the tripe and blanch in plenty of water. Add the tripe to the tomato sauce.

### SALT COD POPCORN

Peel the tripe and cut into 3/4-inch (2-cm) squares. Place in a dryer at 85°F (30°C) for 24 hours. Remove and store in an airtight container until ready to use.
Let the tripe burst into popcorn in oil heated to 350°F (180°C), making sure that it tripled in volume. Drain and season with salt.

## Serving

Ladle the soup in the center of each plate. Place a tablespoon of tripe in tomato sauce on top and finish with a piece of salt cod popcorn.

# Salted veal cheeks with celery root puree

### Ingredients for 4 people
Preparation time: 3 h – Marinating: 24 h

10 fresh veal cheeks*
Salt
Curing spices

*To cook the cheeks, a multi-functional oven or a Roner digital thermostat should be used, pieces of equipment that maintains the water in a container at a set temperature.*

#### PICECUI MUSTARD
7 oz (200 g) picecui (dog rose berries)
1 cup (250 g) white wine vinegar
1 cup (250 g) white wine
3/4 cup (150 g) sugar
Zest of 1 lemon
Zest of 1 orange

2 bay leaves
1 cinnamon stick
5 cloves
1 shallot
1 quince
Salt and peppercorns

#### CELERY ROOT PUREE
8 oz (250 g) celery root, cut into short lengths
Salt, for seasoning
Freshly ground black pepper, for seasoning
Scant 1/2 cup (100 g) extra-virgin olive oil, plus additional, for drizzling
Scant 1/2 cup (100 g) whole milk

### Method

Sprinkle the cheeks with salt, followed by the curing spices. Seal them in a vacuum pack and let marinate in the refrigerator at +35.5°F (2°C) for 1 day. Cook at 200°F (85°C) for 2 hours in the oven.

#### MUSTARD
Cut the berries in half, removing the seeds and washing them carefully under running water to remove any thorny residues.
Boil all the ingredients (apart from the berries) for 5 minutes and then strain. Add the berries and simmer over medium heat for 10 minutes.

#### PUREE
Season the celery root with salt and pepper. Drizzle with extra-virgin olive oil. Seal in a vacuum pack and bake in the oven at 200°F (90°C) for 30 minutes. Open the pack and pour the contents into a food processor. Blend with the milk and extra-virgin olive oil to make a puree. Keep warm.

### Serving

Slice the warm veal cheeks and serve with a generous spoonful of celery root puree and a spoonful of mustard.

# Zamò & Nonino dessert

**Ingredients for 4 people**
Preparation time: 1 h

### ICE-CREAM
Generous 3 cups (625 g) sugar
3 cups (650 g) Vola Vola (raisin dessert wine)
1 1/4 cups (300 g) Vola Vola syrup, (see recipe, below)
2 cups (500 g) milk
1 cup (250 g) fresh cream
Scant 1/4 cup (50 g) egg yolks

### CHOCOLATE AND NONINO
### *ANTICA CUVÉE CUSTARD*
Generous 1 1/4 cups (320 g) cream
1/3 cup (80 g) milk
8 1/2 oz (240 g) couverture chocolate, chopped

2/3 oz (20 g) egg yolks
Generous 2 tablespoons (35 g) aged grappa (Nonino Antica Cuvée)

### NOUGAT
2 oz (60 g) fondant
Scant 3 tablespoons (40 g) glucose
2 tablespoons (30 g) ground hazelnuts
Scant 3 tablespoons (40 g) Jivara cocoa

### SERVING
Dried fruit
Cantucci cookies
Oranges
Grappa

## Method

### VOLA VOLA ICE-CREAM
Heat the sugar and 2 cups (500 g) of Vola Vola until the volume has reduced by half. When it has cooled, it should have a honey-like consistency. Heat the milk and cream and slowly whisk the mixture into the egg yolks, which have been mixed beforehand with the syrup and gently heated in a saucepan to 175°F (80°C). Cover and let infuse, refrigerated, overnight.
The next day, add the remaining 1/4 cup of Vola Vola and churn in an ice-cream machine according to the manufacturer's instructions.

### CHOCOLATE AND NONINO *ANTICA CUVÉE* CUSTARD
Bring the cream and milk to a simmer and pour over the couverture chocolate. Beat in the egg yolks and finally the grappa.

### NOUGAT
Heat the fondant and glucose to 330°F (165°C). Add the ground hazelnuts and Jivara cocoa. Pour the mixture over two sheets of parchment paper to form a thin, even layer. Bake at 250°F (120°C) for 3 minutes. Shape into a low ring.
Marinate the dried fruit in the Vola Vola and the segments of orange, peeled, in the grappa.

## Serving

Arrange a tablespoon of crumbled cantucci cookies and dried fruit marinated in Vola Vola on one side and the orange in grappa on the other side. Place the nougat ring on top of the oranges and a top with a spoonful of the Nonino custard. Place a scoop of Vola Vola ice cream on top of the cantucci cookies and the dried fruit marinade. Serve.

# Peppino (Giuseppe) Tinari

## VILLA MAIELLA RESTAURANT
### Guardiagrele (Chieti)

A force of nature. That is Peppino Tinari, chef and *owner* of the *Villa Maiella* restaurant in Guardiagrele, an evocative historic village at the foot of the Maiella Mountains, in the Chietano hinterland. It is the expression of that instinctive cuisine that the region has offered for centuries. It is not by accident that the first Italian cooking school was founded in the Villa Santa Maria, at the foot of the Sangro River valley, by San Francesco Caracciolo (1563–1608), patron saint of cooks.

The *Villa Maiella* since 1968 has honored the history and evolution of Abruzzi cuisine. Founded as a simple café, it was transformed by Peppino's parents into an inn that featured home cooking, offering regional dishes from rabbit cooked 'under the bricks' to oven-roasted kid with potatoes and *pallottine*, meatballs of horse meat. However it was only in 1984 that Peppino, then twenty-three, began to help in running the restaurant. He was backed by a solid training: first at the *istituto alberghiero* in Roccaraso, where he first learned what it was to be a cook; then for more experience at the *Hôtel Cipriani* in Venice with chef Giovanni Spaventa, whom he considers his second teacher (after Domenico Stanziani) and his second father. Tired of living in Laguna – "I missed my own land… When I worked in Venice, the few times when I returned to Guardiagrele, it was wonderful to smell the aromas of my father's orchard and my mother's kitchen, the smell of the charcoal that burned in the *fornacella* where the sauce was cooking in a clay pot…", he says. – He went back to the family tavern, with his mind set to turning it into a real restaurant. "I told my mother to take away the cutlery with the plastic handles and the hospital dishes, to bring in some copper pots, to redo the kitchen with modern appliances… And my mother supported me." So, with his mother Ginetta and father Arcangelo at his side, he began to run the restaurant and began to form a clientele who still follows him with affection.

In 1985 he founded the *Villa Maiella* – "We called it that because it is the name of the town where it is located, inside the Maiella National Park" – and next to him in the kitchen is his wife Angela: "At first she was a bit frightened to stand at the stove, but over the years she has become better than me, especially with pastries." In 1993 there was a jump in quality: the restaurant was extended and the upper structure was made into a hotel with fourteen rooms.

Today *Villa Maiella* (where Peppino's two sons also work, Pascal in the dining room since 2011 and Arcangelo in the kitchen since 2013) is at the top of the Abruzzi cuisine, and Peppino has received numerous awards including the nomination as *Cavaliere Ufficiale* (Officer and Knight) of the Italian Republic. And the awards are well deserved for his work philosophy: always looking for the best and demanding the most from himself and from others. Peppino is continuously keeping up with the times, always seeking the goal of keeping quality high, and constantly demanding work with a maximum of care and respect for raw materials, which he has turned into practically a cult, from the time the raw materials are brought into the kitchen until they are placed on the table. The same care is also given to the customer.

"Mine is a local cuisine that I would define as personal. A region that I always reinterpret according to new cooking techniques, without excluding traditional methods: if you can use a match, you can also use an automated oven…" However more than innovation, what is important is substance, the defense of genuine flavors. His is an essential cuisine – "when there are three elements in a dish, there are already too many" – within his minimalistic cuisine, there is much research.

The menu chosen for the book begins with the traditional appetizer of *pallotte cacio e uova* (ball with cheese and eggs) and a first course of '*spaghetti alla chitarra* with fresh tomatoes and Maiella herbs', egg noodles softer than usual, that is flavored with raw tomatoes, olive oil, garlic and a bit of thyme, marjoram, oregano, basil, sage and parsley. The second course is a 'leg of lamb with an Aquila saffron sauce', a spice that has for centuries been cultivated in the high plains of the Aquila mountains and a flagship of Abruzzi agriculture. And to finish is '*Parrozzo* parfait': "The *Parrozzo* is a coarse bread, hence the name, in the form of a round loaf made of corn or semolina flour, sweet and bitter almonds, sugar, butter, egg and s of chocolate, which is then covered with chocolate. The recipe comes from a long-lasting bread that the shepherds of Abruzzo used to take with them during the ancient trek from the mountain to the plain and then back following the same path."

## Cheese and egg
fritters

P.**300**

## Chitarrina
with fresh tomatoes
and Maiella herbs

P.**302**

## Lamb shank
with saffron sauce from L'Aquila

P.**304**

## *Parrozzo parfait*

P.**306**

# Cheese and egg fritters

Ingredients for 4 people
Preparation time: 35'

FRITTERS
2 1/2 oz (75 g) day-old bread, soaked in milk
3 whole eggs
1 clove red or white garlic, finely chopped
Pinch of chopped parsley
1 1/4 cups (150 g) freshly grated pecorino cheese
2 cups (250 g) freshly grated semi-aged cow's cheese
Extra-virgin olive oil, for frying

SAUCE
Scant 1/2 cup (100 ml) extra-virgin olive oil
1 clove red or white garlic, lightly crushed
1/3 cup (10 g) finely chopped onion
Sprig of basil
1 cup (250 g) tomatoes, peeled, seeded, and cut lengthwise into thin strips
Vegetable stock
Pinch of salt

## Method

FRITTERS
Squeeze the milk out of the bread. Beat the eggs in a bowl. Add the garlic, soaked bread, parsley, and finally the grated cheeses to make a thick mixture. Let rest for 30 minutes.
Use two tablespoons to shape the mixture into quenelles and arrange on a tray. The mixture should make about 20. (For the less expert cook, make the balls using your hands.)
Heat plenty of extra-virgin olive oil in a large, deep frying pan to 250-275°F (130-140°C). Fry the balls slowly until they puff up and are golden brown. Remove from the oil and let drain on a paper towel-lined baking sheet.

SAUCE
Heat the oil in a pot, preferably earthenware. Add the crushed garlic, then the chopped onion. Discard the garlic when it turns pale gold. Add the sprig of basil and tomatoes. After 5-6 minutes, add the fritters, arranging them evenly in the pot. Cover with the vegetable stock and cook for 5 minutes more. Season with salt to taste and serve.

# Chitarrina with fresh tomatoes and Maiella herbs

Ingredients for 4 people
Preparation time: 45'

PASTA
2 2/3 cups (400 g) flour
4 whole eggs, lightly beaten
Pinch of salt

SAUCE
Scant 1/2 cup (100 ml) extra-virgin olive oil
1 clove red or white garlic, lightly crushed
Handful of finely chopped fresh herbs
1 1/3 lb (600 g) tomatoes, peeled, seeded, and cut lengthwise into thin strips
Parsley, to garnish
Small fried basil leaves, to garnish

## Method

PASTA
Sift the flour onto a wooden surface and shape into a mound. Make a well in the center. Pour the eggs into the hollow, add a pinch of salt, and knead until the dough is smooth and even. Wrap in plastic wrap and let rest for 30 minutes. Roll the dough out with a long pasta rolling pin to 3/4-inch (2-mm) thick. Cut the sheet of pasta on the strings of the chitarra or use a pasta machine and pass the pasta through the cutter. Lay out the pasta on a tray and cover with a cotton cloth.

SALSA
Heat the oil in a large frying pan and add the crushed garlic. Discard the garlic when it turns pale gold. Add the chopped herbs to the pan. Immediately add the tomatoes, season with salt to taste, and cook for 10 minutes. Cook the pasta in plenty of salted water. Drain and sauté briefly in the sauce (given that it is fresh egg pasta, it absorbs a lot of the sauce). Serve at once, garnishing the dish with parsley and fried basil, which has been prepared in advance.

# Lamb shank with saffron sauce from L'Aquila

## Ingredients for 4 people
Preparation time: 1 h 25'

4 Small lamb shanks

HERBS AND AROMATICS
5 oz (150 g) onion
5 oz (150 g) celery
2 sprigs of rosemary
2 sprigs of thyme
4 sage leaves
1 bay leaf
3 cloves garlic
4 juniper berries
Salt and peppercorns, as much as needed
1 quart (1 liter) alcohol-free white wine*
Generous 3/4 cup (200 ml) extra-virgin olive oil

50 saffron strands (soaked in scant 1/2 cup (100 ml) warm water for at least 1 hour before use)
* Bring the wine to a boil in a large pot. Carefully remove the wine from the stovetop, and light alcohol with a match or lighter. Let burn until flame has extinguished naturally, burning off all alcohol.

GARNISH
1 Small pearl barley flan
Vegetable puree (turnip or wild vegetables)
1 Candied tomato

## Method

To prepare the lamb shanks, season them with salt, and brown in a casserole dish to seal the meat. Add the herbs and aromatics and cook them slowly. Then pour in the white wine and half of the saffron water. Cover and bake in the oven for 70 minutes at 325°F (170°C/gas mark 3), checking the level of the cooking liquid occasionally. At the end of the cooking, strain the cooking juices, and add the remaining saffron water. Place pot on the stovetop and simmer until reduced to the desired consistency. Season with salt to taste.

## Serving

Arrange the shank on a plate and drizzle with the sauce. Garnish with the flan, vegetable puree, and candied tomato.

# Parrozzo parfait

### Ingredients for 4 people
Preparation time: 20' - Resting time: 4 h

9 egg yolks
Scant 1 cup (180 g) sugar
2 cups (500 g) cream
4 oz (125 g) chocolate cake*, broken into
pieces
1 3/4 oz (50 g) chocolate

*CHOCOLATE CAKE
1 oz (30 g) almonds
4 tablespoons (60 g) sugar
3 eggs, separated
2 tablespoons (30 g) flour
2 tablespoons (30 g) cornstarch
Scant 3 tablespoons (40 g) butter
2 3/4 oz (80 g) melted dark chocolate
10 toasted almonds

### Method

CHOCOLATE CAKE
Chop the almonds with a tablespoon of sugar. Whip the egg yolks with the remaining sugar, beat them, and add the chopped almond mixture. Sift in the flour and cornstarch. Add 2 tablespoons (30 g) of melted butter. Whip the egg whites and fold them into the mixture. Pour the batter into a buttered cake pan and bake in the oven at 350°F (180°C/gas mark 4) for 40 minutes. Let it cool, then turn the cake out onto a platter. Cover with the melted chocolate and the toasted almonds.

SEMIFREDDO
Use a mixer to beat the egg yolks with the sugar until they turn pale. Meanwhile, beat the fresh cream in a separate bowl until slightly thick. Mix the chocolate cake pieces into the beaten yolks with the chocolate, followed by the cream. Pour the mixture into a semifreddo mold or plastic-lined terrine and freeze for at least 4 hours.
Turn it out of the mold and cut into 1/3-inch (1-cm) thick triangles or slices. Arrange them on a dish and decorate as desired.

# Federico Tonetti

## OSTERIA LE MASCHERE
### Sarsina (Forlì-Cesena)

At *Le Maschere* tavern in Sarsina, a bewitching country founded by the Romans on the highlands of Cesena, good food and good wine are a form of classic theater. Here the great Latin poet and playwright Tito Maccio Plautus would willingly come. Not because the restaurant is in his native land, but because Federico Tonetti, chef and co-owner with Giordana Cattani, head of the dining room, works has the same wit and vivacity. A genuine, passionate and free spirit that every day turns his dishes into cultural experiences: culinary representations founded on history, art, creativity and the good air that one breathes in this part of the Romagna Apennines.

"*Le Maschere,* although well-known, is not just a restaurant, but also a restaurant that has been chosen to be more of a business venture, to follow that difficult path of emotions and feelings, where the cuisine and the table become one in a unique ambiance of human acceptance, where individual differences are harmonized into the personal inspirations that only friendship and natural ingredients can blend into the flavors and panaceas of life", says Federico. Inaugurated in 1990, it is home to all the senses of the soul, even if only for the duration of a dinner. Here, like in the plays of Plautus, "every right of human existence is a fascinating mixed salad, meat that pulses and bleeds, that desires, fish that speak and wine that purifies." And a catharsis is possible: "Everyone is an actor who interprets freely and at his own choice, with the joy of being in a place where one can enjoy a moment of normal daily life with an extraordinary potential for quality, uniqueness, and leisure."

In the kitchen of our host – the term chef does not seem to fit him – for the Appian *gens* of the Val di Savio, with the appearance of a great bearded eater, but with the kind serenity of a philosopher, research and experimentation are not obsessive. Here siphons and sparklings have not yet arrived and may never arrive. What matters is the enhancement of the premium local raw materials and the possibility of eating at reasonable prices. Federico offers "a simple cuisine, tied to the offerings of the region, transforming dignified poverty into a sober gastronomic fancy, healthy and intelligent. A cuisine that is not overdone, but personalized, typical of authentic and guaranteed flavors, capable of marrying with the art of good living."

Born here, since he was a child he has loved to sit in the kitchen to 'experiment': "It's not that I chose to cook; I did it because I'm good in the kitchen, it's not work, it comes naturally to me." After graduating from the hotel institute of Marebello he began a tour of Europe: France, Germany, England, and Spain... always identifying with the life of real people. In the meantime, he passed the seasons in some tourism areas of Italy, from Sestrière to the Emerald Coast. After his professional experience matured abroad, "I surrendered to my impulses and answered the call of my native lands: I came home, to that bunch of family memories and feelings that I think are essential to give meaning to a life worth living." Here then, is the insight to repossess the regional products: "the cuisine is the land that blooms and regenerates in everyone's life."

The menu for this book "to me means being in the territory." As appetizer he chose the *misti-canza* (mixed salad) with aromatic herbs, golden lamb sweetbreads and fried cream. "When you taste and smell the flavors and the aroma of the herbs it is as if you were walking along a path of our badlands..." First course is *cappelletti* as served in Romagna, or stuffed with cheese, candied citrus peel and nutmeg, with sweet onions of Sant'Arcangelo where the Apennines meet between Forlì and Rimini, braised with dried Albana raisins, among the most prized products of the Romagna vineyards, and foie gras: "The meeting of these ingredients communicate the idea that yes, we are bound to the land and we use its excellent products, but we also want to extend to other culinary excellences of Europe." Second course is a pigeon, "a food that is often found in our cooking", stuffed with mushrooms and sausage, toasted liver, poached egg and fried sage. Dessert is an almond basket with English cream and liqueur and sweet cookies, a little known version of the classic *piadina romagnola*. A canvas of flavors, colors and aromas that make a gastronomic show that is 'unparalleled'.

## Mixed salad with herbs

and browned lamb sweetbreads, fried custard
and traditional balsamic vinegar

P.312

## Romagna-style cappelletti

with sweet onion, foie gras,
and Albana passita

P.314

## Stuffed pigeon,

served with liver pate toasts,
poached eggs, and fried sage

P.316

## Almond basket

with vanilla custard and sweet flatbread

P.318

# Mixed salad with herbs and browned lamb sweetbreads, fried custard and traditional balsamic vinegar

## Ingredients for 4 people
Preparation time: 1 h 15'

2 cups (500 ml) + 1 1/4 cups (300 ml) whole milk
1 vanilla pod
Lemon zest
3 egg yolks
Generous 1/2 cup (125 g) sugar
2/3 cup (100 g) flour + 2 tablespoons
14 oz (400 g) mixed salad (such as lettuce, radicchio, lamb's lettuce, curly endive, gentilina, arugula)
5 oz (150 g) herbs (such as chives, tarragon, lovage, cress, chervil, salad burnet, dill, cilantro, mint)
10 oz (300 g) lamb sweetbreads
1 1/4 cups (300 ml) milk
2 eggs
2 tablespoons of olive oil
Edible flowers

## Method

### CUSTARD
Bring the milk to a boil in a small saucepan with the vanilla and lemon zest. Mix the egg yolks with the sugar in a bowl. Add the flour, mixing constantly, making sure that no lumps form. Pour the milk into the prepared egg mixture, whisking constantly.
Return mixture to the heat over low, mixing until the custard becomes fairly thick. Pour the custard onto a sheet of parchment paper; spread to a 3/4-inch (2-cm) layer and let cool.
Wash and chop the mixed greens with the herbs; dry the mixed salad.
Rinse the sweetbreads under cold running water. Blanch in water and milk for about 5 minutes. Let cool.
Make a batter consisting of 2 tablespoons of flour, 2 tablespoons of olive oil, 1 egg, and a pinch of salt.
Cut the sweetbreads into 1/3-inch (1-cm) thick medallions, dip in the flour, followed by the batter. Fry in plenty of olive oil. Cut the chilled custard into diamonds. Dip in the flour, followed by the beaten egg and breadcrumbs. Fry in plenty of oil.

## Serving

Arrange the salad, herbs, and edible flowers on the plate. Place the sweetbreads in the center with a couple of custard diamonds on the side and a few drops of traditional balsamic vinegar.

# Romagna-style cappelletti with sweet onion, foie gras, and Albana passita

## Ingredients for 4 people
Preparation time: 1 h

STOCK
1 1/2 lb (700 g) beef
1 lb (500 g) veal
1 onion
1 carrot
1 stalk celery
Salt
1 bay leaf

PASTA
4 cups (600 g) all-purpose flour
5 whole eggs

FILLING
3 1/2 oz (100 g) Parmesan

1 cup (250 g) Ricotta cheese
2/3 cup (150 g) Raviggiolo cheese
1 egg
Candied citron zest
Nutmeg
Salt and pepper

TO SERVE
Butter
1 sweet onion
1 cup (250 g) foie gras
Scant 1/2 cup (100 ml) Albana passita
Pistachio nuts
Pepper, to taste
Shaved truffle, optional

## Method

STOCK
Put the meat in a large saucepan and cover with cold water. Bring the water to a boil over medium heat, covering it with a lid. When the water comes to a boil, skim the froth, season with salt, and add the whole vegetables, salt, and the bay leaf. Lower the heat, cover again, and simmer for about 2 1/2 hours. Let cool and chill for at least 3 hours. Before using the stock, remove the layer of fat that will have solidified on the surface.

PASTA
Sift the flour onto a wooden surface and shape into a mound. Make a well in the center. Pour the eggs into the hollow and beat them using a fork. Knead until the dough is smooth. Let rest under a cloth for 20 minutes.
Meanwhile, combine the filling ingredients to make a smooth, thick mixture.
Use a long rolling pin to roll out a sheet of pasta until it is fairly thin, almost see-through (or use a pasta machine). Cut into about 3/4-inch (2-cm) squares. Place small amounts of the filling in the center and fold in half diagonally to make a triangle. Take the two ends and join them together to make filled, hat-shaped pasta.

## Serving

Melt the butter in a frying pan. Add the onion, cut into julienne, and add the Albana passita. Let evaporate and add the foie gras, cut into 1/3-inch (1-cm) cubes and brown slightly. Season with salt. Cook the cappelletti in meat stock; drain and toss in the pan. Spoon the cappelletti into a preheated plate. Garnish with chopped pistachios and pepper. If in season, add shavings of truffle.

# Stuffed pigeon, served with liver pate toasts, poached eggs, and fried sage

## Ingredients for 4 people
Preparation time: 1 h

4 pigeon eggs
2 pigeons, boned
3 slices of day-old bread
Scant 1/2 cup (100 ml) brandy
3 1/2 oz (100 g) sausage
3 1/2 oz (100 g) porcini mushrooms
1 egg
1 3/4 oz (50 g) Parmesan cheese
Livers from the pigeons
Salt, to taste
Pat of butter
1 clove garlic
Rosemary, sage, spinach or wild spinach

## Method

### POACHED EGGS
Bring plenty of water to a boil with salt and vinegar in a large pot. Lower the heat as much as possible, break one egg at a time in a dish and carefully add to the water. Boil the eggs for about 3 minutes until the whites are firm and completely enclose the yolk. Use a slotted spoon to drain the eggs and arrange them on a dry tea cloth. Remove any foam from the whites using a sharp knife.

### PIGEON
Season the pidgeon meat with salt and pepper. Soften a slice of bread in 1/4 cup (50 ml) of brandy, then crumble it up and add to the sausage and porcini mushrooms not needed to garnish the dish. Add the egg and Parmesan. Stuff the pigeons with this mixture. Seal them up and arrange on a baking tray with sprigs of rosemary and sage. Bake in the oven at 350°F (180°C/gas mark 4) for 20-25 minutes, basting them occasionally with the white wine and its cooking juices.
Sauté the livers in a frying pan with the onion. Drizzle with 1/4 cup (50 ml) of brandy and let it evaporate. Season with salt to taste. Puree in a blender with a pat of butter and spread on toasts (freshly made); top with the poached eggs.
To finish, sauté the porcini mushrooms (*boletus edulis*) with 1 clove of garlic and keep warm. Sauté the spinach and arrange in the center of the plate. For each serving, form a wreath, alternating the porcini mushrooms and fried sage. Cut half a pigeon into small, thin slices and arrange in a fan shape. Drizzle with the cooking juices and serve with the liver pate toast.

# Almond basket with vanilla custard and sweet flatbread

## Ingredients for 4 people
Preparation time: 1 h 20'

**BASKET**
1 cup (200 g) superfine sugar
2 1/2 cups (240 g) slivered almonds
Mixed berries, to garnish

**CUSTARD**
2 cups (500 ml) whole milk
1 vanilla pod
Lemon zest
3 egg yolks
Generous 1/2 cup (125 g) sugar
2 tablespoons (30 g) flour

Semisweet chocolate shavings
Rosolio

**SWEET FLATBREAD**
6 2/3 cups (1 kg) flour
1 1/2 cups (300 g) sugar
2 tablespoons (30 g) vanilla baking
powder
Generous 3/4 cup (200 g) lard
3 eggs
Lemon zest
1 cup (250 ml) whole milk

## Method

### BASKET
Melt the sugar in a small saucepan. Add the slivered almonds and let them caramelize until the mixture turns a cinnamon color. Pour the mixture onto a sheet of parchment paper, creating interwoven and overlapped circles. Let cool to lukewarm and form them into a basket shape (using an upside-down small bowl as a mold).

### CUSTARD
Bring the milk to a boil in a small saucepan with the vanilla and lemon zest. Mix the egg yolks with the sugar in a bowl. Add the flour, mixing constantly, making sure that no lumps form. Pour the milk into the prepared mixture, whisking constantly. Return to the heat (low), stirring until the custard becomes fairly thick. Let cool to lukewarm and pour into the basket, which has been drizzled with rosolio.

### SWEET FLATBREAD
Sift the flour onto a wooden surface and shape into a mound. Make a well in the center. Add all the remaining ingredients. Knead together and let rest. Shape the mixture into large balls the size of a fist. Roll out with a rolling pin, forming rounds that are 1/3-inch (1-cm) thick. Cook on the typical Romagnolo terracotta *testo* (a circular heated plate). Cut the flatbread into 8 wedges and serve 2 of them per basket. Decorate with mixed berries.

# Gaetano Trovato

## ARNOLFO RESTAURANT
### Colle Val d'Elsa (Siena)

"My dishes are always born in a book, like an architectural design", says chef Gaetano Trovato. So what else could he call his restaurant, as it lies just a stone's throw from the birthplace of Arnolfo di Cambio, the famous Tuscan sculptor and architect? *Arnolfo*, of course, and with great pride.

The restaurant, located in a 16th Century building in the historic district of Colle Val d'Elsa, overlooks the beautiful sea and the peaceful hills of Chianti. The building was recently renovated with the aristocratic simplicity of the architecture of Arnolfo, the spaciousness of long ago with modern elements. "The restaurant – Gaetano continues – was founded in 1982. My mother Concetta and my sister offered home cooking with great attention to the raw materials. My brother Giovanni, who is now the sommelier and dining room manager and I took over in the mid80s, making a radical change in the philosophy." It was a winning decision. Just 26 years old in 1987, thanks to his high regional cuisine and incessant research, he received his first Michelin star and his second in 2000, confirmed again this year.

"My philosophy deals with the evolution of tradition, seen today through the local products." A modern classical style, perhaps finding its origin in the Tuscan Renaissance in which it is immersed. Gaetano always likes to find new ideas, as well as new producers and new gastronomic entities. The cult to raw materials - "I am excited by first class products " – is imprinted on him from the years of his childhood. Of Sicilian origin, the family moved to Tuscany when he was 6 years old. "My grandparents and my parents had a farm in Ragusano where they produced vegetables and oil. Since I was a child I have been used to eating just foods of the season, and of high quality."

Gaetano began his career with the poorest – but most symbolic – food: bread. "When I was in high school I would get extra pocket money in the summer working with an old wood-burning oven, making yeast bread. That experience left an indelible mark on me…" After this beginning as a baker, he had the opportunity for a privileged training: he attended the hotel school in St. Moritz, working at *Kulm's,* the oldest hotel in the famous resort of Engadine, with a stop on the Cote d'Azur under a chef with multiple Micheline stars, and in Paris under a renowned pastry chef, studying their secrets. After various internships in European countries and before starting on his own with his own family restaurant, he had the good fortune to have a beautiful experience with Angelo Paracucchi: "With him every day was a challenge to find the best products offered in the area: a school of life."

Gaetano puts his soul into his work. "The cuisine of the region is an immense treasure that we must preserve, restore and re-launch, like we do with monuments, restating the taste but making it fresher and lighter, more adapted to today." Attention must be paid to both substance and form. He has a humanistic flair: "I don't just write down my ideas for new dishes on paper, before preparing them, but I also pay a lot of attention to presentation. As always - I'm a perfectionist – I personally select the dishes, the cutlery, the glasses and even the tablecloths, checking the best Italian companies."

The menu for this book "are today my expression of the region." As appetizer we have, 'rabbit, apricots and almonds', a dish built of a meat that is especially widespread in Tuscany, which uses the entire animal: the filet, the thighs stuffed with apricots and *foie gras*, and the liver served with a puree of apricot and almond mousse. The first course is 'a cake of ricotta cheese with tarragon and a light tarragon pesto with ricotta flan', a dish that goes back in time to the Medici. "*Tarragon* is an herb from the Crete of Siena since the times of Catherine de Medici, who took it to France to use in her favorite delicacies…" Second course is "the Chianina variation, the most interesting interpretation that we can have of Tuscan cuisine": the classic steak Florentine, revisited without the bone, then made into a tartar with herbs and poached quail egg, served cold with an *aspic* of small vegetables. And to finish on a sweet note, "an Alchermes *zuccotto* made with ice cream and pine nuts from Pisa." *Zuccotto* is a traditional sweet of Tuscany. But here it is reinterpreted by Gaetano, served with a sauce made of Alchermes raspberry liqueur, "a typical Florentine liqueur, made in the pharmacy of Santa Maria Novella using an infusion of cochineal."

# Rabbit

with apricots and almonds

P.324

# Ricotta tortelli

with tarragon sauce and Pecorino flan

P.326

# Chianina beef,

tartare, aspic, and carved steak

P.328

# Zuccotto with Alchermes

and Pisan pine nut ice-cream

P.330

# Rabbit with apricots and almonds

## Ingredients for 4 people
Preparation time: 1 h and 45'

1 locally sourced rabbit, weighing about 3 1/3 lb (1.5 kg), with its liver and kidneys
1 oz (30 g) dried apricots
1 3/4 oz (50 g) fois gras
Scant 1/2 cup (100 ml) brandy
1 small bunch of herbs (such as chives and wild fennel)
Salt and pepper
1 quart (1 liter) extra-virgin olive oil
2 shallots

Scant 1/2 cup (100 ml) white wine
2 cups of beef stock
2 juniper berries
2 cloves
1 cinnamon stick

ALMOND FOAM
Generous 1/4 cup (50 g) blanched almonds
Pinch of soy lecithin
Salt

## Method

### RABBIT
Use a sharp knife to cut the two loins from the saddle and remove the bones from the thighs (or ask your butcher to do this for you). Lay it all out on plastic wrap, fill with the dried apricots, roll it up, and let it rest.
Cut the fois gras into thin strips and add the brandy and chopped herbs. Season with salt and pepper. Marinate it for 30 minutes. Roll the two loins up tightly with a piece of aluminum foil to form two cylinders and arrange them in a baking dish. Bake in the oven for about 12 minutes at 275°F (140°C/gas mark 1). At the end of the cooking time, let cool completely.
To make the sauce, brown the rabbit bones (broken in pieces), 2 chopped shallots, 2 juniper berries, 2 cloves, 1 cinnamon stick in the extra-virgin olive oil in a casserole. Add the wine and let it evaporate. Pour in the stock. Cook for about 1 hour. Strain the sauce through a fine-mesh sieve and keep warm.
Brown the two loins, liver, and the thigh meat split into four parts in extra-virgin olive oil in a frying pan. Season with salt and pepper.

### FOAM
Crush the almonds in a mortar, then mix them into 2 cups of warm water. Let the mixture infuse for about 1 hour. Strain the liquid into a bowl and add the lecithin and a pinch of salt. Whip with a mixer just before serving.

## Serving

Pour the apricot puree onto four warm dishes, then arrange two slices of the thigh, about 3/4 inch (2 cm) high and alternate with three slices of saddle of rabbit. Add a piece of liver, drizzle with the sauce, and garnish with the almond foam.

# Ricotta tortelli with tarragon sauce and Pecorino flan

## Ingredients for 4 people
Preparation time: 55'

### FRESH EGG PASTA
2/3 cup (100 g) semolina flour
2/3 cup (100 g) all-purpose flour
0.07 oz (2 g) egg yolks
1 whole egg

### FLANS
Scant 1/4 cup (50 g) fresh Ricotta
Generous 1/3 cup (50 g) fresh Pecorino, grated
1 egg white
pinch of nutmeg and pinch of salt

### FILLING
Generous 3/4 cup (200 g) sheep's Ricotta
Scant 1/2 cup (100 ml) extra-virgin olive oil
1/2 beaten egg

Small bunch of chopped herbs (such as chives, marjoram, wild fennel)
Pinch of nutmeg
Salt and pepper to taste

### TARRAGON SAUCE
1/2 oz (100 g) tarragon
2 ice cubes
1 3/4 oz (50 g) aged Pecorino
Generous 3 tablespoons (50 ml) Terre di Siena extra-virgin olive oil PDO
Generous 1 tablespoon (20 g) pine nuts
1 pat of cold butter
Salt and pepper to taste
1 3/4 oz (50 g) aged Pienza Pecorino, to be grated over the tortelli

## Method

### PASTA
Sift the flours onto a wooden surface and shape into a mound. Make a well in the center. Pour the eggs into the hollow and knead until the dough is smooth and even. Let rest for 30 minutes in a cool place.

### FLANS
Mix together the Ricotta and Pecorino. Then fold in the lightly whipped egg white with a pinch of salt. Spoon the mixture into buttered individual molds and bake in the oven for 20 minutes in a bain-marie at 275°F (140°C/gas mark 1).

### FILLING
Combine the filling ingredients. Roll out the sheet of pasta using a pasta machine. The sheet must be thin and elastic. Cut it into rounds with a 3-inch (8-cm) diameter pastry cutter. Spoon a walnut-sized amount of the filling in the center, close in a half-moon shape, press down the edges, and join the two ends together.

### TARRAGON SAUCE
In a blender, puree the tarragon leaves with two ice cubes, so that they don't oxidize and turn black. Blend in the Pecorino, olive oil, pine nuts, butter, salt, and pepper.

## Serving

Cook the tortelli in a pot with plenty of salted boiling water for about 2 minutes. Spread a thin layer of the tarragon sauce in the bottom of the dish. Arrange six tortelli on top per person and garnish with the Pecorino flan.

# Chianina beef, tartare, aspic, and carved steak

**Ingredients for 4 people**
Preparation time: 4 h

STOCK
1 1/2 lb (700 g) beef
1 lb (500 g) veal
1 onion
1 carrot
1 celery stalk
1 bay leaf
Salt

BEEF GRAVY (MAKES 1 LITER)
2 lb (1 kg) beef bones with
some meat, broken into
walnut-size chunks
10 oz (300 g) meat scraps,
fat removed
2 1/2 oz (70 g) onions, diced
1 3/4 oz (50 g) celery, diced
1 3/4 oz (50 g) carrot, diced
Small bunch of bouquet
garni (sage, rosemary, stalks
of parsley and a bay leaf)
1 cup (250 g) dry white wine

Generous 1 1/3 cups (350 g)
ripe chopped tomatoes
Peppercorns
2 quarts (2 liters) water
Salt

TARTARE
5 oz (150 g) steak fillet
Small bunch of herbs (thyme,
sage, and rosemary), chopped
Salt, for seasoning
Pepper, for seasoning
Ginger
Juice of 1/2 lemon
1 3/4 oz (50 g) lamb's lettuce
3/4 oz (20 g) watercress
4 quail's eggs
Fleur de sel, for finishing

ASPIC
1 cheek
1 onion, chopped
1 celery stalk, chopped

2 sheets of gelatin
1 quart (1 liter) beef stock
1 1/4 cups (300 ml) beef
cooking juices

CARVED STEAK
1 onion
1 quart (1 liter) red wine
1 clove
1 bay leaf
5 black peppercorns
3 juniper berries
1 cinnamon stick
1 Chianina beef steak,
weighing about 1 lb (500 g),
fat and bone removed
Extra-virgin olive oil
2 cloves garlic
1 sprig of rosemary
Small seasonal vegetables to
accompany the carved steak
Fleur de sel, for finishing

## Method

### STOCK

Place the meat in a large saucepan and cover with cold water.

Bring the water to a boil over medium heat, covering it with a lid.

When the water comes to a boil, skim the froth, season with salt, and add the whole vegetables and the bay leaf.

Lower the heat, cover again, and simmer for about 2 1/2 hours.

Let cool, then strain and chill for at least 3 hours.

Before using the stock, remove the layer of fat that will have solidified on the surface.

### GRAVY

In a cooking pot, put beef bones, meat scraps, fat removed, onion, celery, and carrot, and a small bunch of bouquet garni. Roast it all in the oven, stirring often, until it has turned golden brown.

Skim any fat and pour in the white wine. Add the tomatoes, some peppercorns, and a little salt; pour in the water. Let simmer for 4 hours, skimming the fat continuously. Strain stock through a fine-mesh sieve.

### TARTARE

Use a sharp knife to finely chop the fillet steak and mix with the chopped herbs. Season with salt and pepper, ginger, and lemon juice. Serve the dish alongside the steak, placing the beef tartare in a 2-inch (5-cm) diameter circle, pressing down the meat. Arrange the lamb's lettuce around the meat, garnish with bits of watercress, and place an hard boiled quail's egg on top of each tartare. Season with a pinch of *fleur de sel.*

### ASPIC

Place the chopped onion and celery and the beef cheek with 3 quarts of water in a pot. Bring to a boil and simmer at approximately 250°F (120°C) for about 4 hours. Remove the cheek. Filter the stock, dissolve the gelatin in 1.5 liters of it. Adjust the salt and let cool slightly. Cut the cheek, fat removed, into 4 even pieces and arrange it in four disposable molds with a carrot brunoise and a zucchini. Fill to the brim with the stock and cool in the refrigerator.

### CARVED STEAK

Sauté the coarsely chopped onion in a saucepan. Add the red wine, spices, and bay leaf. Let the wine evaporate almost completely. Pour in the beef gravy and cook over low heat until a runny sauce forms. Strain liquid into a pot and keep warm.

Sear the beefsteak in a hot, heavy, cast-iron pan with extra-virgin olive oil, clove of garlic, and rosemary for about 2 minutes on each side. Bake in the oven for about 3 minutes at 400°F (200°C/gas mark 6). Let rest for about 10 minutes, covering it with foil to keep it warm before carving it. Carve the steak, arrange on warm plates with the sauce underneath. Add seasonal vegetables. Season with *fleur de sel* and extra-virgin olive oil.

# Zuccotto with Alchermes and Pisan pine nut ice-cream

**Ingredients per 8 persone**
Preparation time: 40' – Resting time: 24 h

### BISCUIT BASE
3 tablespoons (45 g) all-purpose flour
3 tablespoons (45 g) ground almonds
3 eggs yolks
Generous 1/4 cup (60 g) sugar

### ALCHERMES DIP
2/3 cup (150 g) sugar syrup
Generous 1/3 cup (83 g) Alchermes
Generous 2 tablespoons (37 g) water

### FILLING
4 egg yolks
1 whole egg
1/2 cup (100 g) sugar
Generous 3/4 cup (200 ml) water
1 cup (250 g) cream, whipped
Grated zest of 1 lemon
Juice of 1/2 lemon

### PISAN PINE NUT ICE-CREAM
Generous 1 1/3 cups (350 g) fresh milk
Generous 1/2 cup (110 g) superfine sugar
1 tablespoon glucose
2 teaspoons (10 g) powdered milk
Scant 1/2 cup (80 g) Pisan pine nuts, well toasted
2/3 cup (150 g) cream

### SAUCE
2 cups (200 g) raspberries
1/2 cup (100 g) sugar
Generous 3 tablespoons (50 ml)
Alchermes, scant 2 fluid ounces

Plain yogurt, for serving
Fresh raspberries, for serving

## Method

### BISCUIT BASE

Beat the egg whites to stiff peaks with the sugar. Fold in the 3 egg yolks, the flour and the ground almonds until well combined. Spread the batter out to 1/8 inch (5 mm) thick on a parchment-lined baking sheet. Bake in the oven for about 10 minutes at 350°F (180°C/gas mark 4). Let cool completely. Line the disposable spherical molds with the biscuit base.

### FILLING

Beat the egg yolks and egg in a bowl with a mixer. Meanwhile, cook the sugar and water in a small saucepan over medium heat to 250°F (120°C). Use a whisk to gradually beat the sugar syrup into the eggs until the mixture has cooled completely. Fold in the whipped cream and grated lemon zest and juice.
Fill the molds lined with the biscuit base and freeze.

### ICE-CREAM

Place the milk, sugar, glucose, and powdered milk in a pan and cook to 175°F (80°C). Toast the pine nuts and stir them into the mixture to infuse for 24 hours. Gently reheat the mixture, strain, setting the pine nuts aside (stir them back into the ice cream at the end). When the ice-cream has become creamy, mix in the whipped cream. Pour the mixture into an ice-cream machine and churn according to the manufacturer's instructions.

### RASPBERRY SAUCE

Place the raspberries and sugar in a saucepan. Bring to a boil and cook until syrupy. Puree and strain the sauce when it has cooled, then stir in the Alchermes.

## Serving

Unmold the zuccotto onto plates with the raspberry sauce and plain yogurt. Decorate the Pisan pine nut ice-cream with fresh raspberries and plain yogurt.

# Pier Giuseppe Viazzi

## ARIANNA RESTAURANT
### Cavaglietto (Novara)

There is no romantic origin of the name *Arianna*', given to the restaurant, but a fun challenge. When the father of chef Pier Giuseppe Viazzi, the current owner of the restaurant with his wife Caterina, who heads the dining room, decided in 1965 to open a business in Cavaglietto, a small rural village in the province of Novara, with a handful of houses o of lakes, rivers and rice paddies, they all took him for a madman. "One day" – said Pier Giuseppe – "going I do not remember where, my father saw the billboard of a nursing home for the mentally ill that was called *Villa Arianna*. From there, he got the idea of the name and he said if anything goes wrong, we'll make it an addition to the clinic."

At first the restaurant was more like a bar, with a pool table, a TV and a few tables to play cards on. Then, slowly, it turned into an inn with a few rooms and a restaurant with good food and generous portions, as it used to be. "In the kitchen was my mother Maria, who liked to cook the typical dishes of the Novara region."

Pier Giuseppe immediately followed in the footsteps of his parents, attending hotel school, then from '75 to '79, he moved around trying to get some 'experience'. "After graduation, my goal was to become a chef in a big hotel, not to work in a restaurant, because I wanted to lead a large kitchen staff." Thus, his first two seasons were at the *Grand Hotel of the Iles of Borromées* in Stresa, then the *Hilton Hotel* in Milan, the international hotel chain, which led him to Stratford-upon-Avon in England, the birthplace of Shakespeare. From there he went to the *Hotel Royale La Baule* in northern France, and then the old *Auberge de Condé* in La Ferté sous Jouarre in the Vallée de la Marne. It is there that he began to see how a great restaurant that makes traditional cuisine runs.

"When I went back to Cavaglietto in the family business, I tried to put into practice what I had learned." For a couple of years he worked with his parents – just his mother and him in the kitchen, his brother and father in the dining room – and they served hybrid cuisines that combined traditional dishes with new. "Then I found myself at a crossroads: either the local cuisine, or a more modern impression that would give preference to local products – cooking, combining and presenting them in a new way – or if this were not possible, availing myself of other raw materials, of the same high quality." But in the end, he chose a kitchen that is part of but not rigidly bound to the territory.

At the end of '85 the entire Viazzi family, who Caterina had joined the year before, took over the restaurant. Later, when his brother Francesco decided to take over a pastry shop on Orta Lake and his parents retired, Pier Giuseppe and his wife were left to run the business. They started to transform the restaurant into the elegant and refined restaurant that it is today, and during the first year of his managing the restaurant, the young chef earned a Michelin star. A few years later he became one of the founders of the Italian association of the *Jeunes Restaurateurs d'Europe* (where he is now an honorary member due to age), an association that brings together young chefs and restaurateurs, uniting them under the motto "talent and passion" as well as respect, interpretation and dissemination of the culinary tradition of their land.

The menu chosen for the book is intimately linked to the territory with a strong personal touch. "It has some courses that either you'll love or you'll hate." As a starter are "frog legs breaded with herbs, but baked instead of fried to make them lighter." This of course is a traditional dish in the region, this being a land of paddy fields and irrigation canals. At one time it was considered food for the poor, but now it's a rare delicacy. First course is "tortelli of Fassone stew topped with gravy. Here we find the traditional Piedmont agnolotti which gives the dish its name, although the shape and filling is different, without using multiple types of meat, but just braised beef." The second course is based on snails, a favorite in Piedmont cuisine: "snails with garlic butter sauce, cooked in a vegetable stock and soaked in *Ghemme,* a full-bodied quality red wine." And finally for dessert we have "eggnog ice cream with sweet *Moscato d'Asti* sauce instead of *Marsala*, paired with a melon cream." Also typical: eggnog, the hot egg cream, sugar and wine found throughout Italian cuisine is considered to be of Piedmonts' origin.

# White bread
P.336

# Herb-breaded
frogs' legs
P.338

# Stewed veal tortelli
with roasted juices
P.340

# Snails cooked in Ghemme wine
with garlic sauce
P.342

# Zabaglione ice-cream flavored
with Moscato d'Asti passito
on pureed melon
P.344

# White bread

Preparation time: 40' - Leavening: 12 h + 30' + 30-60' according to size
Cooking time: 10-20' according to size


FOR HOMEMADE LEAVEN BREAD (BIGA)
2 lbs., 4 oz. (1 kg) bread flour
0,8 oz. (25 g) fresh yeast
Water as needed (about 19 cups, 450 ml)

2 lbs., 4 oz. (1 kg) bread flour
1 oz. (30 g) salt
1 oz. (30 g) sugar
Water as needed (about 38 cups, 700 ml)

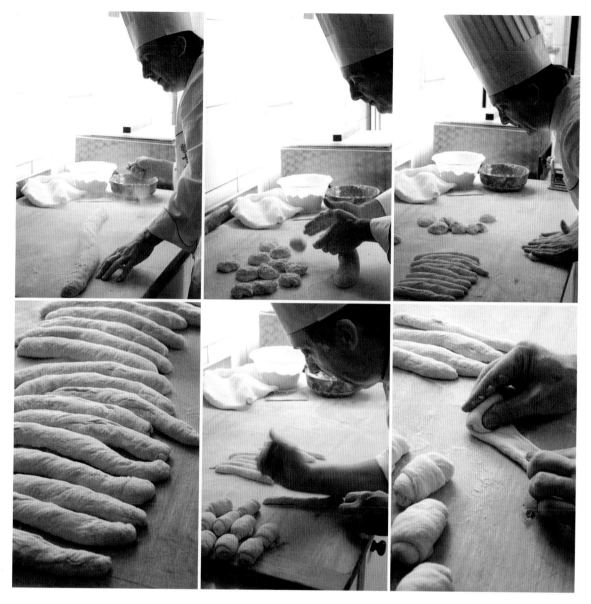

## Method

Crumble the yeast into the flour and knead adding enough water necessary to obtain a firm dough.
Place the dough in a container that can hold at least three times the initial volume and cover it with plastic wrap. Let it rise at room temperature (64 °F approximately) for 12 hours.

Place the ingredients of the second mixture (except salt) in the bowl of the mixer and begin to knead. After about 5 minutes add the homemade leaven bread (Biga) and when it is all mixed well, add the salt. Mix everything well, set it aside covered by a cloth at room temperature for 30 minutes, then divide it into pieces as desired. Shape the bread as desired and let it rise at about 86 °F until the volume has doubled. Bake at 450-480 °F with a little moisture for about 10-13 minutes for small pieces and at 350-390 °F for 18-20 minutes for larger pieces.

# Herb-breaded frogs' legs

### Ingredients for 4 people
Preparation time: 20'

5 oz (150 g) sliced white bread
2/3 oz (20 g) herbs (such as chervil, chives, calamint or mint, parsley)
1 clove garlic
1 lb (500 g) frogs' legs
Salt and pepper
Extra-virgin olive oil

### Method

Break up the bread in a bowl and process with the herbs and garlic.
Season the frogs' legs with salt and pepper and brush with a little
extra-virgin olive oil. Dip them into the herb breadcrumbs. Arrange
the frogs' legs on a baking sheet lined with parchment paper. Bake
in a preheated oven at 475°F (240°C/gas mark 9) for 7 minutes.
Remove from the oven and arrange on serving plates.

# Stewed veal tortelli with roasted juices

Ingredients for 4 people
Preparation time: 2 h 30'

PASTA
1 1/3 cups (200 g) all-purpose flour
2 eggs
2 teaspoons (10 g) extra-virgin olive oil
1 teaspoon (6 g) salt

FILLING
3 1/2 oz (100 g) onion, chopped
1 3/4 oz (50 g) carrot, chopped
1 3/4 oz (50 g) celery, chopped
1 clove garlic, chopped
1 bay leaf
1 sprig of rosemary
Salt and pepper
2 tablespoons (30 g) extra-virgin olive oil
10 oz (300 g) veal shoulder
Scant 1/2 cup (100 g) red wine
1 egg
Scant 1/2 cup (50 g) grated Parmesan

## Method

PASTA
Sift the flour onto a cutting board and shape into a mound. Make a well in the center. Add the eggs, oil, and salt into the hollow and knead until the dough is smooth and even. Let rest for about 1 hour in a cool place.

FILLING
Sauté the vegetables, garlic, and herbs in the oil. Add the meat, cut into large pieces. Add salt and pepper. Pour in the red wine and simmer for 2 hours. Reserve the cooking juices and chop the meat and vegetables in a meat grinder.
Mix the ground meat with the egg and cheese. Roll out the pasta into thin sheets using a pasta machine. Cut it into rounds with a 2 1/2-inch (6-cm) diameter pastry cutter. Fill with the filling and seal the tortelli. Cook the tortelli in plenty of salted water for 4 minutes. Drain and serve with 1/4 cup (60 ml) of the roasted cooking juices.

# Snails cooked in Ghemme wine with garlic sauce

## Ingredients for 4 people
Preparation time: 2 h

48 prepared snails
2 3/4 oz (80 g) shallots
2 3/4 oz (80 g) carrots
2 3/4 oz (80 g) celery
1/3 cup (80 g) extra-virgin olive oil
3 cloves garlic
1 bay leaf
Salt and pepper
Generous 3/4 cup (200 ml) Ghemme wine
3 tablespoons (50 g) butter
1 egg

## Method

Boil the snails in salted water for 30 minutes. Let cool, remove from the shell, and clean, removing them from the black end part.
Finely dice the vegetables and sauté them in the oil with 1 clove of garlic and the bay leaf. Add the snails and season with salt and pepper.
Let them brown for a few minutes. Pour in the wine and let it evaporate. Cover with a lid and cook over low heat for about 1 hour.
Prepare the sauce by emulsifying the butter, cut into cubes, with 1 tablespoon of water and the remaining finely chopped garlic in a saucepan.
Serve the snails with the garlic sauce.

# Zabaglione ice-cream flavored
# with Moscato d'Asti passito on pureed melon

## Ingredients for 4 people
Preparation time: 2 h

ZABAGLIONE
6 egg yolks
1 cup (200 g) sugar
Generous 3/4 cup (200 ml) Moscato
2 cups (500 ml) whipped cream

PUREE
1 melon (cantaloupe), peeled, seeded, and cut into chunks
1/4 cup (50 g) sugar

## Method

ZABAGLIONE
Place the egg yolks in a bowl and add the sugar. Use a whisk to beat the mixture until frothy and increased in volume. Slowly whisk in the Moscato. Whisking constantly, over moderate low heat, bring the zabaglione to 175°F (80°C) in the top of a double boiler filled of water. When the zabaglione starts to thicken, remove from heat and let cool. Then fold in the whipped cream. Pour mixture into a terrine and freeze.

PUREE
Puree the melon chunks with the sugar.

## Serving

Remove ice cream from the terrine. Spoon a ladle of the puree in the bottom of the dish and arrange thin slices of the ice cream on top.

# GLOSSARY

## ACHILLEA

An herbaceous plant characterized by jagged-edged leaves and a slightly bitter taste, Achillea is used to flavor salads, soups, and various liqueurs. Thanks to its beneficial effects on the digestive system, is it also used in the preparation of natural medicines.

## AGAR AGAR

Better known to the Japanese as kanten, agar-agar is a polysaccharide used as a natural gelatin and is obtained from various genera of red seaweed. Agar agar has a high content of mucilage (65%) and of Carrageenas (a gelatinous substance, known as alginate in Pharmacopoeia). The gelatin produced by agar agar has a mild flavor and is very nutritious because it is rich in minerals. It is used in the preparation of gelatin for desserts and aspic because it has the property of not affecting natural flavors. Preparation is quick and easy and requires little cooking; most of the preparation time is taken up by setting, which takes about an hour at room temperature. It is suitable for light refreshing desserts, particularly in summer.

## ALKERMES

This very sweet liqueur has a bright red color, the name of which derives from "qirmiz", meaning scarlet. The Florentine monks of Santa Maria Novella, to whom its origin is attributed, prepared it by marinating cinnamon, cloves, nutmeg, vanilla and aromatic herbs in alcohol together with sugar with rose leaves and jasmine aromas. The characteristic red color was given by cochineal, a food coloring derived from the insect bearing the same name. Subsequently, some variations were introduced, in relation to the type and quantity of the spices used. Today Alkermes, the alcoholic content of which varies between 21 and 32%, is used almost exclusively in cakes and desserts.

## BASTARDELLA (bowl with handles)

A semi-spherical metal bowl (copper, tin plated iron or stainless steel) with two handles, the bastardella is used for beating, cooking and reducing sauces directly over a flame or in double boiler fashion, or for beating mayonnaise or other cold sauces.

## BAVARESE

Made from tea, milk, and alcohol, bavarese is usually served hot and can have numerous variations, such as the addition of an egg yolk, or the substitution of coffee for tea.

## BAVARIAN CREAM

This is the name of an important sweet, with a light and delicate consistency similar to that of a cream or custard, belonging to the group of cold entremets, known as "soft serve dessert." Bavarian cream is easy to make and has a custard and whipped cream base, mixed with isinglass to give the mixture a thicker consistency. Fresh and candied fruit, jam or marmalade, chocolate, vanilla coffee, etc., can be added to this basic mixture. The concoction is then poured into a mold, with a central hole and low sides, which allow the sweet to cool down quickly and uniformly.

## BISQUE

An exquisite sauce made from the carapace of crustaceans, bisque can be used to accompany various fish dishes. The shells, once cleaned, are crushed and toasted with a little oil and coarse salt, so that they release the albumin, which "binds" the dish. After twenty minutes, diced carrot, celery, tomato and onion are added with white wine and cognac. Once the alcohol has evaporated, water is added until it covers everything; the liquid is left to simmer for another twenty minutes. It is subsequently puréed at high speed or pressed through a sieve. Parsley, curry, or saffron is often added to taste.

## BRAISING

A method of cooking used mainly for meat and poultry and extended, with some differences, to include some preparations of fish and vegetables. The term derives from "embers" and refers to the time when the main cooking instrument was the fireplace; today the same result is obtained by putting the dish into a low-temperature oven. In a professional kitchen, braising is done in a special pot that is dedicated for such purpose, the braising pot; in home kitchens a sealed heavy pot or cast iron casserole dish can be used. Generally red meats and game are braised; the meat, typically a joint of reasonable size, can be marinated in wine and vegetables before flouring according to the recipe and searing in oil, lard or bacon fat. Cooking, which must be very slow, should be done in the oven. As far as poultry is concerned, only duck is suitable for braising: the braising pot or casserole is lined with fresh bacon rind and vegetables that have been softened in butter (in which the duck is also lightly fried before proceeding with the cooking). Fish, unlike meat, must not be fried but simply placed on aromatic vegetables soaked in cooking liquid (wine or fumet). Here also, it is advisable to choose fish of a reasonable size, otherwise the rapidity of the cooking would make the exchange of flavors between the fish and the cooking base ineffective. Before braising, vegetables must be parboiled in salted water and subsequently placed in a greased braising pot and put in the oven. The vegetables that are best suited for this way of cooking are leeks, celery, carrots, cardoons and Belgian endive.

## BRUNOISE

A term of French origin which indicates a particular method of cutting vegetables (very finely diced) and also a mixture of vegetables cut in this way. The most common brunoise is onion, celery, carrot, leek, and turnip, to which celeriac and peppers can be added. It can be used raw to add flavor to stews, casseroles and braised dishes or lightly fried in butter to garnish consommé and soups.

## BRUSCANDOLI or BRUSCANSI (shoots or sprouts)

A term used in the Veneto region for two types of wild shoots or sprouts: hop shoots in the province of Padova, and Butcher's Broom in the province of Verona. The shoots are used to make a classic risotto in the style of asparagus risotto, preferably using Vialone Nano rice.

## CHINA CAP

See chinois.

## CHINOISE or CHINOIS

A French word used in international cuisine, it refers to a special steel conical sieve with very fine holes. The Chinois is used to filter sauces, broth, and other cooking liquids. It is different from the mesh strainer because being sturdier it is possible to press the filtered ingredients.

## CIAUSCOLO

A type of sausage with a texture that resembles paté in consistency, ciauscolo is eaten spread on bread. Highly flavored parts of meat are used, such as ham, bacon, and shoulder pork with an adequate addition of fat. The flavors are simple, usually garlic, salt, and pepper crushed in a mortar, sometimes with the addition of a drop of wine. The sausage casing is made of the large intestine. The stuffed sausage is smoked for a couple of days over juniper berries and then matured for 2 to 3 months in a cellar. It is produced in an area extending from the Province of Macerata to a few municipalities in the Ascoli area up to the region of Umbria.

## CLARIFIED BUTTER

Clarified butter is produced by removing most of the water and the casein from normal butter. Clarified butter can be found in shops under the name of concentrated butter, but it is also possible to make it at home. Clarified butter has a higher fat content than traditional butter: almost 100% instead of 86% because it does not contain water. To make clarified butter, take some butter and cook it in a double boiler for around 15-20 minutes.

## COMMIS (chef)

A term used to denote an apprentice or assistant chef of another cook, an assistant reporting to a chef de partie, or a line cook.

## COURT BOUILLON

A French term meaning "short boil" or "reduced broth," court bouillon is a flavored liquid used to poach fish and crustaceans. In its simplest form, it is made with salted water that is flavored with onion, celery and carrot, while in professional cooking there are various versions depending on the type and size of fish to cook.

## FILO

Filo pastry, from the Greek word phyllo meaning "leaf," refers to tissue-thin layers of puff pastry. Characterized by a very short cooking time, it can be baked or friend in a large variety of dishes, and makes an excellent substitution for the roll casings of different international cuisines. Thanks to its versatility, it has found its way into Italian cooking. Unlike most common puff pastries, it is produced without any fat and thanks to its neutral taste it can be used in the preparation of both sweet as well as savory dishes. Traditionally and historically, it has been used throughout the Middle East for sweet pastries filled with hazelnuts and pistachios and dipped in syrup such as Baklava.

## GOOD KING HENRY (Chenopodium bonus-henricus) or POOR-MAN'S ASPARAGUS

An erect, tall, perennial herbaceous plant that grows 11 to 30 inches (30-75 cm) high, Good King Henry has a thick rhizome and a light-colored stem. The numerous wart-like projections give it a slightly floury and sticky appearance. The lower leaves are wedge-shaped and have a long stalk; they are dark green at the top, light and floury at the bottom. The flowers are in the form of a leafless spike at the top of the stem and are formed by small brown-greenish flowers with 5 sepals and stamens. The seeds are black and shiny. This plant is widespread in the hills and mountain areas all over Europe, North America and in Siberia. It flowers from May to August amongst rubble, along fences, and near houses and Alpine huts. The young raw leaves are eaten in salads dressed with oil, pepper, lemon juice and nut kernels. The leaves, lightly boiled in salted water, are cooked like spinach and used in fillings, minestrone, and omelets or cooked in butter. The floral tips can be eaten like asparagus. The plant is rich in iron, mineral salts and vitamins with de-mineralizing, fortifying, anti-anemic, laxative, depurative, skin emollient properties.

## ICE-CREAM MAKER

A multi-functional appliance ideal for preparing and serving ice-cream and sorbets made with fresh fruit, fruit juices and champagne, wine or liqueurs.

## ISOMALT

Isomalt is a sugar substitute, a type of sugar alcohol, primarily used for its sugar-like physical properties. It has only a small impact on blood sugar levels and does not cause tooth decay. It has 2 kcal/g, half the calories of sugar.

## LAVARELLO (Common whitefish)

Also known in Italy by the name of "coregone," lavarello belongs to the Salmonidae. It lives in large lakes. Its flesh is exquisite and it can be cooked in the same was as trout or perch--in the oven or fried in breadcrumbs.

## LOMBO (Loin)

Loin of pork or carré (boned).

## LOVAGE

An aromatic herbal plant that is also called "mountain celery" in Italy, lovage originated in Asia but can now be found all over central Europe. In Italy it is rare to find in the wild, but it is widely cultivated. Its leaves have an aroma that is similar to that of celery but much stronger.

## LYON SHAPED FRYING PAN

A round, shallow metal pan with curved edges and a handle that is generally as long as the pan's diameter. It is still produced today in black metal, a material that is well suited for all types of frying as it is a modest conductor and regulator of heat.

## MANTECARE

In general, this Italian term means to stir and render homogeneous a preparation of a buttery consistency such as ice cream. Nowadays the term is also used for pasta and rice; once cooked and strained, the pasta or rice is transferred to a pan together with sauce where it is also simultaneously mixed with grated cheese for binding, sometimes with the addition of butter or cream.

### MANTECATO

Type of soft ice cream and also a recipe for baccalà.

### MORCHELLA

Also called "sponge mushroom" it is a mushroom family characterized by a very high cap, composed of a network of ridges, and is of varying color from ocher to brown, gray or black. The flesh is white, pleasant-tasting and highly prized and excellent even dried. In classical cooking, the morchella is almost always cooked with cream and used as a pasta sauce and to accompany game; in general, however, it is not widely used in regional Italian cuisine, except for in the Modena area, where it is used to accompany tagliatelle and lasagne.

### NAPPARE

An Italian term that means to spoon sauce or cooking juices onto a composed dish.

### NEPITELLA (Blue cloud)

An herbal aromatic plant, Nepitella is widespread in the wild in meadows and other uncultivated areas. Although similar in appearance, its leaves are not to be confused with those of Basil Thyme or Mint.

### PARFAIT

A French term indicating the classic light ice cream that is as soft as froth. It is prepared directly in the typical conical mold or parfait dish, or in a round cake mold.

### PLANETARIA

The trade name of a pastry making machine for producing uniform dough that can be used in industry and at home.

### QUENELLE

A very common preparation in French and international cuisine, quenlles consist of a "loaf" mixture of fish or meat, sometimes combined with breadcrumbs, and a light egg or fat binding. The mixture is cooked in boiling water or in a creamy béchamel sauce. "Quenelles" are served as an hors d'oeuvre, in soups, or to garnish important dishes.

### RONER

*The RONER, which was designed by Joan Roca and Narcís Caner respectively of the "El Celler de Can Roca" and the "La Fonda Caner," two restaurants in the Province of Girona, keeps water in motion and maintains a constant temperature all around the cooking recipient of a double boiler. Thanks to the Roner it is possible to control very accurately the temperature in low-temperature sous-vide cooking in the 41° F to 212° F (5°C to 100°C) temperature range. It can be adapted to any type of recipient depending on the type and quantity of food to be cooked.*

### ROSTI RING

A stainless steel, ring-shaped bottomless mold of varying diameters, rosti rings are ideal for cutting pastry for ravioli or biscuits, or for plating food in an elegant manner.

### ROUX

Made from a mixture of equal quantities of butter and white flour, roux can be easily prepared at home. When the butter has melted, the flour is added and stirred until it is blended completely. It is then cooked for a few minutes to obtain a white roux and the longer it is cooked, the darker (and more deeply flavored) it becomes. Roux is used to thicken sauces such as Spanish cream and demi glace. It is also the thickening agent for béchamel sauce.

### SAC À POCHE

A cone-shaped bag made of plastic or other waterproof material that is filled with a soft mixture and used to fill or decorate.

### SAUTÉING

The term sauté (literally "jumped" in French, the past participle of "sauter," meaning to fry lightly) indicates a dish prepared mainly by lightly frying the main ingredients (tossing) in a frying pan, over a high flame. Because of the sudden hot temperatures to which the ingredients are subjected, a protective film is formed which seals them and prevents the loss of flavor, aromas and mineral salts. The sautéing technique is most suitable for cooking in a frying pan. It is done over a high flame without the addition of fat or liquid. Using this technique, it is possible to cook fish, vegetables and pasta as well as meat.

### SKIMMING

The act of removing the foam that forms on the surface of a cooking liquid, such as a broth, sauce, or jam. The most suitable instrument for this operation is a skimmer or spoon or ladle with holes.

### STEWING

A method of cooking meat, vegetables and occasionally fish, in liquid, the word in Italian (stufare) derives from "stufa" meaning stove, presupposing slow cooking, and in this sense, it is applied to meat. For vegetables, on the other hand, the term conveys cooking in a small amount of liquid or fat, over a very low flame. For fish the expressions "braising" or "poaching" are normally used.

### TIMBALLO

Also called "dariola," the timaballo is a slightly conical mold, of the same height as the diameter, from 3/4 to 9 inches (2 to 20 cm), and made out of tin-plated iron or stainless steel. The dish called "timballo" should be cooked in the mold by the same name, but in reality the name refers to anything made with pasta or rice, sometimes wrapped in shortcrust or short pastry, usually with a bolognese sauce and placed in various pans and cake tins. Dishes that are defined as "timballo" are the various "timpani," the meat and maccheroni bakes and the Neapolitan lasagna, the sartù and the bomba di riso (rice bomb) from Piacenza.

### ZEST

A term which derives from the French "zoster," zest refers to thin strips of orange or lemon rind separated from the inside of the fruit and the internal white part.

# RESTAURANTS

**AGATA E ROMEO**
www.agataeromeo.it
ristorante@agataeromeo.it
Via Carlo Alberto, 45 • Rome

**AGLI AMICI**
www.agliamici.it
info@agliamici.it
Via Liguria, 252 • Udine

**AL FORNELLO DA RICCI**
ricciristor@libero.it
Contrada Montevicoli • Ceglie Messapica (BR)

**ARIANNA**
www.ristorantearianna.net
info@ristorantearianna.net
Via Umberto I, 4 • Cavaglietto (NO)

**ARNOLFO**
www.arnolfo.com
arnolfo@arnolfo.com
Via XX Settembre, 50 • Colle di Val d'Elsa (SI)

**BALDIN**
www.ristorantebaldin.com
ristorante.baldin@libero.it
P.za Tazzoli 20R • Sestri Ponente (GE)

**BRACALI**
www.ristorante.mondobracali.it
info@mondobracali.it
Via di Perolla, 2 • Ghirlanda • Massa Marittima (GR)

**CAPRICCIO**
www.ristorantecapriccio.it
info@ristorantecapriccio.it
P.za S. Bernardo, 6 (Loc. Montinelle)
Manerba del Garda (BS)

**ENOTECA LE CASE**
www.ristorantelecase.it
info@ristorantelecase.it
Contrada Mozzavinci 16/17 • Macerata

**I BOLOGNA**
www.trattoriaibologna.it
info@trattoriaibologna.it
Via Nicola Sardi, 4 • Rocchetta Tanaro (AT)

**IL DON GIOVANNI**
www.ildongiovanni.com
info@ildongiovanni.com
Corso Ercole I D'Este 1 • Ferrara

**IL SOLE**
www.ilsolediranco.it
info@ilsolediranco.it
P.za Venezia, 5 • Ranco (VA)

**IL VIGNETO**
www.ilvignetodiroddi.com
info@ilvignetodiroddi.com
Località Ravinali 19/20 • Roddi d'Alba (CN)

**LA LOCANDA DI ALIA**
www.alia.it
alia@alia.it
Via letticelli, 55 • Castrovillari (CS)

**LA MADIA**
www.ristorantelamadia.it
info@ristorantelamadia.it
Corso F. Re Capriata, 22 • Licata (AG)

**LA PURITATE**
Via Sant'Elia, 18 • Gallipoli (LE)
+39 0833 264205

**LE MASCHERE**
www.lemaschere.it
info@lemaschere.it
Via Cesio Sabino, 33 • Sarsina (FC)

**LUIGI POMATA**
www.luigipomata.com
info@luigipomata.com
Viale Regina Margherita, 14 • Cagliari

**MALGA PANNA**
www.malgapanna.it
info@malgapanna.it
Strada de Sort, 64 • Moena (TN)

**PARIZZI**
www.ristoranteparizzi.it
info@ristoranteparizzi.it
Via della Repubblica, 71 • Parma

**PERBELLINI**
www.perbellini.com
ristorante@perbellini.com
Via Muselle, 130 • Isola Rizza (VR)

**ROMANO**
www.romanoristorante.it
info@romanoristorante.it
Via Giuseppe Mazzini, 122 • Viareggio (LU)

**TORRE DEL SARACINO**
www.torredelsaracino.it
info@torredelsaracino.it
Via Torretta, 9 • Loc. Marina d'Equa
Vico Equense (NA)

**VECCHIA TRATTORIA DA TONINO**
www.vecchiatrattoriadatonino.com
vecchiatrattoriadatonino@gmail.com
C.so Vittorio Emanuele II, 8 • Campobasso

**VECCHIO RISTORO DA ALFIO E KATIA**
www.ristorantevecchioristoro.it
info@ristorantevecchioristoro.it
Via Tourneuve, 4 • Aosta

**VILLA MAIELLA**
www.villamaiella.it
info@villamaiella.it
Località Villa Maiella, 30 • Guardiagrele (CH)

**ZUR ROSE**
www.zur-rose.com
info@zur-rose.com
Via Josef Innferhofer, 2 • San Michele - Appiano (BZ)

# ALPHABETICAL INDEX OF RECIPES

# PHOTO CREDITS

All photographs by FOTO RCR, studioparma@fotorcr.it, except:

pages 10-11 courtesy of Max & Douglas
pages 14-15, 16, 17 courtesy of Academia Barilla

WS White Star Publishers® is a registered trademark
property of De Agostini Libri S.p.A.

© 2009, 2014 De Agostini Libri S.p.A.
Via G. da Verrazano, 15
28100 Novara, Italy
www.whitestar.it - www.deagostini.it

Revised Edition

Translation by Helen Farrell
Editing by Sarah Huck

ISBN 978-88-544-0854-8
1 2 3 4 5 6    18 17 16 15 14

Printed in China